BRANDING BHAKTI

FRAMING THE GLOBAL BOOK SERIES

Hilary E. Kahn and Deborah Piston-Hatlen, series editors

BRANDING BHAKTI

KRISHNA CONSCIOUSNESS AND THE MAKEOVER OF A MOVEMENT

NICOLE KARAPANAGIOTIS

INDIANA UNIVERSITY PRESS

This book is a publication of

Indiana University Press
Office of Scholarly Publishing
Herman B Wells Library 350
1320 East 10th Street
Bloomington, Indiana 47405 USA

iupress.org

Manufactured in the United States of America

First printing 2021

Library of Congress Cataloging-in-Publication Data

Names: Karapanagiotis, Nicole, author.
Title: Branding Bhakti : Krishna consciousness and the makeover of a movement / Nicole Karapanagiotis.
Description: Bloomington : Indiana University Press, 2021. | Series: Framing the global | Includes bibliographical references and index.
Identifiers: LCCN 2020039577 (print) | LCCN 2020039578 (ebook) | ISBN 9780253054890 (paperback) | ISBN 9780253054883 (hardback) | ISBN 9780253054906 (ebook)
Subjects: LCSH: International Society for Krishna Consciousness—United States. | International Society for Krishna Consciousness—India. | Branding (Marketing)
Classification: LCC BL1285.835.U6 K37 2021 (print) | LCC BL1285.835.U6 (ebook) | DDC 294.5/512—dc23
LC record available at https://lccn.loc.gov/2020039577
LC ebook record available at https://lccn.loc.gov/2020039578

For my parents, Maria and Athanasios,
and for Shantanu

CONTENTS

ACKNOWLEDGMENTS

A published book, with its glossy cover and well-edited prose, hides the immense work and hardship taken to produce it—the years of long days (that stretch into nights) at the computer, the isolation that stems from the solitary nature of writing, the fatigue and self-doubt, and the general putting aside of one's life that is required to finally push the manuscript past the finish line.

No one deserves a bigger thank-you for helping me through this process than my husband, Shantanu Bagchi. Shantanu knows this book inside and out, because he fully lived it with me and because he engaged with me in near-daily conversation about it. Not only did he make this book better with his keen observations, editorial insights, and thoughtful suggestions, he also made its existence possible with his constant support, encouragement, friendship, and confidence in me. He also made my life better in so many day-to-day ways during the writing process: he encouraged impromptu and fun activities to keep our life from becoming too overscheduled and robotic, he did the lion's share of the household chores, and he sat on the porch with me to share pensive reflections on life and pints of IPA. Most importantly, though, during the writing of this book and well beyond, he has filled my life with love and the deepest of friendships. Shantanu, thank you for being my warm place, my remover of mustard. Your partnership has been the true joy of my life.

My parents, Maria Karapanagiotis and Athanasios Karapanagiotis, also deserve an enormous thank-you for keeping me afloat during the writing process. Writing is hard, and on more occasions than I can count, they were there to patiently listen to my complaints and then to offer me their advice in the form of reminding me not to take myself too seriously and to come over for dinner or coffee. My debt of gratitude to them, though, extends far beyond the writing of this book. As blue-collar immigrants from Greece, my parents likely never imagined that their only child—the first in the family to attend college—would go on to become a professor of South Asian religions or that she would write and publish a book on the Hare Krishnas. But they instilled in me a set of traits that set me on this path in ways that they likely never foresaw and for which I'm eternally grateful. In particular, they encouraged me toward a deep curiosity and sense of adventure as a young adult, and they emboldened me to believe that any idea I had, no matter how far-fetched, could become a practical reality if I was willing to stick to it and be inventive enough. They also showed me that they would support me no matter how far off the beaten path I went.

There are many others without whom this book would have been impossible. Chief among them are the ISKCON devotees themselves, who were nothing short of generous, gracious, and incredibly warmhearted during this process. They rolled out the red carpet for me all over India and across the United States, giving me up close and personal access to their new projects and centers, their temples, their media control rooms, and even their intimate gatherings. More than this, they gave me more hours of their time than I ever would have expected, letting me interview them formally and informally, letting me hang out with them at their various religious spaces, and letting me crash their retreats and, in many cases, their homes. They were also incredibly willing to engage with me in what I thought would have been difficult and controversial conversations over the course of this project, and they always did so with an exceptional reflexivity and openness. Though there are far too many devotees to thank here by name, I hope that those who worked closely with me on this project know my appreciation for them. I would, however, like to give a special thanks to the three gurus at the center of this book: Devamrita Swami, Radhanath Swami, and Hridayananda Das Goswami. Their participation in this project made it possible, and I am grateful to them for taking so much time out of their busy schedules to sit down, talk, and spend time with me.

This book would also have been impossible if not for the generous support that I received from Rutgers University, Camden. In particular, Dean Kriste Lindenmeyer of the College of Arts and Sciences gave me generous research funding. I also received a substantial fellowship from the Rutgers University, Camden, Digital Studies Center. Without the funding from these sources, the ethnographic work of this book—and therefore this book itself—would not have been possible. I am also grateful to have received a Rutgers University Research Council Award, which I used to support the production of the book's index.

Still, there are many others deserving of my appreciation, notably my many teachers. Thanks are due to my two graduate advisors, David L. Haberman and

Rebecca J. Manring, for giving me a firm foundation within which to understand Hinduism—its texts, its rituals, its theologies, and its many diverse traditions. I would also like to thank them, along with my many teachers at the American Institute of Indian Studies (AIIS) Jaipur, the American Institute of Indian Studies (AIIS) Pune, and at University of Wisconsin, Madison's South Asia Summer Language Institute (SASLI) program, for teaching me—and encouraging my continued study of—the languages that have enabled me to read Hindu texts and conduct ethnographic research within Hindu communities. Richard Nance and Robert Ford Campany at Indiana University were also instrumental in my graduate studies and deserve recognition here as well. At the University of Florida, I was benefitted by my undergraduate advisor, Vasudha Narayanan, who shepherded me into the field of Hinduism and who graciously allowed me to write my undergraduate thesis with her—a thesis that, as she likes to remind me, I handed in to her at her home, at night, an embarrassing number of pages over length and mere hours before it was due. David Hackett, also at the University of Florida, deserves a thank-you as well, since it was for his senior capstone ethnography project that I first began my study of ISKCON—visiting the Gainesville Hare Krishna House with my roommates and friends almost two decades ago.

Jennika Baines, my editor at Indiana University Press, offered keen editorial advice on this project, and I thank her for having such tremendous confidence in and enthusiasm for my project right from the outset. She deserves gratitude, too, for the humanity that she brought to the acquisitions process, which is not something that I, as a first-time author, expected from a university press editor. Two anonymous reviewers of this book also deserve much thanks; their thoughtful suggestions pushed me to dig deep into areas and questions that I would not have otherwise thought about, and I thank them for the spirit of scholarship and collegiality in which they offered them. Still others deserve a mention here. My family in India—Maitreyee Bagchi, Arnab Roy, Sandeep Bagchi, and Rita Bagchi—enthusiastically awaited the publication of my book, as did Jamie Raleigh, whom I consider my sister. Special thanks also go to my best friend, Clemisha Garnet, who partook in her fair share of conversations with me about religion, Hinduism, and conceptions of "the real" throughout our lifelong friendship. Clemisha also joined me on my adventures to study ISKCON as an undergraduate at the University of Florida, and it is my hope that the spirit of the discussions we had over Krishna Lunch (by day) and Taco Bell (by night) has made its way into this book. Last but not least, thanks also go to my beloved "research assistant," Nestor. Of course, as my research assistant, Nestor always slacked on the job, basically just sitting underneath my desk snoring away as I wrote. But he has added so much warmth and joy to my life for the past eight years, and he really is the best dog in the world.

I have a number of colleagues with whom I have worked over the years whom I would also like to acknowledge. At Rutgers are my colleagues John Wall, Stuart Charmé, Craig Agule, Eric Chwang, Margaret Betz, Melissa Yates, Sharon Smith, Jim Brown, Robert Emmons, Nyeema Watson, and Michael D'Italia. At Georgia Southern, I was lucky to work with Hemchand Gossai, Caren J. Town, Mary Villeponteaux, Gautam Kundu, and Finbarr Curtis, among others. A shout-out also goes to my graduate school colleagues and life-long friends, including Aimee Hamilton, Geoffrey Goble, Cuong Mai, Amy Hirschtick, Nicole Willock, Erik Hammerstrom, Brad Storin, Diane Fruchtman, Cheryl Cottine, and Jessica Carr.

Importantly, thanks also go to my students at Rutgers, Camden, who have gone along with me for all sorts of intellectual and ethnographic adventures over the past few years and who have brought to the table an inquisitiveness and infectious enthusiasm that have sustained me in my work as an academic. The landscape of Philadelphia, Pennsylvania, and Cherry Hill, New Jersey, will always be marked in my mind by memories of the many religious centers we have explored together. A few students in particular—from Rutgers and Georgia Southern—deserve special recognition, as they have had an extraordinary impact on my life as a teacher (and some have over the years also become my friends): Suzanne Shurling, Justin Miller, Pamela Delarosa, Krystal Lovell, Lacy Belham, Michael Belham, Thomas Hutchison, James Shay, Elijah Crouch, Emily Olsen, Chase Bryson, Hawa Fuseini, Ariel Bru, Omar Khasawneh, Richard Kuiters Hurtado, Krithi Kannan, Ernest Nelson, Joshua Green, Adam Soliman, and Christian Jung. And, as promised, I'd also like to give a special shout-out to the students in two classes in particular: Asian Religions at Georgia Southern and Selling God in the Digital Age at Rutgers, Camden. The students in these classes have offered me many insights into my work along the way.

In many ways, this is a book about people who hope—in particular, people who hope for a different future than the one their religious movement has seen in recent decades. In my own personal life, the past few years have caused me to reflect on the nature and value of hope myself, in ways that have been unexpected and deeply life-changing. I'm grateful to all who have walked this path with me.

Nicole Karapanagiotis
Wilmington, Delaware
February 14, 2020

NOTE ON TRANSLITERATION

In this book, I have used diacritical marks for transliterations of all words from Sanskrit and Hindi (such as *mūrti*, *yukta vairāgya*, *rathayātrā*, etc.). I have omitted diacritics, however, for words that frequently appear in English (such as *guru* and *karma*), as well as for terms that frequently appear in scholarship on Hinduism and ISKCON (such as *Krishna*, *Vaishnava*, *Brahman*, *darshan*, and *puja*). I have also omitted diacritical marks for proper names, such as those of people, places, gods, and goddesses. Finally, when citing direct quotations, or an author's name in which a diacritical standard different from my own is used, I have followed the author's own convention in my diacritical markings.

For definitions of any unfamiliar, non-English terms, the reader is encouraged to consult the glossary at the end of the book.

Unless otherwise noted, all translations in this book are my own.

BRANDING BHAKTI

INTRODUCTION

Each day, for better or worse, I start my morning with a cup of coffee and a quick check of Facebook. Too groggy to begin working or to get ready for my grueling commute in Philadelphia rush-hour traffic, I like the five minutes I get on Facebook: it allows me to wake up and get a quick debriefing of the goings-on in the world through the various news channels I've friended and the informative, witty, and sometimes narcissistic posts of my family and friends.

As I sip my coffee and scroll through the mundane status updates, images, and advertisements, I see many different posts: my aunt is playing poker, my friend from middle school made artisanal waffles for her children's breakfast, Beyoncé is rumored to be pregnant with baby number two, and Hillary Clinton made a political advertisement video that many of my friends have shared. But on this day, shuffled in the mix of advertisements, updates, news articles, stories about celebrity Twitter feuds, and pictures of my friends' kids, stands a beautiful beaming image of Sri Parthasarathiji. Sri Parthasarathiji is a form of the Hindu god Krishna and is the central deity of the Sri Sri Radha Parthasarathi Temple in New Delhi, India. In his form this morning, Sri Parthasarathiji appears on my News Feed as a striking high-resolution image. Adorned in an ornate, multicolored flower and jeweled outfit, he is playing his infamous flute, which he holds beneath a garlanded turban. His black body is fully adorned in jewels and flowers and is also stenciled with body paint—his hands a glowing red, and his arms and cheeks ornamented with pink-flowered vines. Although the image is two-dimensional, it still manages to appear lifelike on my screen. Sri Parthasarathiji's eyes are of central presence in the image, and he stands with a faint smile, ready to capture his audience.

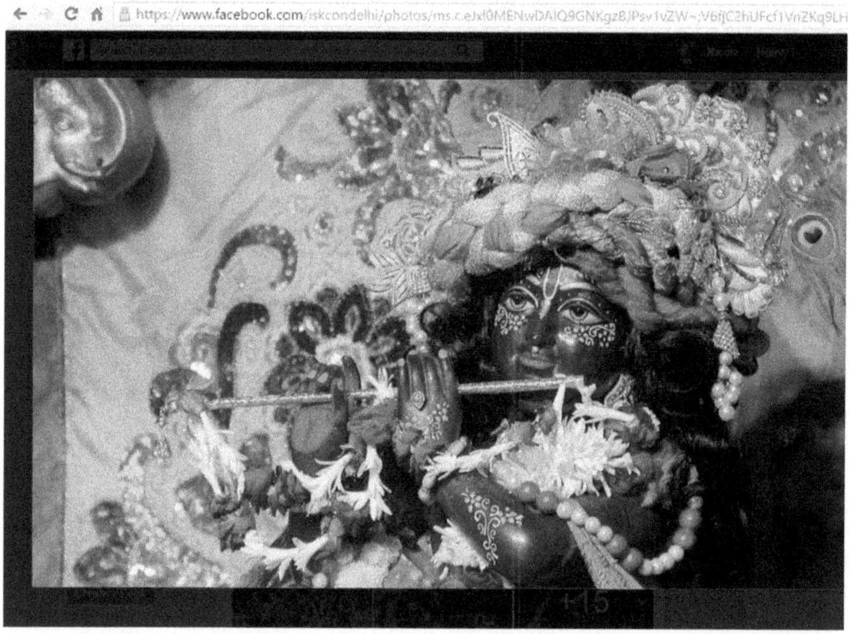

Figure 0.1 Sri Parthasarathiji. International Society for Krishna Consciousness (ISKCON) Delhi Facebook page. Screenshot by author.

Gazing at the Facebook image of Sri Parthasarathiji this morning, it seems to be more than just an image; rather, it is also a digital *bhakti* (devotion) event of a sort. Beneath the image is a sequence of 302 comments. The first of these comments reads, "श्री कृष्ण गोविंद हरे मुरारी, हे नाथ नारायण वासुदेवा, राधे कृष्णा-राधे कृष्णा, ॐ" (*Shri Krishna Govinda Hare Murari, He Nath Narayana Vasudeva, Radhe Krishna-Radhe Krishna Om*). This series of words is a veritable callout to Krishna through the use of his many names—Govinda, Murari, Narayana, Vasudeva, and so on—along with the name of his beloved divine consort, Radha. There are many other comments beneath the image just like this one. Most of these comments are vocative, devotional exhortations, calling out to Krishna and Radha by name: "Jai Shree Krishna," "Hare Krishna," "Radhe Krishna," and "Radhey Krishna to all."[1]

The Sri Sri Radha Parthasarathi Mandir, which is also known by the name of ISKCON of Delhi (or International Society for Krishna Consciousness of Delhi), posts many images of Sri Parthasarathiji on Facebook. They also post a great many images of him with Radha. Typically, these image posts receive roughly forty thousand "likes" each and also receive a great number of

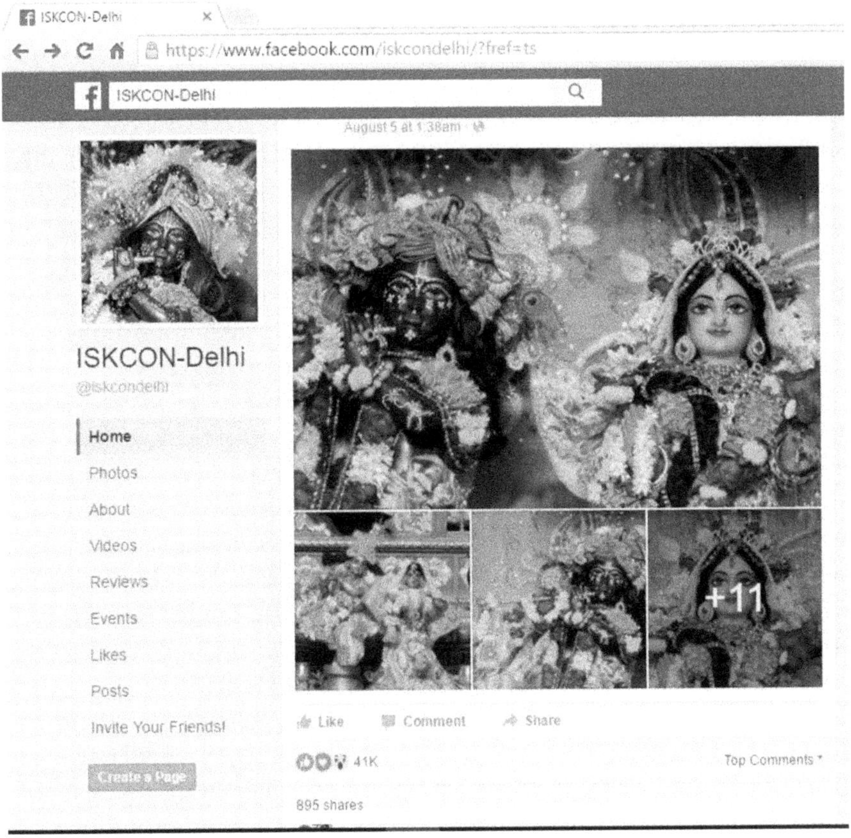

Figure 0.2 ISKCON Delhi Facebook page. Screenshot by author.

enthusiastic comments. Some of these comments are devotional calls to Krishna or to Radha (such as "Radhe Radhe!"), while others are emoji replies—hands raised in praise and hands bowed in "namaste," for example. Many of them are prayers or petitions, some even bearing the great pain or hardship of the poster. "मैं उदासी आज भी मेरे चेहरे से झलकती है, पर *ऐ श्याम सुंदर* तेरी कृपा से अब दर्द में भी मुस्कुराना सीख गया हूँ मैं" (*Maiṁ udāsī āj bhī mere cehare se jhalakatī hai, par *ai Shyam Sundar* terī kṛpā se ab dard meṁ bhī muskurānā sīkh gayā hūṁ maiṁ*), one user wrote.[2] This comment, translated to English, says that "even though today there are flashes of sadness on my face, by your grace, Oh, Shyam Sundar [a name of Krishna], I'm learning to smile through the pain."

Across India, in the bustling city of Mumbai, another ISKCON temple—ISKCON Juhu—also regularly posts images of Krishna that appear on my

Facebook feed as I sit at my desk in Wilmington, Delaware. Although the two temples share a geographical divide of about 1,200 kilometers, the digital forms of Krishna that they post often appear on my Facebook feed just a few scrolls apart. One such image that I see posted by ISKCON Juhu is a close-up image of Sri Rasabihariji, yet another form of Krishna and the central deity of the ISKCON Juhu temple.[3] This image is a high-resolution close-up of Sri Rasabihariji, and in it, he is gazing off into the distance and smiling in seeming delight. In his photo, Sri Rasabihariji stands garlanded in beautiful shades of red, yellow, green, and orange. He wears a shiny jeweled necklace, and there are flowers strung on and interwoven throughout his accessories, adding a striking contrast to the long, curly black locks that flow from beneath his crown.

Just like the images posted by ISKCON Delhi, this image has received a great number of "likes," "loves," and "wows"—200,000 of them, in fact. Further, it has been shared on Facebook by 6,685 people. Finally, just like the photo of Sri Parthasarathiji, the image of Sri Rasabihariji has numerous enthusiastic devotional comments (1,659 in total). These comments include vocative exclamations of Krishna's (and Radha's) various names, such as "Hare Ram" and "Jai Shree Radhe," as well as exhortations to others to also call out these names. "Dil se bolo hora Krishna. Radhey Gobind," one comment implores. Another reads: "Exclaim 'Krishna Radhey Govinda' from your heart."[4]

Posts like these, which feature up close digital *darshan* images of Krishna, dot my Facebook feed.[5] They are shared by ISKCON temples and individual devotees not only in Delhi and Mumbai but also in Vrindavan and Mayapur, India; Alachua and Towaco, United States; and London in the United Kingdom, to name just a few.[6] They even adorn the websites of many ISKCON temples and groups across the world, as well as their Instagram and other social media pages and platforms.[7]

Now, fast-forward to another world altogether, yet one that also nonetheless appears on my Facebook feed. This time I see a post of an entirely different order: a *Huffington Post* video of a young man named Jay Shetty. The title of the video is *Changing the World Starts with You,* and it identifies Jay Shetty as a "motivational philosopher." In the video, Shetty speaks to the camera from what appears to be an outdoor veranda of sorts.[8] Wearing a green T-shirt and a big smile, he has a spiked hairdo and a neck tattoo and is a mastermind behind the camera. At the writing of this book, Jay Shetty's video had already received over thirty-one million views on Facebook alone.[9]

The exact message of the video is hard to pin down, but it seems to be most focused on one main point, namely that although humanity has become advanced in so many ways, it has simultaneously become less advanced—even

Figure 0.3 Sri Rasabihariji. ISKCON Juhu Facebook page. Screenshot by author.

injured—in others. For example, Shetty mentions that although we have gone to the moon, have built big, elaborate, expensive homes, have created wide and extensive highway systems, and can connect with each other via numerous social media apps, mobile phones, and the internet, our connection with each other has decreased, our judgement has decreased, our depression and loneliness have increased, and our morals have declined. The video, in other words, shines light on a purported problem: the lack of meaning, reflection, happiness, and "real" connection characterized by life in the modern "western world."

Like so many of Shetty's other videos, this one is meant to be an encouragement—a veritable wake-up call—for people in the "modern west" to have a realization, to change the direction of their lives, and to begin to solve their problems. Shetty, however, doesn't give his viewers concrete solutions to these problems—a fact about which some of his viewers complain. He does, however,

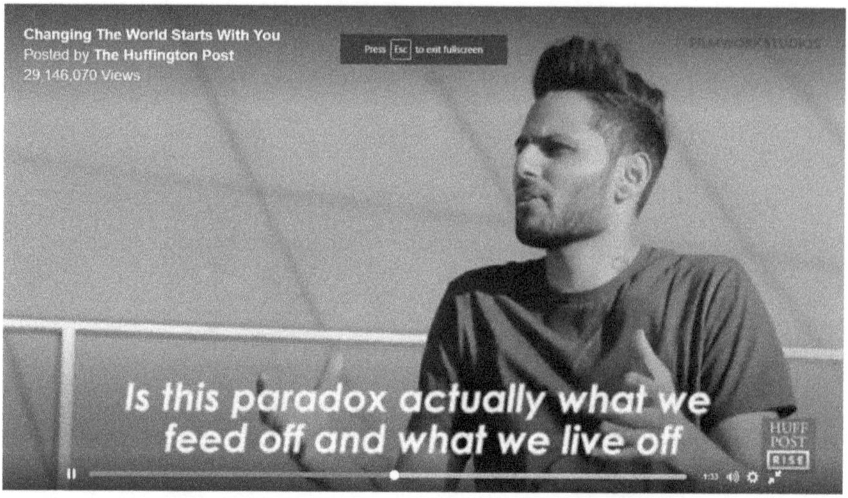

Figure 0.4 Jay Shetty in his *Changing the World Starts With You*. Screenshot by author.

implore them with a few general suggestions. Quoting Albert Einstein, for example, Shetty notes that "the problems we have today can't be solved with the same thinking we used when we once created them." Instead, he claims, "we need to research alternative teachings. We need to deep down dig into those ancient books of wisdom. We need to go back to understanding if there's anything written in those creased pages of time that can reveal more knowledge and more wisdom of how we can transform our experience of life today, otherwise this paradox means that every step forward we take means that we're taking three backwards every time."[10]

Beyond the suggestion to dig deep into ancient texts—and interestingly, Shetty does not mention which ones—he gives another set of suggestions for the viewers, instructions that he combines with images of people meditating and doing yoga. These suggestions include that the viewers take time to "pause and reflect," to become "more aware," to cultivate "a different perspective," and to develop more "empathy." And, for the most part, his viewers seem to love his advice, with one viewer even commenting that Shetty is "arguably the most articulate human being the world has seen."[11]

Like the posts of Jay Shetty, also available on Facebook are the posts, articles, and program advertisements of Gadadhara Pandit Das (or just Pandit Dasa or Pandit, as he is known). Pandit is a savvy "reflectively minded" motivational speaker in New York City. Like Shetty, Pandit shares media—pictures, articles, and videos—to his various digital media sites, urging the reader/viewer toward greater reflection, mindfulness, and well-being in life. Pandit's media tend to

Figure 0.5 Jay Shetty's *Changing the World Starts With You*. Screenshot by author.

Figure 0.6 Jay Shetty's *Changing the World Starts With You*. Screenshot by author.

be about the importance of balance, including work-life balance, the balance of food (for him, eating vegetarian food), and the balance achieved by meditation. And like Shetty, Pandit has earned a great deal of repute for himself, having been invited to speak at Chase, Intel, Google, Bank of America, and even TEDx. Pandit is a talented orator who seems to captivate audiences wherever he goes. He is also a sought-after columnist, writing regularly for the *Huffington Post*, with occasional pieces for NPR and the *New York Times*, as well.

Figure 0.7 Jay Shetty's *Changing the World Starts With You*. Screenshot by author.

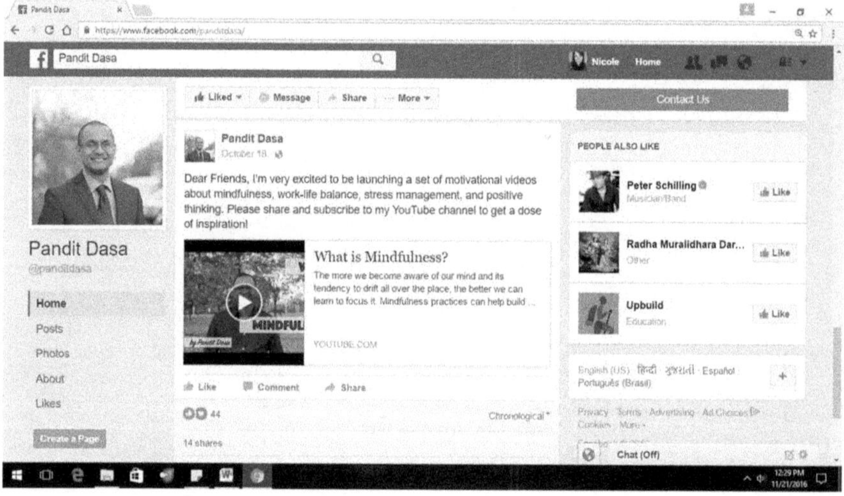

Figure 0.8 Public Facebook page of Pandit Dasa. Screenshot by author.[12]

The digital media shared by Jay Shetty and Gadadhara Pandit Das differ dramatically from the media featuring close-up, digital *darshan* images of Krishna in his *mūrti* (embodied) forms. But there is one important feature that all of these media share in common: they are all media created and spread with the aim and hope of drawing people to the International Society for Krishna Consciousness (ISKCON), or the Hare Krishna movement, as it

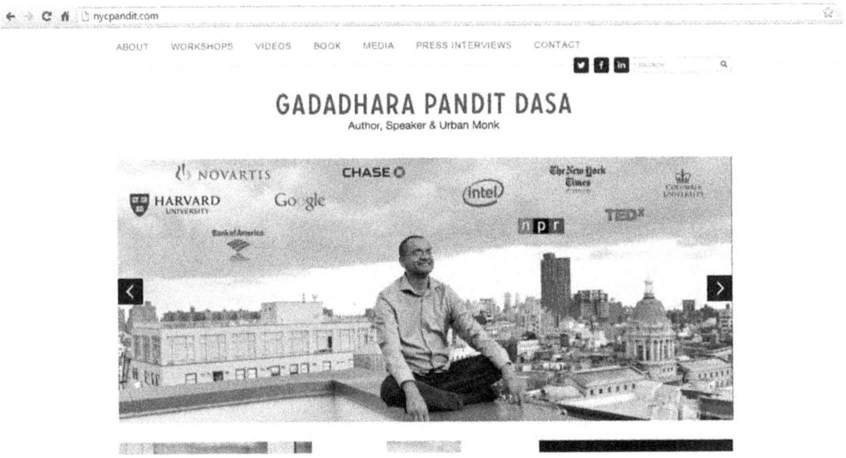

Figure 0.9 Pandit Dasa's first website, "NYC Pandit." Screenshot by author.[13]

is more colloquially known. That is, although you would never know it from their videos and media posts and although it seems that their viewers and followers are also unaware of it, Shetty and Pandit are fully committed ISKCON preachers. Jay Shetty, who is also known by the devotional name Ganashyam Priya Das, is based out of ISKCON's Bhaktivedanta Manor in London, where he lived as a *brahmacārī* (celibate monk) until at least 2012. Gadadhara Pandit Dasa, too, lived as a *brahmacārī* in ISKCON for upwards of fifteen years.[14] And although he is no longer a *brahmacārī*, Pandit continued to reside full-time in an ISKCON-affiliated center in New York until his recent marriage, and he still worships and preaches there. Just like devotees at ISKCON of Delhi, Juhu, New Jersey, etc., who routinely share *darshan* images of Krishna, Shetty and Pandit are trying to attract people to ISKCON through the various digital images and image posts that they share—image posts featuring yoga, mindfulness, and meditation for work-life balance.

But if both Shetty and Pandit are active and devoted members of ISKCON whose videos are posted with the aim of ultimately drawing people toward Krishna and the Hare Krishna movement, why do their media look so dramatically different from those posted by so many other ISKCON devotees with similar aims? Why is it that while ISKCON media traditionally make use of images and temple scenes of Krishna's embodied forms, his playful mythological engagements (*līlā*), and his associations with Radha and his childhood cowherd friends, the media posted by Shetty and Pandit showcase images of people meditating, doing yoga, and/or otherwise sitting in corporate settings "mindfully" listening to lectures? Why does it look like Shetty and Pandit are promoting a mix of American Buddhism and postural yoga, rather than theistic devotion (*bhakti*) to Krishna?

As a devotee in London, Shetty is a part of an ISKCON team known as Urban Monk, a group whose primary role is "attractively repackaging Krishna consciousness for the 'Apple generation.'"[15] According to an article written about him and his Urban Monk team, Jay Shetty "emerg[ed] from Cass Business School with a first class degree in Management Science [and] turned down lucrative job offers in London to move into Bhaktivedanta Manor's ashram full-time."[16] Soon after doing so, "he teamed up with five other young devotees . . . [and] the team has been working together on relevant, accessible and innovative preaching for the past two years."[17] This "innovative preaching" aims to reach audiences from "academic and corporate backgrounds" by creating a "cutting edge visual identity"—that is, by making Krishna Consciousness seem widely appealing, "rather than something that's only practiced by some strange, unique breed of people."[18] And as discussed previously, reach audiences far and wide, it does: with Shetty at the helm, Urban Monk has been able to get wide attention on social media through videos, livestreams, and articles on *Huffington Post*. And just like Pandit—who also refers to himself as an *urban monk* (having penned a book by that same name)—Jay Shetty presents this "attractively packaged Krishna Consciousness" to wide audiences.[19] He conducts his "innovative preaching" not only at universities but also at corporations such as JP Morgan, Ernst & Young, Bank of America, Deutsche Bank, and British Sky Broadcasting Group.[20]

This is a book about ISKCON's new innovative preaching. Going well beyond just the media and preaching enterprises of Jay Shetty and Gadadhara Pandit Dasa, I aim to show that the work of devotees like them is just the tip of a very large iceberg within the ISKCON movement: a small reflection, that is, of a large and growing effort that is revolutionizing the way ISKCON is branded for the public. Known traditionally for their orange robes, shaved heads, ecstatic dancing on the streets, and exuberant Hindu-style temple worship, many contemporary ISKCON groups are radically rebranding their public presentation and reconfiguring their style of worship in order to change the public face of their movement. The aim of this book is to explore with the reader this radical reconfiguring of ISKCON—including its roots and its many manifestations—within both the United States and India.

Throughout this book, I trace the seeds of ISKCON's new rebranding efforts to historical events that surrounded the movement beginning in the 1980s—events during which the devotional base of ISKCON shifted from one of mostly non-Indian converts to one primarily comprised of Indian Hindus (the so-called "Hinduization" of ISKCON).[21] I show that ISKCON's rebranding and reinvention efforts are a direct response to these historical events, and I argue that through these efforts, ISKCON devotees are attempting to attract "westerners" (whom they define as non-Indian converts) to their movement by branding it as mindfulness, yoga, and meditation. This book is an ethnographic study of the innovative and complex ways in which they are doing so: primarily through the construction and promotion of a completely reenvisioned and redesigned ISKCON worship-scape. This new worship-scape is radically different from ISKCON's traditional one of temples, theistic ritual worship of embodied forms (*mūrtis*) of Krishna, dancing, and boisterous singing-parades. Instead, it is one centered in mindfulness institutes, posh yoga studios, corporate work-life balance programs, urban spiritual "lounges," edgy mantra clubs/lofts, and rural meditative retreat facilities. These new centers and programs are ushering in great diversity to the contemporary landscape of the global ISKCON movement, making it much more heterogeneous than in decades past. And taken together, they reflect the multiple, shifting, and conflicting ways in which the ISKCON movement is positioning itself for growth in the global religious marketplace.

THE STORY OF ISKCON

As a tradition, ISKCON is perhaps best known as the Hare Krishna movement: the religious group whose saffron-robe-clad followers can be seen dancing joyfully in the streets while ecstatically singing the names of the Hindu god Krishna. As scholars such as Ferdinando Sardella, Thomas J. Hopkins, Jason Dale Fuller, Sukanya Sarbadhikary, Shukavak N. Dasa, Kenneth Russell Valpey, Varuni Bhatia, and many others have detailed, the ISKCON movement has its origins in Bengal Vaishnavism, or those Krishna-worshipping traditions that evolved around the sixteenth-century charismatic saint Chaitanya in what is now West Bengal, India.[22]

Although the ISKCON movement originated in India,[23] it wasn't until it arrived in the United States that it burgeoned into the worldwide movement that it is today. As the story goes, in 1965, Abhay Charan De (1896–1977) left his home in India at the behest of his guru, Bhaktisiddhanta Sarasvati (1874–1937), and boarded a freight ship to the United States in hopes of starting a worldwide devotional movement. The journey to the United States was arduous for the sixty-nine-year-old Abhay Charan De (or A. C. Bhaktivedanta Swami Prabhupada, as he is better known). In fact, legend has it that he suffered two heart attacks en route. But his commitment to his cause was so great that he carried on his journey nonetheless—anxious but faithful—until he reached the shores of the new land that was to become the home base for his "western preaching." In so doing, he saw himself to be fulfilling not only the request of his guru but also the wishes (and predictions of) Chaitanya himself, whom he believed had foreseen the spread of Krishna *bhakti* to the western world.

Arriving in New York City in 1965, alone and near penniless, Swami Prabhupada is said to have sat down in Tompkins Square Park chanting the names of Krishna; one by one, he began to draw curious and interested people to himself. Beginning in this way, during his time in the United States, Swami Prabhupada was able to draw American youth to the ISKCON movement in droves.[24] Throughout his days in the United States, Prabhupada (as he is affectionately known) preached a movement of unremitting devotion to Krishna, tempered by a communal lifestyle and a rigorous program of chanting and asceticism. As his initial disciples narrate the story, American youth were attracted to ISKCON not only because of the charisma and religious devotion of Prabhupada himself but also because of ISKCON's philosophy of high thinking and simple living, its communal lifestyle, and its exuberant worship programs. These worship programs included temple residential setups whereby devotees would engage in the daily worship of embodied forms (*mūrtis*) of Krishna according to strict Vaishnava *puja* standards. Devotees also spent their days chanting and singing Krishna's names (in the form of the famous Hare Krishna *mahā mantra*), reading Prabhupada's translations of key Vaishnava texts (such as the *Bhagavad-Gītā* and *Bhāgavata Purāṇa*), and associating with Prabhupada and each other over devotional conversations and sanctified meals (*prasādam*).

TROUBLED TIMES AND THE SHIFT TO "HINDUIZATION"

Although Bhaktivedanta's ISKCON movement has enjoyed global success and was initially successful in the United States, the movement faced a series of problems (especially in the United States and Western Europe) starting in the 1980s. These problems are myriad and have been discussed at length by noted scholars of ISKCON.[25] They will also be discussed in detail in chapter 1 of this book. For now, suffice it to say that by most accounts, these hard times had largely to do with two interrelated factors. The first factor was financial. During the 1980s, the ISKCON movement was litigated with several major lawsuits and cult accusations.[26] These lawsuits were brought against devotees by the anti-cult movement, as well as by some parents and families of devotees who alleged that their relatives had been mistreated (some grossly) within the movement. The settlement of these suits—many of which did not resolve in favor of ISKCON devotees—left the movement in a serious financial pinch. This pinch was exacerbated by a number of other factors, including legislation in the United States that obstructed devotees' revenue channels by prohibiting them from selling books in public places (such as airports).

The repercussions of these lawsuits and legislation changes were not merely financial, however. Almost as damaging (if not more so) than the financial woes they caused were the public relations nightmares that they initiated. Having been associated in the media with the negativity involved in these lawsuits and their concomitant accusations of "brainwashing," child abuse, public nuisance, and even murder, ISKCON devotees in the 1980s and 1990s had a serious image problem on their hands. Many Americans feared the ISKCON movement, and ISKCON devotees lacked the financial means (as well as the strength) to continue reaching out to them on the scale that was necessary to change their public image.

Faced with the need for both money and legitimacy in the eyes of the public, ISKCON devotees found themselves in a tremendous bind. And in this time of immense need, devotees made the decision to reach out to the Indian Hindu diaspora community for their assistance.[27] This decision was a complex one—as we will see throughout this book—but was based on the belief that the Indian community could provide ISKCON with exactly what it needed: money and cultural capital. It was also a decision that, over time, would come to dramatically alter the sociological makeup of the ISKCON movement. This is because as the Indian Hindu community continued to increase their financial support of ISKCON, they also naturally began to petition for increased roles at ISKCON's administrative tables, as well as an increased say in the management of the movement and its programs.[28] Moreover, they also began to attend ISKCON's programs in increasing numbers and to bring their families, friends, and peer groups to ISKCON's weekly worship events and calendrical festivals. Fast-forward twenty-five years, and the ISKCON movement today (not only in the United States but also around the world) is largely, if not almost exclusively, comprised of Indian Hindu members. This demographic shift—coupled with the religious and sociological changes it is believed to have ushered into the movement—has been dubbed the "Hinduization of ISKCON."[29] It has been discussed most notably in the works of E. Burke Rochford Jr. but also in its various forms by scholars such as Nurit Zaidman, Travis Vande Berg, Fred Kniss, and others.[30] Moreover, as we shall see, it is a shift in the movement that is frequently discussed in ISKCON internal sources (such as the *Sampradaya Sun*, *Jagannatha's Chakra*, and *ISKCON News*) and is described therein as a matter with which contemporary devotees struggle greatly.[31]

APPROACH AND ORGANIZATION

This book chronicles devotees' complicated struggles and fears as they attempt to come to terms with what they see to be the dramatic changes in their movement arising from this "Hinduization." In one regard, this book is backward-looking, and in it I examine in detail the "Hinduization" of ISKCON (chap. 1). More than just providing a descriptive account of this sociological shift, however, I examine the impact that it has had on the movement, especially in terms of devotees' fears and concerns about ISKCON's future. These fears, I argue, are based in a theology (which devotees trace from Prabhupada all the way back to Chaitanya) that a successful ISKCON movement is necessarily a universal one—that is, one that has a globally representative constituency (chap. 2). Put simply, present-day ISKCON devotees believe that their movement has failed because it is only successful among people from one region of the world, when they believe Prabhupada's dream was to create a movement with a global, multinational, multiracial, and multiethnic constituency.

Following chapters 1 and 2, the remainder of the book looks forward to the future and examines the ways in which contemporary ISKCON devotees are endeavoring to transform their now largely demographically homogenous movement into one that has a universal religious appeal and global constituency. Toward this end, this book addresses two broad, yet interrelated questions: How do religious groups reinvent themselves in order to attract new audiences? And more specifically, how do they reinvent their messages and recast their rituals in order to diversify their congregations and make them more multinational, multiracial, and multiethnic? In the ISKCON case, the key to making their movement more diverse is the successful attraction of people whom devotees refer to as "westerners," or non-Indian converts; and devotees go to tremendous—often radical—lengths to attract them. ISKCON devotees use the term *westerner* to refer to anyone who is not of Indian descent, including individuals of East Asian heritage, such as those from Japan, China, and Korea. Clearly this term betrays an overly simplistic and troubling categorization of people. I will historically contextualize and problematize the use of this term in chapter 2.

Although there are many ways in which one could approach the book's central questions, I approach them both ethnographically and through the theoretical lens of marketing. This book is an ethnographic investigation of the ways in which ISKCON devotees are engaging in innovative and complex marketing strategies so as to most effectively pitch their movement to westerners. Put differently, this is a book about religious storytelling; it is a book about the stories devotees tell about ISKCON so that they can not only attract westerners but also remake the movement's public image so that it resonates with what they perceive to be westerners' religious desires and existential wants and needs.[32] As I showcase throughout this book, these religious self-stories are not just told through words but are also told through images; they are not just told in temples or meditation centers but are also told across a variety of print, digital, and social media. The stories I trace, in other words, are what I refer to as ISKCON religious brands, and the storytellers I study are the ISKCON practitioners whom I call the *Krishna Branders*: those ISKCON gurus, devotees, and initiates who are rebranding the ISKCON movement as mindfulness, yoga, and meditation in order to attract more westerners. These Krishna Branders are a diverse group of devotees (many of whom are of Indian heritage themselves), and they include ISKCON gurus who are direct disciples of Prabhupada as well as these gurus' own worldwide disciples and students.[33]

In recent years, scholars have paid increased attention to the intersection of religion and marketing—or the various ways in which, and reasons for which, religious groups market themselves, their messages, and their practices for the public. These studies usually begin with discussions of "competition," arguing that if religious groups want to compete for the attention of potential followers, then they "must present [themselves] as a valuable commodity, [as a set of] activit[ies] that is worthwhile in an era of over-crowded schedules."[34] They must compete, in other words, for both our time and our attention against everything else in our over-packed lives, including work, school, chores, friends, family, and pursuits of hobby.

But more than just competing with our work, chores, and family time, religious groups must also compete with each other for our attention, time, and commitment. As scholars have noted, with the turn to globalization and with access to information being so readily available at people's fingertips, would-be religious practitioners now have more access to information about religion than ever before. As Lorne L. Dawson and Douglas E. Cowan have argued, this is especially the case since the rise of the internet. In fact, scholars have noted that as of 2004, 25 percent of American people had used the internet to gather information about religion[35] and more than three million people in the United States get religious information online *each day*.[36] This easy availability of religious information, coupled with a relative freedom to choose one's religion, to switch religions, or to shop for religions,[37] has led to increased competition between religious groups in the religious marketplace.[38] As Mara Einstein argues, "As people are increasingly prone to shop, religions will not only have to increase the level of marketing and promotion in order to be heard among so many competing forces, but they will also be increasingly prone to create a product that religious consumers will buy."[39] And those products, which Einstein argues are different *brands of faith,* are different packages that religious groups and institutions put together—marketable image products, if you will—to distribute their products most effectively.

With increased attention to the notions of competition, promotion, and branding, scholars of religion and marketing have highlighted the fact that the success of religious groups does not lie alone in their doctrine or in the experiences they afford to their practitioners. Rather, it also relies on "their sales representatives" and "their marketing techniques"—that is, on their ability to successfully pitch their messages into packages that people are captured by and attracted to.[40] Shayne Lee and Phillip Luke Sinitiere make a strong case for this point in their book, *Holy Mavericks: Evangelical Innovators and the Spiritual Marketplace.* Studying the "supply-side of religious vitality," Lee and Sinitiere argue that "religious suppliers thrive in a competitive spiritual marketplace [when] they are quick, decisive, and flexible in reacting to changing conditions, savvy at packaging and marketing their ministries, and resourceful at offering spiritual rewards that resonate with the existential needs and cultural tastes of the public."[41] In other words, Lee and Sinitiere argue that savvy, customer-focused marketing is essential for growth and competitive advantage in a religious economy. And they give the name "holy mavericks" to those religious suppliers (preachers, pastors, ministers, etc.) who do it especially well.

Situated in theories of religion and marketing such as these, chapters 3, 4, and 5 of this book take the reader through three new ISKCON brands, each of which is a distinct attempt within the movement to build and promote a set of programs and centers that will attract westerners. Each of these brands is administered by a globally prominent ISKCON guru and his worldwide disciples, and each is promoted through a mix of digital and social media, as well as new and innovative outreach and worship spaces on the ground. Chapter 3 examines the centers and promotional activities of the ISKCON guru Devamrita Swami and his global disciples. Since 1994, Devamrita Swami and his disciples have been constructing new ISKCON worship spaces all over the world that explicitly cater to the tastes of westerners. These new spaces completely turn away from traditional ISKCON temples and instead consist of meditation "lofts" and mantra "lounges" located in urban centers of places such as Wellington, New Zealand; Toronto, Canada; and Philadelphia, Pennsylvania. Through the construction and promotion of these new lofts and lounges, I argue, Devamrita Swami and his disciples are branding ISKCON as an edgy meditation- and mindfulness-based social club: one that provides visitors and regulars alike a space in which to practice a variety of meditation forms and gather for broad-based philosophical discussion and healthy vegetarian meals in a fellowship environment.

Chapter 4 examines the enterprises, multimedia branding campaigns, and programs of the hugely popular ISKCON guru Radhanath Swami and his worldwide disciples. In particular, it examines Radhanath Swami's rustic Govardhan Eco Village in rural Maharashtra, India, his upscale Bhakti Center in downtown Manhattan, and the work of his many disciples in Chowpatty, Mumbai, and Washington, DC. Through an examination of these centers and the myriad retreats and programs that they advertise and support, I argue that Radhanath Swami and his disciples are reaching out to westerners by branding ISKCON as the theological heart of postural yoga. As I will show, this is a complex and widespread brand, and is one that Radhanath Swami promotes and maintains through a fascinating interplay of the conceptual and the material: by developing intricate theologies of *bhakti* (devotion) as interpreted through Patañjali's *Yoga Sūtras* (what I call the conceptual arm of the brand) and by building and administering a number of ISKCON temples that are housed inside yoga studios and yoga retreat centers (what I call the material arm of the brand). Through this two-armed brand, Radhanath Swami and his disciples are able to bring in a wide variety of western yoga teachers and yoga enthusiasts to their events, retreats, and yoga-teacher training programs.

Chapter 5 examines the newest brand of ISKCON—the ISKCON submovement called Krishna West. Started by ISKCON guru Hridayananda Das Goswami, Krishna West is an ISKCON brand that aims to attract more westerners to ISKCON by creating a "western Hare Krishna movement"—that is, one that is completely stripped of all traces of "Indian culture." For advocates of Krishna West, including Hridayananda Das Goswami and his disciples, this removal of "Indian culture" entails not just changing the way the movement is digitally branded or the centers it constructs to attract newcomers. Rather, it also involves changing the clothing that devotees wear (from traditional Hindu devotional dress to jeans and Oxford shirts), the food they eat and serve to others (from Indian-inspired vegetarian dishes to pizza), and the musical instruments they use in praise of Krishna (from harmoniums and *mṛdaṅga* drums to guitars and pianos).[42] It also involves paring Krishna West centers down to what they (Hridayananda Das Goswami and Krishna West advocates) see to be the essence of the ISKCON movement: the chanting, the philosophy, and the sanctified food.

An important set of questions that runs throughout these chapters concerns the relationship between the new brands of ISKCON—the meditation clubs, yoga programs, and Krishna West centers that aim to attract westerners—and the traditional temples and communities that have historically characterized the ISKCON movement. How do devotees bridge the gap between these new brands and the movement's traditional worship spaces? That is, how do devotees transition the westerners from the yoga and meditation centers to the traditional temple communities that characterize the majority of the ISKCON landscape? How do they entice the westerners who come to practice yoga and meditation to participate in the Vaishnava temple practices of deity *darshan* and *puja*?[43]

These questions are complicated ones and, as we shall see, are addressed differently by the different groups of Krishna Branders that I discuss in this book. Devamrita Swami accomplishes this transition by creating lofts and lounges that are intentionally designed to obscure their ties to ISKCON so that they can be religiously and socially comfortable spaces for westerners. And it is precisely through these religiously and socially comfortable environments that he and his disciples gradually introduce traditional ISKCON to the western newcomers whom they believe would never be sold on it otherwise. Radhanath Swami, on the other hand, accomplishes the transition from yoga to devotional Vaishnavism through in-depth theological instruction: convincing the yogis at his programs that the true heart of postural yoga is devotion to Krishna. Finally, proponents of Krishna West take an entirely different approach, arguing that efforts like those of Devamrita Swami and Radhanath Swami do not work. This is because, Krishna West proponents claim, westerners are not interested in participating in, or worshipping at, ISKCON temples. Instead, Krishna West advocates argue that if ISKCON wants to not just attract but also reliably *retain* westerners, then the movement must be completely reinvented: ISKCON must create a set of spaces and centers where westerners will want to stay and participate for the long haul.

As I discuss throughout this book, the questions of whether and how ISKCON's new brands connect to the traditional movement showcase not only the different ways that Krishna Branders groups understand and enact religious marketing but also the various ways in which they visualize what is possible for a congregationally diverse ISKCON. This book includes a sustained examination of these questions.

GATHERING PIECES FOR THE NARRATIVE: REFLECTIONS ON METHOD

My methodological approach in this book is a multimodal and multi-sited ethnography. According to George E. Marcus, multi-sited ethnography is a methodology that "moves out from the single sites and locations of conventional ethnographic research designs... [and] defines for itself an object of study that cannot be accounted for ethnographically by remaining focused on a single site of intensive investigation."[44] As Marcus notes, this multi-sited research is designed around the establishment of connections between locations that the ethnographer herself draws in presenting her argument to the readers.[45]

Marcus argues that there are several ways in which an ethnographer might establish the critical connection between the sites that hold her ethnography (and her argument) together. For example, she might "follow and stay with the movements of a particular group of initial subjects" across a variety of locations (what Marcus calls "following the people").[46] This is the approach taken by Amanda J. Lucia in her groundbreaking *Reflections of Amma*.[47] Alternatively, an ethnographer might "follow the thing" by tracing a material object across spaces and contexts. Finally, she might "follow the metaphor"—a mode of ethnography in which "the thing traced is within the realm of discourse and modes of thought, [and] the circulation of signs, symbols, and metaphors guides the design of the ethnography."[48]

In conducting the ethnographic research for this book, I followed both the metaphor and the people.[49] In particular, my approach was to follow the three different ISKCON brands and to trace them across the various locations in which they were both created and spread. I began this tracing online, and I conducted netnographic research on a variety of ISKCON digital sites, including a number of social media pages; temple, center, and devotee websites; new media apps; and online platforms created to host live-feed and web brand services. At its most basic level, this netnographic research involved content analyses of these various sites. But as digital ethnographers such as Christine Hine and others have aptly pointed out,[50] well-conducted netnography is never just a study of that which appears online; rather, netnographic "researchers need to consider participants' local off-line environments, as well as . . . how participants blend their on-line and off-line lives and social contexts both sequentially and simultaneously with their on-line participation."[51] In other words, the posts, sites, platforms, and comments that we see online do not exist in a vacuum, nor are they separable from the offline people who put and arrange them there. Therefore, in my research for this book, my examinations of the ISKCON brands online were supported by in-person ethnographic fieldwork (2014–2018) that I conducted with the devotees in the United States and India who create and manage these brands. In this vein, I met with the devotees in charge of crafting and maintaining many of the digital and social media pages and apps that I discuss in this book. I also spent time with them in their offices and control rooms to get a behind-the-scenes look at the methods of their work, as well as their marketing motivations.[52] In this sense, then, following the metaphor and following the people were not distinct inquiries. This is because it is the people themselves who create, maintain, and spread the metaphor (here, the online brands).

The new ISKCON brands that I examine in this book are not only online, however. Instead, the Krishna Branders are also largely rebranding the movement on the ground through the construction of physical centers that are both extensions of, and supports to, the online brands they design. Therefore, just as I studied the ISKCON brands online in connection to the people who created them, I also studied the new ISKCON brands' physical spaces and offline branding enterprises along with the people constructing and managing them on the ground. In this capacity, I engaged in extensive participant observation at a number of ISKCON-affiliated yoga and meditation centers, programs, "lounges," and events in India and the Northeastern United States (2014–2018). These centers included the Bhakti Center of New York City, the Mantra Lounge in Philadelphia, Bhakti Yoga DC, and the rural Maharashtrian Govardhan Eco Village, just a few hours outside of Mumbai. During my visits to these centers (and their sponsored programs and events), I both witnessed and participated in a great many yoga, mindfulness, and meditation classes, as well as courses and programs on vision boarding, stress management, and even playing the guitar. I also attended a number of group dinners, get-togethers, and public presentations, along with several events held at college campuses. In addition, I attended a several-day-long yoga retreat in the rustic woods of Lanexa, Virginia, jointly hosted by ISKCON DC and Bhakti Yoga DC.

It is important to note, however, that following the people in this project meant more than just ethnographically engaging with them in the locations in which they administer and promote the new ISKCON brands. To really "follow the people," the researcher must aim to understand those she studies, not just in the capacity to which their work relates to her research questions but also in the contexts and locations that support them as fully embedded social actors. Therefore, in addition to the fieldwork I conducted at the newly branded ISKCON spaces, yoga centers, etc., in my study of the Krishna Branders, I also conducted much fieldwork at traditional ISKCON temples. Although the Krishna Branders are engaged in creating and administering new ISKCON brands for the sake of recruiting westerners to the movement, they are also fully committed members of (and often residents in) traditional ISKCON temple communities. Therefore, understanding the work that they do—as well as the circumstances of and motivations for it—meant understanding them in their roles as devotees at ISKCON temples.

For this book, I conducted participant observation fieldwork at a number of traditional ISKCON temples in India and the United States (as I will discuss in detail in the chapters to follow). Primary among them were ISKCON of Juhu, Chowpatty, Mayapur, Vrindavan, and Delhi, in India, and ISKCON of DC, Philadelphia, and New Jersey, in the United States. The length of my fieldwork at each of these temples varied from a few weeks at one time to once a week (or once every few weeks) over a several-year period (2014–2018). At these temples, I was a participant observer in programs ranging from morning *āratīs* and *Bhāgavata Purāṇa* classes to evening and weekend services, feasts, and festivals. Moreover, during my visits I freely gave of my time to assist devotees in various volunteer tasks. For example, I helped devotees make garlands for the deities, helped sell sarees and Vaishnava trinkets at temple gift shops, assisted in setting up for festivals, and even gave family tours of a manufactured "Vrindavan village" that I myself helped to construct and design. These volunteering opportunities allowed me to get to know devotees intimately; they also helped me give something back to the communities who had so graciously hosted me in my work.

Equally important, it bears mentioning that in ethnographically "following the people," I often interacted with devotees outside of the formal edifices of ISKCON temples, centers, and sponsored programs. Throughout my research, I was warmly welcomed into a number of spaces and activities beyond official ISKCON sites and events. These included intimate programs at devotees' homes, social get-togethers, and even late-evening conversations around campfires. This unexpected and up close association with devotees (Krishna Branders and otherwise) allowed me to see dimensions of the movement and devotees' lives within it that I would have been otherwise unable to see. It also allowed me to understand devotees' hopes for ISKCON's future, as well as their concerns about its present, in a very intimate way. It is my hope that I am able to translate some of this interior world for the reader in the pages of this book. Finally, my methodology also involved many structured interviews with leading branders in the global ISKCON movement, including those gurus whose brands of ISKCON I discuss at length in chapters 3, 4, and 5: Devamrita Swami, Radhanath Swami, and Hridayananda Das Goswami, respectively. These interviews ranged in length from three hours to thirty minutes, and many were conducted over multiple sittings. I also conducted formal interviews with the disciples and associates who help make their brands possible. The majority of these interviews were conducted in person, although some were also conducted via Skype, email, telephone, or WhatsApp. Most conversations and interviews in this book were audio recorded (with permission of the interviewee); for those conversations that were not recorded, I relied on copious notes that I took during conversations.

Finally, in addition to that discussed above, my ethnography included two more formal dimensions that are worth mentioning. First, my methods included interpretive use of a great many digitally recorded ISKCON sources, including many hours of video-recorded ISKCON lectures and numerous ISKCON audio recordings and podcasts. The voices in these sources are interwoven throughout this book, along with the other ethnographic ones I discussed above. Second, my methodology made analytic use of both ISKCON and greater Vaishnava primary textual (print) sources in Sanskrit, Hindi, and English.[53] Like devotees' own narrative accounts, these textual sources are woven into the book's story to help shed light for the reader on the different positions and programs discussed herein.

What follows in this book is the composite result of all of the above research—a set of investigations that took me from Delaware to New York, from Washington, DC, to New Jersey, and all across North and Central India and back home again. Through its pages, I hope to introduce the reader to the various new brands and branders of ISKCON, along with the shifting interior worlds of the ISKCON movement that produce them. More than this, I hope to give the scholar of religion, as well as the curious reader, a new organizational schema with which to understand the ISKCON movement and its landscape in all of its contemporary heterogeneity and complexity—a schema that situates the recent growth of the movement's new and nontraditional centers and programs within the theoretical lenses of marketing. It is to this examination that I now turn, beginning first with a brief look at the historical circumstances that set the stage for ISKCON's new western-focused marketing.

NOTES

1. ISKCON Delhi Facebook page. *Darshan* album from February 8, 2016. Accessed August 7, 2016. https://www.facebook.com/iskcondelhi/?fref=ts. Throughout this book, I only cite Facebook (and other web and social media) pages that are public—that is, directly accessible to anyone who clicks to follow the page or searches the page on Google, Bing, or other search engines. As such, I have not made use as source data for this book any digital sources that are private (e.g., that are an individual's own personal pages), nor have I included material from digital or social media that are password protected, require friending to access, and so on. Moreover, although the sites I use are public and although scholars typically consider public social media sites, posts, and comments to be unrestricted public statements, I nonetheless try to anonymize the authors

of these public statements to the best of my ability throughout my book. This anonymization applies both to those whose statements are digital, as well as those devotees with whom I conducted other ethnographic fieldwork. I make exceptions to this anonymization only if the individual in question is a large-scale public personality.

2. ISKCON Delhi Facebook page.

3. Krishna is believed to take many different forms. Some of these forms are mythological, meaning that they are described in various Hindu religious texts, epics, stories, and the like, and are believed to have existed at some point in the mythological past. Others of these forms are material, meaning that they have tangible presences here in the world and are made of matter (stone, wood, paint, etc.). Krishna can also take digital forms. See Nicole Karapanagiotis. 2018. "Of Digital Images and Digital Media: Approaches to Marketing in American ISKCON." *Nova Religio: The Journal of Alternative and Emergent Religion* 21, no. 3: 74–102. See also Nicole Karapanagiotis. 2019. "Automatic Rituals and Inadvertent Audiences: ISKCON, Krishna and the Ritual Mechanics of Facebook." In *Digital Hinduism*. Xenia Zeiler, ed. New York: Routledge Press.

4. ISKCON Juhu Facebook page. *Darshan* post from July 9, 2016. Accessed August 8, 2016. https://www.facebook.com/iskconjuhu/?fref=ts. It is probable that the image got more total shares than this given number because the post likely got re-shared from some of its initial shares.

5. In her now classic work, *Darśan: Seeing the Divine Image in India,* Diana Eck defines *darshan* as "seeing and being seen" by the divine. Diana L. Eck. 1996. *Darśan: Seeing the Divine Image in India*. New York: Columbia University Press. If *darshan* is classically defined as seeing and being seen by the divine as mediated by (materially) embodied forms, then *digital darshan* can be defined as seeing and being seen by a god (or goddess) as mediated by digital forms and on the digital technologies and networks (e.g., the internet) that they utilize. As the newest form of *darshan,* digital *darshan* is hosted by both temple communities and individual devotees alike and includes digital forms of the divine that are posted and shared on and across temple websites, devotees' personal websites, and a variety of social media sites including Facebook, YouTube, and Instagram. Nicole Karapanagiotis. "Digital Diaspora of Viṣṇu: Vaiṣṇava Digital *Darśan(s)* and the Internet." Forthcoming in *Vaiṣṇavisms: Many Varieties of the Worship of Viṣṇu*. Archana Venkatesan and Gavin Flood, eds. Oxford: Oxford University Press. See also Nicole Karapanagiotis. 2013. "Cyber Forms, *Worshipable Forms*: Hindu Devotional Viewpoints on the Ontology of Cyber-Gods and Goddesses." *International Journal of Hindu Studies* 17, no. 1: 57–82; Phyllis K. Herman. 2010. "Seeing the Divine Through Windows: Online Puja and Virtual Religious Experience." *Online—Heidelberg Journal of Religions on the Internet* 4, no. 1: 151–178; Madhavi Mallapragada. 2010. "Desktop Deities: Hindu Temples, Online

Cultures and the Politics of Remediation." *South Asian Popular Culture* 8, no. 2: 109–121; Heinz Scheifinger. 2010. "Om-Line Hinduism: World Wide Gods on the Web." *Journal for the Academic Study of Religion* 23, no. 3: 325–345; and Heinz Scheifinger. 2009. "The *Jagannath* Temple and Online *Darshan*." *The Journal of Contemporary Religion* 24, no. 3: 277–290. See Karapanagiotis 2019 for a detailed discussion of Facebook posts of Krishna within the ISKCON movement.

6. Karapanagiotis 2019; Karapanagiotis 2018. ISKCON digital *darshan* pages on Facebook include (all accessed December 17, 2016): ISKCON Vrindavan Daily Darshan Facebook page. https://www.facebook.com/iskconvrindavandailydarshan/?fref=ts; ISKCON Vrindavan Facebook page. https://www.facebook.com/vrindavan.tv/; ISKCON Mayapur (Public Group) Facebook page. https://www.facebook.com/groups/167861299929466/; ISKCON Alachua Facebook page. https://www.facebook.com/alachuatemple/?fref=ts; ISKCON New Jersey Facebook page. https://www.facebook.com/iskconofnj/?fref=ts; and ISKCON London Facebook page. https://www.facebook.com/iskconlondon/?fref=ts. There are also a number of ISKCON Facebook pages/groups that are unaffiliated with particular temples but that nonetheless post frequent *darshan* images of Krishna across their social media and websites. For example, Darshan Deities Around the World has a Facebook page and a Tumblr. See https://www.facebook.com/darshanglobal/?fref=t and http://darshanglobal.tumblr.com/.

7. Karapanagiotis 2018.

8. *Changing the World Starts with You*. Video by Jay Shetty. *Huffington Post* Facebook page. Accessed August 9, 2016. https://www.facebook.com/HuffingtonPost/videos/10153699398631130/.

9. As of August 9, 2016.

10. Ibid.

11. Ibid.

12. This is Pandit's newly launched public Facebook page. Previously, Pandit was using his personal Facebook page for marketing purposes. Private pages not cited here.

13. Gadadhara Pandit Dasa. "NYC Pandit." Accessed October 2015. http://www.NycPandit.com. Page now redirects to Pandit's new site, "Conscious Living with Pandit Dasa." Accessed August 9, 2016. http://www.consciouslivingnyc.com/.

14. Personal communication by telephone with Gadadhara Pandit Dasa, June 17, 2015.

15. Madhava Smullen. 2016. "Urban Monks Present Spirituality for the Apple Generation." ISKCON News.Org, May 20. Accessed August 9, 2016. http://iskconnews.org/urban-monks-present-spirituality-for-the-apple-generation,3524/.

16. Ibid.
17. Ibid.
18. Ibid.
19. Gadadhara Pandit Dasa. 2013. *Urban Monk: Exploring Karma, Consciousness, and the Divine.* New York: Pankaj Srivastava (Gadadhara Pandit Dasa).
20. Smullen 2016.
21. E. Burke Rochford Jr. 2007. *Hare Krishna Transformed.* New York: New York University Press.
22. Ferdinando Sardella. 2013. *Modern Hindu Personalism: The History, Life, and Thought of Bhaktisiddhānta Saravatiī.* Oxford and New York: Oxford University Press; Thomas J. Hopkins. 1989. "The Social and Religious Background for Transmission of Gaudiya Vaishnavism to the West." In *Krishna Consciousness in the West.* David G. Bromley and Larry D. Shinn, eds. Lewisburg: Bucknell University Press and Associated University Presses; Jason Dale Fuller. 2005. *Religion, Class, and Power: Bhaktivinode Thakur and the Transformation of Religious Authority Among the Gauḍīya Vaiṣṇavas in Nineteenth-Century Bengal.* PhD Dissertation: University of Pennsylvania; Sukanya Sarbadhikary. 2015. *The Place of Devotion: Siting and Experiencing Divinity in Bengal-Vaishnavism.* Oakland: University of California Press; Shukavak N. Dasa. 1999. *Hindu Encounter with Modernity: Kedarnath Datta Bhaktivinoda Vaiṣṇava Theologian.* Los Angeles: Sanskrit Religions Institute; Kenneth Russell Valpey. 2006. *Attending Kṛṣṇa's Image: Caitanya Vaiṣṇava Mūrti-Sevā as Devotional Truth.* London and New York: Routledge; Varuni Bhatia. 2017. *Unforgetting Chaitanya: Vaishnavism and Cultures of Devotion in Colonial Bengal.* New Delhi: Oxford University Press. See also Federico Squarcini and Eugenio Fizzotti. 2004. *Hare Krishna.* Salt Lake City: Signature Books; Kim Knott. 1986. *My Sweet Lord: The Hare Krishna Movement.* Wellingborough: The Aquarian Press. Finally, several essays in Edwin F. Bryant and Maria L. Ekstrand's well-researched volume also highlight the history of the ISKCON movement. Edwin F. Bryant and Maria L. Ekstrand. 2004. *The Hare Krishna Movement: The Postcharismatic Fate of a Religious Transplant.* New York: Columbia University Press.
23. Of course, it was not known as India when the ISKCON movement originated.
24. Many books discuss the early years of the ISKCON movement as well as its official founding in the United States. These include Squarcini and Fizzotti 2004; E. Burke Rochford Jr. 1985. *Hare Krishna in America.* New Brunswick: Rutgers University Press; Knott 1986; Graham Dwyer and Richard J. Cole, eds. 2007. *The Hare Krishna Movement: Forty Years of Chant and Change.* London and New York: I.B. Tauris; and Bromley and Shinn 1989. For more recent examinations of the ISKCON movement in the United States, see Bryant and Ekstrand 2004 and Rochford 2007.

25. See, for example, Rochford 2007; Bryant and Ekstrand 2004; and David G. Bromley. 1989. "Hare Krishna and the Anti-Cult Movement." In *Krishna Consciousness in the West.* Bromley and Shinn, eds.

26. Rochford 1985, 2007; Bromley 1989.

27. Rochford 2007.

28. Ibid.

29. Ibid.

30. Nurit Zaidman. 1997. "When the Deities are Asleep: Processes of Change in an American Hare Krishna Temple." *Journal of Contemporary Religion* 12, no. 3: 335–352; Nurit Zaidman. 2000. "The Integration of Indian Immigrants to Temples Run by North Americans." *Social Compass* 47, no. 2: 205–219; and Travis Vande Berg and Fred Kniss. 2008. "ISKCON and Immigrants: The Rise, Decline, and Rise Again of a New Religious Movement." *The Sociological Quarterly* 49: 79–104.

31. *Sampradaya Sun.* Accessed June 5, 2016. http://www.harekrsna.com/sun/. *Jagannatha's Chakra.* Accessed June 5, 2016. http://www.chakra.org/. Access date 6/5/2016; *ISKCON News.* Accessed June 5, 2016. http://iskconnews.org/.

32. Shayne Lee and Phillip Luke Sinitiere give the term *holy mavericks* to religious marketers whose success is based in their catering to the existential tastes of their would-be followers. Shayne Lee and Phillip Luke Sinitiere. 2009. *Holy Mavericks: Evangelical Innovators and the Spiritual Marketplace.* New York and London: New York University Press.

33. *Krishna Consciousness Branders* might be a more apt term to describe the Krishna Branders, since it is Krishna Consciousness or ISKCON itself (and not Krishna) that they are rebranding. However, for the sake of ease on the reader, I have chosen the shorter *Krishna Branders* neologism.

34. Mara Einstein. 2008. *Brands of Faith: Marketing Religion in a Commercial Age.* New York: Routledge.

35. Lorne L. Dawson and Douglas E. Cowan. 2004. "Introduction." In *Religion Online: Finding Faith on the Internet.* Lorne L. Dawson and Douglas E. Cowan, eds. New York: Routledge.

36. Elena Larsen. 2004. "Cyberfaith: How Americans Pursue Religion Online." In *Religion Online.* Dawson and Cowan, eds. These numbers have likely greatly increased since 2004.

37. Robert Wuthnow. 2005. *America and the Challenges of Religious Diversity.* Princeton and Oxford: Princeton University Press.

38. Wuthnow. 2005; Wade Clark Roof. 1999. *Spiritual Marketplace: Baby Boomers and the Remaking of American Religion.* Princeton and Oxford: Princeton University Press; Roger Finke and Rodney Stark. 2005. *The Churching of America 1776–2005: Winners and Losers in Our Religious Economy.* New Brunswick and London: Rutgers University Press.

39. Einstein 2008, xi.

40. Finke and Starke 2005, 9. Many recent books have examined the marketing of particular religious traditions. For example, Jeff Wilson's *Mindful America* examines the marketing of Buddhist mindfulness in the United States (2014), Andrea R. Jain examines the selling of yoga (2015), and Heather Hendershot investigates how Evangelical Christians make use of a vast range of modern media as they try to sell their message far and wide (2004). Still others have examined the marketing of religious traditions more generally, such as Jeremy Carette and Richard King's *Selling Spirituality* and R. Laurence Moore's now classic *Selling God*, which looks at religion and commercial culture across American religious history. Jeff Wilson. 2014. *Mindful America: The Mutual Transformation of Buddhist Meditation and American Culture.* Oxford and New York: Oxford University Press; Andrea R. Jain. 2015. *Selling Yoga: From Counterculture to Pop Culture.* Oxford and New York: Oxford University Press; Heather Hendershot. 2004. *Shaking the World for Jesus: Media and Conservative Evangelical Culture.* Chicago and London: University of Chicago Press; Jeremy Carette and Richard King. 2005. *Selling Spirituality: The Silent Takeover of Religion.* Abingdon and New York: Routledge; R. Laurence Moore. 1994. *Selling God: American Religion in the Marketplace of Culture.* New York and Oxford: Oxford University Press.

41. Lee and Sinitiere 2009, 3.

42. A harmonium is an instrument that resembles an accordion but is played while seated.

43. ISKCON devotees refer to *mūrtis*, or embodied forms of Hindu divinity, as deities.

44. George E. Marcus. 1995. "Ethnography in/of the World System: The Emergence of Multi-Sited Ethnography." *Annual Review of Anthropology* 24: 95–117.

45. Ibid., 105.

46. Ibid., 106.

47. Amanda J. Lucia. 2014b. *Reflections of Amma: Devotees in Global Embrace.* Berkeley and Los Angeles: University of California Press, 28.

48. Marcus 1995, 108.

49. My methods take much inspiration from the well-executed approach of Amanda J. Lucia (Lucia 2014b), who successfully followed the followers of Amma.

50. Christine Hine. 2015. *Ethnography for the Internet: Embedded, Embodied and Everyday.* London: Bloomsbury; Christine Hine. 2000. *Virtual Ethnography.* Thousand Oaks, London, and New Delhi: SAGE Publications.

51. Lori Kendall. 1999. "Recontextualizing 'Cyberspace': Methodological Considerations for On-Line Research." In *Doing Internet Research: Critical Issues*

and Methods for Examining the Net. Steve Jones, ed. Thousand Oaks, London, and New Delhi: SAGE Publications, 60.

52. For those few devotees with whom I could not meet in person, there was Skype, email, and mobile phone communication.

53. I also examined a number of ISKCON periodicals online, such as the *ISKCON Communications Journal*. Accessed October 15, 2016. http://content.iskcon.org/icj/contents.html; *ISKCON News*. Accessed June 5, 2016. http://iskconnews.org/; and *Dandavats*. Accessed August 11, 2016. http://www.dandavats.com.

ONE

A BRIEF HISTORY OF ISKCON

1965–Present

At 9:00 a.m. on the blistering summer morning of August 13, 1965, the Scindia Steam Navigation Company's cargo carrier the *Jaladuta* departed from Calcutta (Kolkata) to New York. The ship was to make the arduous journey across the world, traveling across the turbulent waters of the Red Sea and the Atlantic Ocean before arriving in New York Harbor a full month later. While the ship was primarily used for cargo, it also had a small passenger cabin. Aboard this ship, in the tiny passenger cabin space, was sixty-nine-year-old A. C. Bhaktivedanta Swami Prabhupada. Although the accommodations were meager, they were more than satisfactory for the elderly swami, who noted in his August 13, 1965, journal entry that "the cabin is quite comfortable, thanks to Lord Sri Krishna."[1] This was the first time that the swami had been out of India, and he packed with him for the journey just the bare essentials: his complimentary ticket, some books and pamphlets, a small suitcase, an umbrella, and some dry cereal to eat in the event that the ship was not equipped with any vegetarian fare.

According to ISKCON's hagiographical accounts of A. C. Bhaktivedanta Swami Prabhupada (known affectionately within the movement as Srila Prabhupada), the elderly guru's whole life had led him up to the moment when he boarded the *Jaladuta*. In his birth year of 1896, for example, an astrologer is said to have predicted that when Prabhupada "reached the age of seventy, he would cross the ocean, become a great exponent of religion, and open 108 temples."[2] By the mid-seventies, it seemed to his followers that he was well on his way to fulfilling this prediction; by 1975, Prabhupada had opened ISKCON temples and communities in thirty US cities and six Canadian ones. He had also opened eleven communities in Western Europe and twenty-nine across

Australia, Africa, India, Asia, and Latin America.[3] By 2007, just forty-one years after ISKCON was legally registered as an official, tax-exempt, religious institution, the movement claimed to have roughly one million adherents worldwide.[4]

Today, ISKCON enjoys widespread, global success. Official reports, as recent as July 2016, indicate that there are currently 650 ISKCON centers, temples, schools, and colleges worldwide. Besides centers, temples, and educational institutions, however, ISKCON also owns and manages 110 vegetarian restaurants, as well as 65 farms and eco-villages around the world. What is more, ISKCON devotees run an estimated 3,600 home-study (*bhakti vṛkṣa*) groups each week, as well as a number of regular programs at universities and colleges, parks, and other public meeting spaces.[5]

Along with the programs that they host at fixed locations such as temples, farms, and homes, devotees within ISKCON today also run a number of itinerant programs. As of 2016, for example, devotees had executed an estimated 260,000 kilometers' worth of *padayātrās* (foot journeys) whereby they walk the streets of cities and towns around the world while singing the names of Krishna, dancing, pulling his *mūrtis* on carts, and/or distributing ISKCON literature. As noted in ISKCON's bicentennial report, "one hundred and fifty *padayatra* teams, with approximately 10,000 participants, have walked [the] 260,000 km (161,000 miles). This is almost 6.5 times the Earth's circumference. Padayatra Worldwide has visited 52,000 towns and villages in 110 countries since its inception in 1976."[6]

ISKCON is also flourishing in terms of its number of worldwide practitioners. According to ISKCON's most recent official report, 95,000 people have taken formal initiation into the movement since 1966.[7] But there are many more participants in the ISKCON movement than this number suggests. This is because the number of formally initiated devotees does not include those devotees who, although not officially initiated, have nonetheless been attending and participating in ISKCON's programs for years—many of whom even volunteer their time in service to the movement on a weekly or even daily basis. It also does not include those congregational members who attend the temple on Sundays and/or during holiday and festival events (of which ISKCON holds 6,000 yearly). This is why, in their July 2016 bicentennial count, ISKCON's Governing Body Commission (GBC) estimated that the actual number of people who worship at ISKCON each year is around nine million—and many on the GBC feel this number is conservative.[8]

This magnitude of ISKCON's devotee/participant base is palpable to anyone who visits ISKCON's programs around the world. At a recent Janmāṣṭamī festival I attended at ISKCON of DC, for example, there were an estimated

Figure 1.1 A *padayātrā* within the walled streets of ISKCON Mayapur, December 22, 2015. Groups are also known as *saṅkīrtan* parties. Photograph taken by author. Mayapur, West Bengal, India.

Figure 1.2 Standing room only at ISKCON, Vrindavan, January 2, 2016, at a regular Saturday afternoon program. Photograph taken by author. Vrindavan, Uttar Pradesh, India.

Figure 1.3 A large crowd gathers in the temple room of ISKCON, Vrindavan, on January 2, 2016, for a regular Saturday afternoon program. Photograph taken by author. Vrindavan, Uttar Pradesh, India.

Figure 1.4 A packed house at a home program in Potomac, Maryland, on June 8, 2015. Photograph taken by author. Potomac, Maryland, United States.

Figure 1.5 Crowds gather for *darshan* at ISKCON Juhu on Sunday, January 10, 2016. Photo taken by author. Mumbai, Maharashtra, India.

8,000 people in attendance. The attendance at the celebration was so great, in fact, that the temple had to spend $10,000 just to provide parking and parking services to the guests. And it is not just DC that draws these large numbers; festivals in Spanish Fork, Utah, also draw participants in the several thousands. In New Delhi, devotees line up for miles just to see Krishna in his *mūrti* (embodied) forms on important festival days. I have attended many ISKCON festivals and events, in fact, where attendance was so large, security guards had to be hired to enforce crowd control.

ISKCON temples and centers do not just draw large groups of people during festival or event occasions, however. Instead, there are large groups of gathered attendees during regular program times, as well. Between 2014 and 2018, for example, I attended jam-packed programs at varying times at ISKCON centers around the world, from Sunday afternoon programs in Philadelphia to morning programs in Mayapur; from evening guest lectures in New Jersey and Delaware to unstructured Saturday afternoons in Mumbai and New Delhi.[9] And attendance at ISKCON's Vrindavan hub is immense throughout all days and times of the calendrical year—so great, in fact, that a booming hotel industry has arisen in the small temple town just to accommodate the pilgrims who travel both nationally and internationally to visit the temple. By all accounts, ISKCON is doing better than ever.

Given these success statistics, it might seem curious that ISKCON is currently administering a major set of rebranding campaigns all around the globe, aggressively aimed at attracting westerners to the movement through mindfulness institutes, posh yoga studios, urban spiritual "lounges," and rural meditative retreat facilities. Why, given ISKCON's success, is this dramatic rebranding seen as necessary at all? And why are devotees so focused on attracting westerners in particular to the movement? This chapter tells the story of the events that unfolded within the ISKCON movement that set the stage for this new western-focused rebranding effort. As we will see, this story involves a complex set of circumstances, both historical and sociological, that produced what devotees today regard as a demographically imbalanced movement—an imbalance that, as we will learn in chapter 2, they believe both challenges some of ISKCON's central theological principles and undermines Prabhupada's mission for his movement's success. In order to tell this story, however, we must first back up and trace the history of the ISKCON movement, beginning on September 19, 1965—the day that A. C. Bhaktivedanta Swami Prabhupada stepped off the *Jaladuta* at the New York Harbor.[10]

ISKCON's Early Days: 1965–1977

It is hard to imagine a sixty-nine-year-old swami walking the streets of Manhattan, on his own in a foreign culture, with his heart set on spreading a movement of love of Krishna. But in many ways, this was the trend du jour during the time of Prabhupada's arrival in the United States. In fact, many gurus had arrived from India during the 1960s and 1970s, each hoping to spread his own particular spin on the ultimate Hindu salvific goal of *mokṣa* (liberation).[11] For example, arriving in the United States around the same time as Prabhupada (late 1950s) was Maharishi Mahesh Yogi, the infamous guru who popularized a path of religiosity called Transcendental Meditation.[12] There was also Swami Satchidananda, the well-known guru who started Yogaville in rural Virginia.[13] And finally, there was Swami Muktananda, the teacher who popularized the Siddha Yoga movement in both the United States and around the world on his first world tour in 1970.[14]

As scholars and devotees alike have noted, however, during his early years in the United States, Prabhupada set himself and his ISKCON movement apart from the other Indian gurus and their paths in many ways. First and foremost, Prabhupada's movement theologically departed from those offered by his peers. Rather than being a nontheistic system of yoga or meditation, Prabhupada's ISKCON was a highly structured, staunchly ascetic, and adamantly theistic Vaishnava devotional movement. In terms of specific teachings, Prabhupada presented to his early disciples the idea of the divine in the form of Krishna, a Hindu god whom he repeatedly taught was a person, albeit the Supreme one.[15] Moreover, he taught his early followers that they are "not their bodies" and also that their souls are "part and parcel" of Krishna's divine nature. Perhaps most importantly, he taught them that they could realize their relationship to Krishna not through a quiet set of yogic meditations but through a joyful, and often boisterous, set of celebratory devotions.

The religious philosophy that Prabhupada presented to his followers was an interpretive formulation of the Acintyabhedābeda school of Vedānta: a theology (attributed to Chaitanya) that was systematized by the Vrindavan Goswamis in the sixteenth century and that forms the basis of the Gauḍīya Vaishnava traditions.[16] Within this theology, the soul is believed to be both the same as and different from the divine. More than this, the Acintyabhedābeda school of Gauḍīya Vaishnavism holds that the point of religious practice is not to merge with the divine but rather to realize the soul's eternal and loving relationship to it and to live out that relationship in perpetuity. This relationship is established through ritual, although the specific forms of practice vary across the different Gauḍīya traditions.[17]

For Prabhupada, these ritual practices meant following a set of "regulative principles," which included the prohibition against eating meat, engaging in illicit sex,[18] gambling, and ingesting any intoxicants, including alcohol, tobacco, and caffeine. They also meant chanting the names of Krishna on *japa mālās* (prayer beads) for roughly two hours daily, as well as worshipping *mūrtis* (embodied forms) of Krishna (often referred to as "deities" in ISKCON). This worship of embodied forms included daily *puja* ceremonies and *āratī* (fire lamp) offerings at ISKCON temples, as well as a routine of collective gatherings there in order to sing and dance before the deities, to cook for them, and to otherwise host them as divine guests. During its early days in the United States, therefore, ISKCON very much functioned as a theistic devotional movement—one that was fully situated in Vaishnava Hindu religious roots. More than this, Prabhupada's ISKCON was also fully situated in Indian Hindu cultural norms. As Larry D. Shinn and David G. Bromley put it, "By 1970, the Krishna movement had become more regularized in terms of its devotional practices and temple lifestyles and thoroughly 'Indianized' in terms of its adoption of lactovegetarian diet and Indian cultural customs. Disciples wore common dress (e.g., white *dhotis* and saris or ochre robes), practiced traditional Indian rituals (e.g., regular chanting of sixteen rounds, required attendance at early morning deity worship, community reading of scriptures), and had a common appearance (e.g., shaven heads for men and covered heads for women, and traditional marks and beads)."[19]

EVANGELISM

By presenting his disciples with not only a new and exciting religious tradition but also an all-encompassing meaning system, worldview, lifestyle, and set of cultural customs into which they could plug themselves, Prabhupada was able to quickly develop a large, committed, and fast-growing core of American disciples. More importantly, Prabhupada was able to grow this disciple base exponentially during the 1960s and 1970s by effectively enlivening his followers to become evangelists for the movement they had just joined. Prabhupada had come to the United States, he often said, to save the Western world from "demoniac ways," and to spread love of Krishna "to every town and village" around the world.[20] And his new American disciples were the instruments by which he set out to accomplish this.

For these reasons, a primary aspect of participation in the early ISKCON movement was the expectation that devotees would actively try to spread the movement to the public, or "preach," as devotees put it. There were many ways in which Prabhupada encouraged his disciples to engage in preaching. For example, Prabhupada encouraged his devotees to chant Krishna's names exuberantly in the streets, dancing ecstatically in public display while doing so. This practice is known as *saṅkīrtan*.

According to Neal Delmonico, "*Kirtana* means 'praising' or 'glorifying,' and *sankirtana* means loudly praising or glorifying. *Sankirtana* often takes the form of the congregational singing of Krishna's names with the accompaniment of various kinds of instruments (drums, cymbals, harmoniums, and so forth). As the singing becomes emotionally charged, various kinds of dancing often break out as well. *Sankirtana* is generally a public performance, in that it is often carried out in public areas such as the streets and the squares of villages, towns and cities."[21]

Besides *saṅkīrtan*, however, devotees also engaged in public preaching in a variety of other ways. For example, devotees orchestrated public devotional "parades" known as *rathayātrās*, during which they would pull Krishna's *mūrtis* on chariots throughout the streets of major cities, thereby effectively putting the public into direct contact with Krishna through his embodied forms.[22]

More than anything else, however, devotees were encouraged to engage in preaching by helping their guru establish ISKCON temples all around the world, as far and wide as possible. And with a zeal for their new movement and a love for Swami Prabhupada, ISKCON's earliest disciples, in fact, went hard to work for their elderly guru. Using a variety of innovative methods to draw the attention of newcomers, Prabhupada's early disciples sold flowers at airports, danced and sang in the streets and in a number of public venues, sold books in public places (a central ISKCON practice also called *saṅkīrtan*), and hosted public events and concerts. They also sold jewelry and other handmade trinkets in bookstores, fairs, and even tattoo parlors. Through these methods, early ISKCON devotees were able to introduce outsiders to the movement and invite them to attend ISKCON rituals and events. Moreover, through these activities, they were also able to collect a sizable amount of money. They used this money, in combination with their own savings and other donations, to open temples all over the United States—temples that would be the basis for both the participation in, and the further spreading of, the ISKCON movement.

By all accounts, the efforts of early ISKCON devotees and their beloved guru Swami Prabhupada were a wild success. By the mid-seventies, Prabhupada and his disciples had established ISKCON temples and centers all over the world and had made new followers nearly everywhere they went. Finally, in 1976, Prabhupada and his disciples opened the massive Krishna-Balarama temple complex in the sacred Vaishnava town of Vrindavan. The opening of this temple complex, which would come to forever change the landscape of Vrindavan,[23] was a hugely symbolic moment for ISKCON. This is because Vrindavan was the very last place in which Prabhupada had lived before embarking on his life-altering journey to the United States aboard the *Jaladuta*. Having traveled from Vrindavan all the way around the world and back again, A. C. Bhaktivedanta Swami Prabhupada (and the ISKCON movement that his disciples helped him establish and spread) had come full circle.

ISKCON FALLS ON TROUBLED TIMES: 1977–PRESENT

During Prabhupada's lifetime, the ISKCON movement seemed to flourish with an almost unbridled success. However, following the aged guru's death in 1977, the movement experienced a series of problems that thwarted its initial momentum and also subsequently paved the way for devotees' shift toward western-focused marketing.

It is well known that with the passing of a religious tradition's central figure or guru comes a period of the "routinization of charisma"—a phase of time that "introduces the need for mechanisms of coordination, supervision, and delegation" among devotees to replace the organizational power, control, and inspiration once wielded by the central figurehead.[24] When Prabhupada died in 1977, his disciples—most of them very young—were left in charge of the movement. This was a complex situation on a variety of levels. To begin with, Prabhupada's early disciples were still relatively unfamiliar with the theological and ritual intricacies of their own tradition. More than this, however, they were also administratively inexperienced; most of them completely lacked the managerial skills required to run a large and growing multinational organization such as ISKCON. As a result, Prabhupada's young disciples found themselves in a sink or swim situation and experienced their fair share of troubles and failures.

Chief among these troubles was a series of significant lawsuits launched against the ISKCON movement during the 1970s and 1980s. The first case involved Robin George, a young woman who had become active in ISKCON during her high school years. Following her graduation, George moved out of her parents' home and into an ISKCON temple; however, she did not tell her parents which temple. Fearing the worst, and frantic to find their daughter, the George family searched high and low for her. Their efforts were neither quiet nor private but instead included the very public practices of "picketing temples; writing letters to police officials, the FBI, ambassadors of foreign nations, Krishna temple leaders around the country and Prabhupada himself; appearing on radio and television shows and giving interviews with the print media; and traveling to temples where they thought she might be found."[25] Although Robin eventually left the movement on her own, the public relations (and financial) damage to ISKCON had already been done; by 1977, the Georges had filed a lawsuit against ISKCON for brainwashing, false imprisonment, emotional damage, libel, and even wrongful death (the George family blamed the death of Robin's father on the emotional trauma he had experienced as a result of Robin's involvement with ISKCON). The case went to trial in 1983 and initially was settled for $32,500,000, although this was later reduced to $9,700,000.[26] In 1993, the case finally reached a confidential settlement, after much legal back-and-forth between ISKCON and the George family.[27]

ISKCON was also embroiled in a legal battle with the family of Edward Shapiro. Edward Shapiro was a Brandeis University student who, like Robin George, had moved into an ISKCON temple in 1972 against his family's will. Like the George family, the Shapiros tried repeatedly to sway their son to leave ISKCON; they even took extreme measures, such as using physical restraint and forcibly cutting off their son's Vaishnava *śikhā* (tuft of hair). The Shapiro family also took their case to the courts, but it was eventually dismissed.[28]

Despite the fact that the Shapiro case was dismissed in the courts, it nonetheless had a significant negative impact on the ISKCON movement. Just like the George case had been publicized on the radio and in other media, including the popular *People* magazine and the *Los Angeles Times*,[29] the Shapiro case also drew negative attention from various media outlets. Moreover, it was a case that was widely known to the local publics in the areas in which it occurred and was litigated. It therefore did much public relations damage to ISKCON, which was already struggling with its public image.

But by far the biggest and most significant legal battles that were fought against ISKCON involved the litany of child-abuse accusations, charges, and legal proceedings brought against devotees beginning in the 1970s and persisting (in litigation at least) through the turn of the millennium. The charges in these cases were especially grave and included allegations that ISKCON devotees had physically, emotionally, and physically abused children—some as young as three years old—in the movement's *gurukulas* (traditional schools), where the children were supposed to be educated and protected. These charges were troubling not only because of how serious they were but also because of the sheer number of children they involved; at its final count, the number of plaintiffs included a total of 535 students from all over the world. And these children were said to have been abused in not just one but several of ISKCON's schools.

Like the George and Shapiro cases, ISKCON's child-abuse cases were brought to the courts. In the end, the lawsuits they involved cost the ISKCON movement $9.5 million in settlements, with students receiving compensation ranging from $2,500 to $50,000 each.[30] These child-abuse cases—which also involved charges of racketeering—ended up causing significant financial damage to the ISKCON movement, completely bankrupting several of its temple communities. They also, understandably, sank the ISKCON movement into a near-unrecoverable public relations crisis.

ISKCON's child-abuse cases bankrupted the movement in ways beyond just the financial and public relational, however. For a great many devotees, the charges of child abuse also caused a spiritual bankruptcy within their movement. For those devotees who had put their full trust, as well as their lives, into the hands of ISKCON's leaders, learning of the child abuse that had occurred within ISKCON led to a crisis of faith—if not in the strength of the teachings of Prabhupada, then certainly in the institution and leaders that he had left behind. Following the initial accusations of child abuse, therefore, there was a growing disenchantment within ISKCON—a disenchantment that was only exacerbated by problems on a number of other fronts. These problems included accusations of the mistreatment of women, as well as controversies over the role and power that Prabhupada intended for the men whom he'd chosen to be gurus after his death.[31]

Most prominent of these guru governance debates was the so-called *ritvik controversy*. While some devotees felt that Prabhupada had appointed gurus so that they could initiate new devotees on their own, others contended that these gurus were intended only to be *ritviks*—proxies for Prabhupada, who was himself, even after his death, the only authorized initiating guru. Although this controversy might seem to be nothing more than philosophical hairsplitting, it was nonetheless significant within the movement because it both showcased and produced devotees' diminishing trust of the movement's leaders and leadership structure, as well as the institution of ISKCON more generally. It even led to a schism within the movement, with many followers of the *ritvik* position creating the ISKCON Revival Movement (IRM) in the late 1990s.[32]

Collectively, all of these events contributed to devotees' growing disenchantment with the movement and a loss of faith in the institution of ISKCON.[33] As many devotees lost heart, some left ISKCON, while others simply moved out of the temples to continue their practices on the outside. More significantly, perhaps, is the fact that during this period, devotees didn't just move out of the temple due to disillusionment; many also left due to the temples' lack of financial resources. Having lost so much money in lawsuits, ISKCON temples had few resources left with which to support full-time residents. As a result, many temple residents were forced to move out and find full-time jobs. This exodus of devotees from the temples only further exacerbated the financial problem, however.[34] As E. Burke Rochford Jr., puts it, "The dramatic decline in temple residents, combined with the limited contributions of ISKCON's congregations, left local ISKCON temples with a critical shortage of labor and other resources."[35] With a decline in full-time resident devotees, in other words, also came a decline in ISKCON's full-time workforce, and along with it, a decline in book sales and the sale of other devotional goods: both of which meant a significant loss of revenue for temples. This revenue shortage, combined with the near financial ruin that ISKCON had suffered at the hands of lawsuits, settlements, and resulting bankruptcies, left the movement in an extremely difficult economic situation. And together with the public relations problems the movement was facing, ISKCON was having a difficult time not only surviving but also recruiting. The road to a hopeful and sustainable future seemed grim.

THE "HINDUIZATION" OF ISKCON

Feeling themselves to be anxious and, in many ways, out of options, ISKCON devotees turned for help to the one group that had long been their biggest supporters and allies in the United States: the Indian Hindu diaspora community.

In a land far away from home, the Indian Hindu diaspora community sensed a religio-cultural affinity with ISKCON devotees. As Diana L. Eck notes in *Darśan*, "As Hindu communities became established in the United States, they developed many different patterns of religious life."[36] In so doing, "some new Hindu immigrants found a ready-made home in one of the Kṛṣṇa temples of ISKCON, the International Society for Kṛṣṇa Consciousness, where elaborate daily and weekly cycles of *pūjā* and *āratī* were already being practiced. They could participate in the observance of a cycle of festivals and help pull the chariot of Jagannātha Kṛṣṇa through the streets in the annual Rathyātrā festival."[37]

In other words, new to the United States and finding themselves in an unfamiliar setting, many Hindu immigrants took religio-cultural comfort in ISKCON temples and felt an affinity to the ISKCON devotees with whom they shared much religious practice. Despite being culturally different from the American disciples of Prabhupada, in other words, Indian Hindu immigrants nonetheless felt a kinship with ISKCON devotees and had found a home in their temples and centers. Therefore, when ISKCON devotees called on them for help beginning in the 1980s, the Hindu diaspora community reciprocated graciously.

There were many ways in which diaspora Hindus assisted ISKCON during these years of struggle. Of the most important among them was the work they did to offer the movement an air of legitimacy in the eyes of the American public. During ISKCON's hardest years, many Americans considered ISKCON to be a cult. The lawsuits and child-abuse scandals played a major role in this perception. However, also to blame was the fact that ISKCON devotees simply seemed to the American public to be too "other"; they lived a communal lifestyle, had a worldview that was radically different from many Americans', and engaged in sometimes pushy public proselytizing activities like giving out flowers and books in airport corridors.[38] Also at the root of this "cult" perception was devotees' appearance; although saffron- and white-colored *dhotīs* and colorful sarees are forms of dress popular in India, Americans were not accustomed to this clothing style, especially on people who were not of Indian descent. Devotees' manner of dress, therefore, seemed deeply strange, especially when coupled with the hairstyle worn by many male devotees (heads completely shaven but for a small tuft of hair in the back). As Bir Krishna Das Goswami puts it:

> There's many aspects . . . of our movement . . . ya know, things like *dhotīs* and other things like that that are quite shocking for Western people. I mean, I always tell this story . . . my first impression of the Krishna

Conscious Movement . . . not only were [devotees] jumping up and down . . . [but they were also] wearing bed sheets with bald heads. . . . From a western perspective, try to understand if you look at us from an outsider's perspective, in many cases, we look extremely weird. I mean, even if you look at the *dhotīs* that we wear, I mean, at least the household *dhotīs* and the *Brahmacārī dhotīs*, they look to a certain extent to be adult diapers, you understand? Just the way they're tucked in and everything like that.[39]

In order to combat this "cult" perception, ISKCON leaders asked diaspora Hindus to go to bat for them in the public arena. These Hindus answered the call in two ways: by appearing on behalf of ISKCON in the courtroom and by petitioning on devotees' behalf to the local government. Through these court appearances and government petitions, ISKCON devotees hoped that the Hindu community could convince the public that ISKCON was not a strange cult but rather a form of Hinduism. Through this association with Hinduism, ISKCON aimed to gain a greater deal of cultural cachet and legitimacy; for although Hinduism was a minority religion in the United States, it nonetheless carried with it a cultural credibility in the eyes of Americans.[40] If ISKCON was Hindu, therefore, it wasn't a dangerous cult or even a group with "weird-looking" followers; rather, it was a legitimate religious group with long-standing historical roots. Aligning themselves with Hinduism and Hindus was an opportunity that ISKCON devotees felt they could not forego.

But ISKCON devotees did not just reach out to the Indian Hindu diaspora community for legitimacy; most importantly, they also reached out to them for money. In fact, it was financial assistance that ISKCON devotees needed most from diaspora Hindus. According to E. Burke Rochford Jr., one of the chief ways in which the ISKCON movement solicited financial aid from the Hindu diaspora community was through the establishment in 1991 of the ISKCON Foundation. As Rochford notes, "The foundation's primary mission was to raise money to support ISKCON's communities by actively encouraging the involvement of Indian Hindus in ISKCON temples."[41] In order to generate this money through the foundation, however, ISKCON governing bodies knew that they had to be strategic. As such, they created advisory boards comprised of "influential and affluent Hindus,"[42] who would not only be in charge of soliciting these donations but were also powerful and influential enough to actually engender them. And engender them they did; by "making use of personal contact with potential donors, as well as phone calls and a direct mail campaign involving thousands of Hindus across North America, the ISKCON foundation successfully mobilized the support of a significant number of Hindus. . . . As a result, temple revenues increased substantially in many locations."[43]

Although it is difficult to ascertain the exact numbers, by most accounts it was almost entirely through the donations of the Hindu diaspora community that ISKCON was able to bounce back to financial solvency. While some temples reported that roughly two-thirds of their revenue came from Indian Hindu contributions, others reported that 95 percent of their temple's revenue came from the donations of Indian Hindus.[44] As Hridayananda Das Goswami noted in a lecture entitled "Ideal Vedic Culture," in the beginning of the movement, the devotees used to sell all sorts of paraphernalia in order to earn money. For example, they used to sell candles, records, books, art, and so on. "And then," he said, "they discovered the ultimate paraphernalia: the Hindu. I don't mean to say that the preaching to Hindus was insincere, I mean, they're great souls, they're Vaishnavas, they're certainly, ya know, very beloved members of our spiritual family. But they also—the Hindus that came to the West—tended to be successful. And so ISKCON basically in the West reinvented itself for its best customers."[45]

Being that the Indian Hindu diaspora community was both successful and willing to help out, ISKCON devotees willingly accepted the funds they donated to financially restore the movement. As economists are wont to say, however, there is no such thing as a free lunch. Over time, the Indian Hindus who solicited money for ISKCON through the ISKCON Foundation and other donation campaigns—as well as those who themselves donated to them—were no longer satisfied with simply soliciting and donating money on behalf of ISKCON. Rather, they also began to attend ISKCON temples and temple functions in greater numbers and with greater frequency and to bring their friends and families along with them. Most importantly, however, as both their donations and their attendance increased, so too did their desire for more involvement in the movement—in particular, in its administrative roles and positions. Being as they were the movement's largest donors, in other words, these diaspora Hindus understandably wanted a voice in the movement's governance; they wanted a say in the movement's rituals, events, and organization, and they wanted a hand in directing its future.

Since Indian Hindu community members were the biggest donors to the ISKCON movement, ISKCON devotees had no choice but to oblige them in their requests for more administrative power. This was especially the case if devotees wanted these donations and support to continue into the future. Beginning in the 1990s, therefore, ISKCON devotees started to hand over various administrative roles to interested and influential Indian Hindus. Although this trend began slowly at first, as it continued through the 2000s, it began to pick up momentum. As more Indian Hindus donated money, more of them became involved in executive and managerial roles. Over time, as the number of both

Indian Hindu participants and administrators grew, Indian participants in the ISKCON movement soon came to significantly outnumber ISKCON's non-Indian disciple base—a base that itself had not been growing during these decades because of ISKCON's negative public image issues.

ISKCON devotees speak frequently of this demographic shift in their movement, both in casual conversations at temple and home gatherings and more formally in ISKCON periodicals. Consider, for example, the following statement written for ISKCON's *Sampradaya Sun* by a devotee recounting his experience at a recent ISKCON festival: "I came back from the 2011 Mayapur Festival" he notes, "and as usual, it was packed with devotees. . . . But as with my previous visit to ISKCON in Mayapur, in 2008, I was hard pressed to see any real showing of American, EU, UK and non-Indian devotees there. So that's the situation—a lopsided membership in ISKCON in the USA and UK and elsewhere. No one seems alarmed! . . . 'All I see is Indians.' . . . 'Where are the Western devotees?' Almost nowhere, that's where!"[46]

There are many aspects of this comment that are troubling. To begin with, it is, of course, more than just a little ironic to complain that an Indian-originated religious movement is largely demographically Indian, and it is especially ironic given that the festival about which this comment was written took place in India. This comment might also strike the reader as ungracious, and rightly so; after all, if it were not for Indian Hindu donations and congregational presence, the ISKCON movement would have all but died out in many parts of the world. Finally, and most importantly, the strongly biased tenor of this comment—particularly the author's palpable emotional alarm at the number of Indians at the event relative to westerners—is startling. I will discuss the origins of comments such as these at length in the next chapter. For now, suffice it to say that this devotee is not the only one to make such comments regarding ISKCON's congregational demographic shift or to perceive the movement's congregant base as demographically imbalanced. Instead, such statements are frequent (though they do vary in tenor) and appear regularly in periodicals written and produced by ISKCON devotees. Consider, for example, the following statement by Uravashi Patel, who writes about the demographic shift for *Jagannatha's Chakra*: "Visiting the Bhaktivedanta Manor," she writes, "you are forgiven to think that you are coming to a 'Hindu Mandir,' as perhaps 95 percent or more are Hindus who attend the programs. Any westerner will definitely feel out of place. I have been told there was once a thriving devotee community of hundred [*sic*] or more Westerners living around the Manor. They have almost all moved away because there was no need for them anymore."[47]

These statements, and many others like them, highlight devotees' recognition of the demographic shift within ISKCON, whereby the movement's congregational base has changed from one of mostly non-Indian converts to one of almost exclusively Indian participants. This demographic shift—coupled with the religious and cultural changes it is believed to have ushered into the movement—is widely known as the *Hinduization of ISKCON.* Scholars of ISKCON have written about it extensively, noting not only that it has occurred in recent decades but also how it came about,[48] as well as the ways in which it is playing out in the social dynamics of many contemporary ISKCON communities.[49] ISKCON devotees, too, write frequently about the Hinduization of ISKCON. Just a cursory glance through databases of ISKCON periodicals reveals a number of articles on the topic published in ISKCON sources such as *Dandavats*, the *Sampradaya Sun*, and *Jagannatha's Chakra*. These articles include "The Hindufication of ISKCON," "The Hinduization of ISKCON?," "Surrounded By Indians," "The Need for Diversity," and "A Disciple's Perspective on the Hinduization of ISKCON," to name just a few.[50] In these articles, devotees make frequent reference to the number of Indian participants and attendees at ISKCON temples and functions, relative to the number of western devotees they find at them. They also discuss the reasons why they see this shift to have unfolded. According to one devotee:

> In the early 1980's, when Tamal Krishna Maharaj was the GBC and "Zonal guru" of Texas, he developed a number of new strategies for preaching in North America.... One of these was his idea that in order for ISKCON, the Hare Krishna Movement, to be genuinely accepted by the American public we would have to "merge" with the culture and lifestyle in certain respects and get rid of the current misrepresentation the movement had in the media of being a cult. In other words, devotees should be seen as socially responsible and acceptable.... So the Indian community was an obvious target for support.... There was many a discussion on how to get the Indians involved in the temples for their financial assistance as well as for good public relations. Guess what? This cultivation of the Indian community worked so well that the Indians did get involved, so much so that they got involved not just in assisting temples financially, but in temple management as well—and to the extent that, when there were no more Westerners left or willing to manage the temples, they took over, 80%+ over. Now the Indian temple managers get together and discuss how to get Westerners coming to the temples again! Sounds ridiculous, but it's true. The full circle has come around.[51]

These Indian temple managers who gather to brainstorm ways to get westerners to come to their temples again are part of a broader undertaking within ISKCON aimed at reattracting westerners back to the movement. This undertaking, and the Krishna Branders who run it, has as its goal to rebalance the perceived demographic imbalance in the global ISKCON movement caused by the Hinduization of ISKCON and to turn ISKCON into a movement that is more ethnically, nationally, and racially diverse. But why is this diversity a goal for which the Krishna Branders are willing to strive so intensely? In the next chapter, I explore the philosophical and theological foundations that underscore this drive to make ISKCON a more diverse movement—foundations that devotees trace not only back to Prabhupada but all the way back to Chaitanya himself.

Before concluding the chapter, however, I would like to pause for a moment to inquire about the perspectives of the Indian community members who are associated with the ISKCON movement, in particular those who encounter ISKCON's newest rebranded programs that actively seek to attract westerners. What do they think of the rhetoric that there are too many Indians in the ISKCON movement or that the movement is demographically "imbalanced" and therefore needs to be diversified?

For starters, it is safe to say that many of those in this community feel a degree of ingratitude coming from the Krishna Branders who complain that there are too many Indians in ISKCON, especially since—as discussed above—it is almost entirely through the donations of the Indian community that the ISKCON movement is financially solvent at all. Further, it is likely that many in the Indian community feel this way despite not knowing the full history of the bailout of ISKCON at the financial hands of Indian donors; one only needs to glance at the names typed on the plaques on the walls of ISKCON's worldwide temples, announced as sponsors at ISKCON's Sunday feasts, or mentioned as donors on ISKCON's various community newsletters to get a sense of the degree to which Indian donors fund and sustain the movement. It must be hurtful for many, then, to hear that the Krishna Branders are developing and running programs and projects designed to draw in more westerners so as to "balance" the movement's demographics.

Additionally, besides feeling that the Krishna Branders possess an ingratitude about them, members of the Indian community might also feel that there is a degree of racism to the Krishna Branders' rhetoric and programming. This is because, to the large majority of Indians who come into contact with the ISKCON movement, ISKCON is *a Hindu movement*: ISKCON devotees worship Krishna, who is a Hindu god; they practice *puja* and *darshan*, which are Hindu religious practices; and they organize their lives around texts such as the *Bhagavad-Gītā* and the *Bhāgavata Purāṇa*, which are Hindu religious texts. With all of these ties to the Hindu traditions, it therefore makes sense that ISKCON is full of people of Indian descent, and to hear the Krishna Branders complain otherwise likely strikes many within the Indian community as troubling, if not racist and colonial.[52]

It is important to bear in mind, however, that on the ground, Indian perspectives on the Krishna Branders and their programming are not always as clear-cut as this. For starters, Indians—including those who encounter ISKCON's new western-focused rebranding efforts—are a vastly diverse and heterogeneous group, and one cannot generalize across them as if their perspective on this, or any other issue, is unified. Further, many of the Krishna Branders themselves are of Indian descent, and they share views with their other Krishna Branding peers regarding ISKCON's "imbalanced" demography (and they also work alongside them to change it). Because of this, one must be careful not to presume that the Indian community and the Krishna Branders are necessarily distinct or even mutually opposed. Instead, the Krishna Branders are a diverse group of ISKCON devotees who work together in their endeavor to turn ISKCON into a movement that is more ethnically, nationally, and racially diverse.[53] The next chapter explores the philosophical, theological, and historical roots of their desire to do so.

NOTES

1. Satsvarūpa Dāsa Goswami. 1983. *Prabhupāda: Messenger of the Supreme Lord*. Mumbai: The Bhaktivedanta Book Trust, 1. This hagiographical text is the official biography of A. C. Bhaktivedanta Prabhupada within the ISKCON movement.

2. Ibid., viii.

3. E. Burke Rochford Jr. 2007. *Hare Krishna Transformed*. New York: New York University Press, 14.

4. Ibid., 12. The date of 2007 reflects the date of publication of Rochford's book, wherein these statistics were reported.

5. Mukunda Goswami and Krishnarupa Devi Dasi, eds. 2016. *The Hare Krishnas: Celebrating 50 Years*. ISKCON Communications International, 6–7. This magazine is the official commemorative periodical for the fiftieth anniversary of ISKCON and is produced by ISKCON Communications International. It contains a set of statistical data for the movement to which I refer throughout this chapter as ISKCON's bicentennial report. This report contains both the most recent and the most accurate statistical counts for the movement, according to ISKCON's International Minister of Communications Governing Body Commissioner.

6. Ibid., 7.

7. Ibid., 6.

8. Personal communication with ISKCON's International Minister of Communications Governing Body Commissioner.

9. E. Burke Rochford Jr. and Kenneth Valpey have noted that attendance at daytime programs at American (Rochford) and other western (Valpey) ISKCON temples has dwindled to record lows. See Rochford, 2007; and Kenneth R. Valpey. 2013. "Interview with Dr. Kenneth R. Valpey." In *Hare Krishna in the Modern World*. Graham Dwyer and Richard J. Cole, eds. London: Arktos Media, Ltd. This decline in attendance, Rochford argues, is due to a shift in the ISKCON movement from a residential model of participation to a more congregational one. Now, rather than living in the temple, most devotees reside in their own homes outside of the temple and only visit the temple during nonworking hours. This accounts for the lack of attendance during the weekdays. It is important to note, however, that despite this shift, ISKCON temples in the United States are—in my experience—typically very full during weekend programs, not only for the Sunday feast days or festival occasions but also during other weekend programs such as invited speaker programs. These temples are also well-attended on some weeknights. Therefore, the lack of attendance at these temples during the day is not suggestive of an overall lack of attendance. Finally, the daytime emptiness that characterizes American temples does not at all characterize ISKCON temples in India, which I have seen are full for all of their programs, including those in the morning and midday.

10. The history that I discuss in this chapter is one that unfolds primarily in the United States (although I also reference the United Kingdom and India). It focuses on the United States in order to establish the historical and sociological circumstances that gave rise to the Krishna Branders groups, not to imply that ISKCON's history unfolded exclusively in the United States or that the movement is centered there. Chapter 2 traces the roots of the movement prior to its establishment in the United States.

11. Thomas A. Forsthoefel and Cynthia Ann Humes, eds. 2005. *Gurus in America*. Albany: State University of New York Press.

12. Cynthia Ann Humes. 2005. "Maharishi Mahesh Yogi: Beyond the TM Technique." In Forsthoefel and Humes 2005, 63.

13. The Pluralism Project, Harvard University. "The Rush of Gurus." Accessed February 11, 2017. http://pluralism.org/religions/hinduism/hinduism-in-america/the-rush-of-gurus/.

14. Lola Williamson. 2005. "The Perfectability of Perfection: Siddha Yoga as a Global Movement." In Forsthoefel and Humes 2005, 149. The gurus who came to the United States from India also tended to draw similar crowds of seekers:

"Bhaktivedanta's early disciples," Larry D. Shinn and David G Bromley suggest, "were indistinguishable from those of other Asian gurus in America in the 1960s in terms of their countercultural affectations." Larry D. Shinn and David G. Bromley. 1989. "A Kaleidoscopic View of the Hare Krishnas in America." In *Krishna Consciousness in the West*. David G. Bromley and Larry D. Shinn, eds. Lewisburg, London, and Toronto: Bucknell University Press and Associated University Presses, 14.

15. Prabhupada spoke of Krishna as the "Supreme Personality of Godhead." Although this translation to English is perhaps a bit awkward, this rendering is a direct translation of the Sanskrit term *Puruṣottama*, that Being depicted in the fifteenth chapter (15.16–15.18) of the *Bhagavad-Gītā* who is identified as the "Ultimate Person" because he is beyond both the *kṣara* (changing) and *akṣara* (unchanging) dimensions of existence. (*dvāv imau puruṣau loke kṣaraścākṣara eva ca kṣaraḥ sarvāṇi bhūtāni kūṭastho'kṣara ucyate* [15.16] . . . *yasmāt kṣaram atīto'ham akṣarād api cottamaḥ ato'smi loke vede ca prathitaḥ puruṣottamaḥ* [15.18].) Ramananda Prasad. 1995. *The Bhagavad-Gītā*. Delhi and Fremont: Motilal Banarsidass and The American Gita Society. Although many Vaishnavas interpret *Puruṣottama* to mean the Supreme Being whose body subsumes both the *kṣara* (changing) and *akṣara* (unchanging) world, the traditional ISKCON gloss on *Puruṣottama* tends to highlight Krishna's transcendental superiority over the *kṣara* and the *akṣara*, rather than his ontological inclusion of them.

16. Gauḍīya Vaishnavism refers to the schools of Vaishnavism that stem from the sixteenth century Bengali mystic Chaitanya. The Vrindavan Goswamis were a group of six theologians commissioned by Chaitanya to set up Vrindavan as a religious center and to lay a cohesive philosophical framework to Chaitanya's Gauḍīya Vaishnava movement.

17. Sukanya Sarbadhikary's *The Place of Devotion* is a lucid and lively examination of differences between Bengali Vaishnavisms. See Sukanya Sarbadhikary. 2015. *The Place of Devotion: Siting and Experiencing Divinity in Bengal-Vaishnavism*. Oakland: University of California Press.

18. Traditionally, illicit sex within ISKCON referred to any sexual act that is not intended for procreation. This historically included even a prohibition against non-procreative sex within the confines of marriage. However, in recent years, many devotees (at the "OK" of their gurus) have loosened this prescription somewhat, identifying illicit sex as sex outside of marriage.

19. Bromley and Shinn 1989, 14–15.

20. Kim Knott. 2000. "In Every Town and Village: Adaptive Strategies in the Communication of Krishna Consciousness in the UK, the First Thirty Years." *Social Compass* 47, no. 2: 153–167. As Knott notes, those in ISKCON often discuss Chaitanya's prediction that his name would be sung "in every town and village." Devotees cite this prediction as both proof that their movement was destined to

grow worldwide as well as an injunction that they need to work to spread it as far and wide as possible. As such, scholars such as Knott have noted that ISKCON is at heart an inherently evangelical movement. This evangelical spirit might be the feature of the Hare Krishna movement that most distinguishes it from other Vaishnava traditions.

21. Neal Delmonico. 2007. "Chaitanya Vaishnavism and the Holy Names." In *Krishna: A Sourcebook*. Edwin F. Bryant, ed. Oxford and New York: Oxford University Press, 549. The names of Krishna are widely held throughout ISKCON, as in other forms of Gauḍīya Vaishnavism, to be *svarūpa* (forms) of Krishna. Jiva Goswami famously states this in his *Bhagavat Sandarbha* with his well-renowned formulation *bhagavat-svarūpam eva nāma* (the name is the very form of God). This theology of the name is articulated in a number of Vaishnava primary textual sources. For a discussion of this theology and the sources that produce it, see Delmonico 2007. See also Barbara Holdrege. 2015. *Bhakti and Embodiment: Fashioning Divine Bodies and Devotional Bodies in Kṛṣṇa Bhakti*. London and New York: Routledge; and Norvin Hein. 1994. "Chaitanya's Ecstasies and the Theology of the Name." *Journal of Vaiṣṇava Studies* 2, no. 2, 7–27.

22. Both *saṅkīrtan* and *rathayātrā* can be understood as "automatic rituals" within ISKCON. Since ISKCON devotees believe that both the name of Krishna and the form (*mūrti*) of Krishna are Krishna himself, they also believe that putting the public into contact with these names or forms automatically stirs the public's hearts with love towards Krishna (even if such stirring is subconscious and even if such contact is inadvertent). See Karapanagiotis, Nicole. 2019. "Automatic Rituals and Inadvertent Audiences: ISKCON, Krishna and the Ritual Mechanics of Facebook." In *Digital Hinduism*. Xenia Zeiler, ed. New York: Routledge Press. ISKCON devotees also believe that Krishna can take *digital forms* and that these forms are also fully Krishna himself. As such, many devotees believe that these digital forms can also automatically stir the hearts of all who see them. There is a subset of ISKCON devotees, however, who believe that digital forms of Krishna do not work automatically to rouse love of Krishna in those identified as "western newcomers." For a full discussion of the complexities of this issue, see Karapanagiotis, Nicole. 2018. "Of Digital Images and Digital Media: Approaches to Marketing in American ISKCON." *Nova Religio: The Journal of Alternative and Emergent Religion* 21, no. 3: 74–102.

23. Charles R. Brooks. 1989a. "A Unique Conjecture: The Incorporation of ISKCON in Vrindaban." In Bromley and Shinn 1989. For a full-length discussion of ISKCON in Vrindavan, as well as an examination of the relationship between western devotees and Vrindavan residents, see Charles R. Brooks. 1989b. *The Hare Krishnas in India*. Delhi: Motilal Banarsidass Publishers.

24. Irvin H. Collins. 2004. "The 'Routinization of Charisma' and the Charismatic: The Confrontation Between ISKCON and Narayana Maharaja." In *The Hare Krishna Movement: The Postcharismatic Fate of a Religious Transplant*. Edwin F. Bryant and Maria L. Ekstrand, eds. New York: Columbia University Press, 216. Collins is citing Roy Wallis. 1982. "Charisma, Commitment and Control in a New Religious Movement." In *Millenialism and Charisma*. Roy Wallis, ed. Belfast: The Queen's University, 116. Bryant and Ekstrand's edited volume makes an important set of contributions to the study of this issue within ISKCON, and the interested reader is encouraged to consult it for essays on the topic. Bryant and Ekstrand 2004.

25. Bromley 1989, 266.

26. Ibid., 268.

27. Eugene V. Gallagher. 2004. *The New Religious Movements Experience in America*. Westport and London: Greenwood Press, 110.

28. Bromley 1989, 265.

29. See Carl Arrington. "In a Landmark Case, Ex-Krishna Robin George Sues the Cult and Wins Big: $9.7 Million." *People Magazine*, September 12, 1983. Accessed February 19, 2017. http://people.com/archive/in-a-landmark-case-ex-krishna-robin-george-sues-the-cult-and-wins-big-9-7-million-vol-20-no-11; and Eric Lichtblau and Matt Lait. 1992. "Court Orders Retrial of O.C. Krishna Case." *Los Angeles Times*, January 31. Accessed February 19, 2017. http://articles.latimes.com/1992-01-31/news/mn-1099_1_supreme-court.

30. Rochford 2007, 96.

31. See, for example, the essays in Bryant and Ekstrand 2004.

32. Rochford 2007, 171–172. See also the essays in Bryant and Ekstrand 2004.

33. See, for example, the essays in Bryant and Ekstrand 2004.

34. Squarcini and Fizzotti discuss the shift in the ISKCON movement's congregational model in their book *Hare Krishna*, calling it the "most influential development in the thirty-year history of the religion's social life." Squarcini, Federico, and Eugenio Fizzotti. 2004. *Hare Krishna*. Salt Lake City, UT: Signature Books, 29.

35. Rochford 2007, 179.

36. Eck, Diana L. 1996. *Darśan: Seeing the Divine Image in India*. New York: Columbia University Press, 78.

37. Ibid., 78.

38. E. Burke Rochford Jr. 2004. "Airport, Conflict, and Change in the Hare Krishna Movement." In Bryant and Ekstrand 2004.

39. Bir Krishna Dasa Goswami. 2014. "Krishna West Overview by Bir Krishna Dasa Goswami, Part 1." YouTube video, April 15. 0:23–4.01. Accessed February 19, 2017. https://www.youtube.com/watch?v=bShPRTP1IJw.

40. For a discussion of a similar set of circumstances in Britain (surrounding the Bhaktivedanta Manor), see Malory Nye. 2015. *Multiculturalism and Minority Religions in Britain: Krishna Consciousness, Religious Freedom, and the Politics of Location*. London and New York: Routledge.

41. Rochford 2007, 186.

42. Ibid., 187.

43. Ibid., 187.

44. Ibid., 187.

45. Hridayananda Das Goswami. 2015. "Ideal Vedic Culture—Krishna West Istagosthi with H. D. GOSWAMI." Daniel Laflor YouTube channel, September 29. 1:00–1:03:30. Accessed February 24, 2017. https://www.youtube.com/watch?v=YottYzI98_M.

46. Jaya Madhava Dasa. 2011. "Is ISKCON Shrinking or Growing?" *The Sampradaya Sun-Independent Vaishnava News*, April 3. Accessed May 20, 2020. http://www.harekrsna.com/sun/editorials/04-11/editorials7165.htm. Jaya Madhava Dasa cites a conversation with Kavichandra Maharaj.

47. Urvashi Patel. 2006. "The Need for Diversity." *Jagannatha's Chakra: Discussions*. http://www.chakra.org/discussions/IntJun08_06.html. Accessed February 20, 2017. In discussions of the Hinduization of ISKCON, the terms *Hindu* and *Indian* are often conflated.

48. E. Burke Rochford Jr., is the scholar who is best known for writing about the Hinduization of ISKCON (most notably in Rochford 2007), specifically in the United States.

49. Zaidman, Nurit. 1997. "When the Deities Are Asleep: Processes of Change in an American Hare Krishna Temple." *Journal of Contemporary Religion* 12, no. 3: 335–352; Zaidman, Nurit. 2000. "The Integration of Indian Immigrants to Temples Run by North Americans." *Social Compass* 47, no. 2: 205–219; Berg, Travis Vande, and Fred Kniss. 2008. "ISKCON and Immigrants: The Rise, Decline, and Rise Again of a New Religious Movement." *The Sociological Quarterly* 49: 79–104; Rochford 2007. Malory Nye also discusses the "Hinduisations" of ISKCON in *Multiculturalism and Minority Religions in Britain* (2015). Various devotees and scholars are also interviewed regarding their perspectives on Indian and non-Indian devotees in Graham Dwyer and Richard J. Cole's edited volume *Hare Krishna in the Modern World* (2013). Finally, it is important to note that although Hinduization has significantly affected the demographics of the global ISKCON movement generally, it has not affected all ISKCON communities evenly, nor has it affected all ISKCON communities. Communities in areas without an Indian population, for example, tend to be exceptions to the general trend.

50. Ragaputra Das. 2005. "The Hindufication of ISKCON." *Jagannatha's Chakra*. Accessed February 20, 2017. http://chakra.org/discussions/IntMar31

_05.html; Hare Krsna Dasi. 2004. "The Hinduization of ISKCON?" *Jagannatha's Chakra*. Accessed February 20, 2017. http://www.chakra.org/discussions/IntFeb12_04.html; Jaya Madhava Das. 2014. "Surrounded by Indians." *The Sampradaya Sun-Independent Vaishnava News*, January 10. Accessed May 20, 2020. http://www.harekrsna.com/sun/editorials/01-14/editorials11247.htm; Patel 2006; Dayananda Das. 2006. "A Disciple's Perspective on the Hinduization of ISKCON." *Jagannatha's Chakra*. Accessed February 20, 2017. http://www.chakra.org/discussions/IntApr15_06.html. See also Urvashi Patel. 2005. "Response to the Article 'The Hindufication of ISKCON.'" *Jagannatha's Chakra*. Accessed February 20, 2017. http://www.chakra.org/discussions/IntMay04_05.html; and Jaya Madhava Das. 2006. "The Hinduization of ISKCON?" *Dandavats: Discussion*. Accessed May 20, 2020. http://www.dandavats.com/?p=127. The comment thread following this latter article is an interesting set of primary texts in itself.

51. Jaya Madhava Das. 2013. "The Hare Krishna Movement Without Krishna/Prabhupada—Part 4." *The Sampradaya Sun-Independent Vaishnava News*, August 19. Accessed May 20, 2020. http://www.harekrsna.com/sun/editorials/08-13/editorials10516.htm.

52. Prabhupada's public understanding of ISKCON's relationship to Hinduism is a complicated matter, as is ISKCON devotees' current self-understanding of the movement's relationship to Hinduism. While Prabhupada is consistently reported to have said that ISKCON is not Hinduism (a stance many of his contemporary followers maintain), he did align his movement with Hinduism on occasion. Likewise, contemporary ISKCON devotees often identify the movement as Hindu, depending on the necessity of the circumstance. For an excellent analysis of ISKCON's complex public relationship with Hinduism in contemporary Britain, see Nye 2015. Vineet Chander has also produced an excellent study that traces ISKCON's alignment (or lack thereof) with Hinduism across a variety of social, historical, and spatial circumstances. Vineet Chander. 2016. *The Washerman's Dog: Reflections on Liminality and ISKCON's Engagement with the Hindu Diaspora* (unpublished manuscript). Presented at The Worldwide Krishna Movement: Half a Century of Growth, Impact, and Challenge Conference. Harvard University, Cambridge, MA, April 22–24. Jan Brzezinski has also written an excellent analysis of Prabhupada's complex position with respect to Hinduism. See Jan Brzezinski. 1998. "What Was Srila Prabhupada's Position: The Hare Krishna Movement and Hinduism." *ISKCON Communications Journal* 6, no. 2: 27–49. See also Gavin Flood. 1995. "Hinduism, Vaishnavism, and ISKCON: Authentic Traditions or Scholarly Constructions?" *ISKCON Communications Journal* 3, no. 2: 5–15.

53. It is the case, however, that many of the most powerful Krishna Branders are westerners (by ISKCON's definition of the term). This is consistent with

the prominent place of westerners across a number of ISKCON's ventures (in ISKCON, prominence often derives from proximity to Prabhupada, and generally speaking, most of Prabhupada's direct disciples were westerners). For a discussion of this phenomenon more broadly, see Amanda J. Lucia. 2014b. *Reflections of Amma: Devotees in Global Embrace*. Berkeley and Los Angeles: University of California Press.

TWO

CONTEXTUALIZING THE KRISHNA BRANDERS

During one of my visits to ISKCON of Philadelphia, I sat down for *prasādam* (sanctified food) on a cold winter evening in a small upstairs room filled wall-to-wall with people. This upstairs room was a tucked-away classroom of a sort, one in which devotees and guests gather informally to eat and socialize and formally to discuss a range of devotional topics. On this particular evening, a group of guests, devotees, and I sat on the floor and shared a meal of ground cauliflower, rice, and *pūrīs* (fried bread puffs), and we chatted over topics ranging from the personal (devotees' conversion stories) to the conceptual (what it means to host the deities in the temple as living embodiments of Krishna). As I left for the evening, ready to head home, a Black woman dressed in a colorfully adorned saree, which she wore conservatively wrapped around the full frame of her face, stopped me in the hall, eager to catch me on my way out. "There is something I forgot to tell you that is really important," she said. "ISKCON used to be a lot more international. A lot has changed over the past twenty years or so, I don't know if you have noticed. It is all Indians now, but it wasn't always like this."

Like the devotees discussed in chapter 1, this devotee in Philadelphia expressed a deep sadness about the fact that ISKCON has become what she perceives to be an imbalanced or demographically homogenous movement. Chapters 3, 4, and 5 of this book detail the programs of the Krishna Branders, who, having recognized the demographic changes in the ISKCON movement, are launching and administering a series of innovative marketing and branding strategies, initiatives, and programs all over the world in hopes of attracting westerners to ISKCON and making the movement once again more ethnically, racially, and nationally diverse. But before we explore who the Krishna

Branders are and the rebranding campaigns that they operate, we must first look into the bigger and more basic question raised at the end of the previous chapter: Why is this diversity a goal for which the Krishna Branders so intensely strive?

In order to answer this question, we need to travel back in time to understand Prabhupada himself, long before he ever stepped off of the *Jaladuta* in New York Harbor. We must also understand the religious mission for the ISKCON movement that he and his predecessors developed well before he even decided to come to the United States, for it is this mission, I argue in this chapter, that underscores and motivates the present-day actions of the Krishna Branders. It is to this historical discussion that I now turn, beginning first with an examination of the historical context of Swami Prabhupada (1896–1977), as well as the two prominent Vaishnava figures who most influenced his religious life: Bhaktisiddhanta Sarasvati (1874–1937) and Bhaktivinoda Thakura (1838–1914). The mission of these three religious figures together, I show, is what drives the contemporary Krishna Branders in their efforts to attract more westerners to ISKCON.

CONTEXTUALIZING A. C. BHAKTIVEDANTA SWAMI PRABHUPADA

A. C. Bhaktivedanta Swami Prabhupada was born Abhay Charan De into a Bengali Vaishnava family in 1896 in what is now Kolkata (Calcutta), India. Traditional ISKCON stories about De describe him as having been introduced to the formal worship of Radha and Krishna by his family from an early age and as having been a pious person from boyhood.[1] These hagiographical stories recount, for example, that De not only visited the neighboring Radha-Govinda temple daily as a child in order to make offerings to the deities but also that he learned to play the *mṛdaṅga* (cylindrical drum) at an early age and received his very own *mūrti* (embodied form) of Krishna at just six years old.

Although he grew up immersed in Vaishnava religious practices, during his college years, De turned away from religion and instead focused his attention on politics. While attending the Scottish Church College in Calcutta, for example, he became a "strong sympathizer of Gandhi's and was politically active with the Congress Party."[2] ISKCON sources note his involvement in Gandhi's political cause of noncooperation with the British rule was so intense, in fact, that in 1920, he quit college—as a statement of protest—and refused to accept his diploma, despite completing all of the requirements necessary for his degree. Following this act of protest, De took a position as a manager at a chemical factory owned by Dr. Kartick Chandra Bose, a close family friend.[3] It was at this time that he met Bhaktisiddhanta Sarasvati, the man who was to become his guru.

Swami Prabhupada and Bhaktisiddhanta Sarasvati

Swami Prabhupada met the Vaishnava ascetic Bhaktisiddhanta Sarasvati in 1922. Born Bimal Prasad Datta in 1874 Calcutta, Bhaktisiddhanta Sarasvati—like Prabhupada—is described in ISKCON sources as having been instilled with Vaishnava religious values and practices from an early age. When he was in just the seventh grade, for example, Bhaktisiddhanta is said to have been given a religiously powerful *japa mālā* (prayer beads) from the famous Jagannath temple in Puri and was initiated into the practices of *harināma* (chanting the name of Krishna). Further, sources note that Bhaktisiddhanta was also given an embodied form of the avatar Kurma at a young age and was instructed in formal Vaishnava ritual worship so that he could be entrusted with its care.[4]

Although Bhaktisiddhanta was, in these ways, similar to many other religiously trained youth of his time, several features of his religious life stand apart from those of his contemporaries. Traditional accounts describe Bhaktisiddhanta as having been an exceedingly disciplined young man. This discipline stands out as one of the foremost features of his hagiographical accounts, especially within the ISKCON movement. For example, Bhaktisiddhanta is often said to have abstained from the consumption of mangoes for his entire life as an act of self-chastisement for having mistakenly eaten a mango as a child without first offering it to the deities. Bhaktisiddhanta also took a vow of celibacy at the age of seventeen—a vow he is said to have maintained for the duration of his life.[5] Finally, in 1918, Bhaktisiddhanta entered into the renounced order of *saṃnyāsa*, a highly respected Hindu stage of life wherein an individual formally relinquishes their previous identity and societal standing in order to live a permanently celibate life of a single-focused devotion to religious pursuits.[6]

Besides showcasing his highly disciplined and ascetic bent, however, the act of entering into *saṃnyāsa* also showcased another important aspect of Bhaktisiddhanta Sarasvati's life: the degree to which he was a religio-social maverick during his day. This is because unlike other Hindus who entered into *saṃnyāsa* by formal initiation, Bhaktisiddhanta conferred the order upon himself. As Ferdinando Sardella puts it in his historical account of Bhaktisiddhanta Sarasvati, "Those that aspire to take *saṃnyāsa* generally find an established member of that community and seek initiation from him. Not so Bhaktisiddhānta. In his characteristically singular style, he simply sat down before a picture of Gaura Kiśora dāsa Bābājī [his guru] and invested that order upon himself. And from that day forward to the end of his life he not only adopted the dress and symbols of a Vaishnava renunciate, but strictly adhered to the vows and personal sacrifices that the life of a *saṃnyāsin* demands."[7]

One might surmise that it was the distinctive nature of Bhaktisiddhanta's religious style that drew the otherwise religiously uninterested Abhay Charan De to be so captivated by him.

The Meeting

Swami Prabhupada first met Bhaktisiddhanta Sarasvati at a lecture that the latter delivered in 1922. Prabhupada attended the lecture at the request of his friend, Narendranath Mallik,[8] and sources note that it was a lecture that Prabhupada only begrudgingly attended. This is because Prabhupada had not only become disillusioned with religion during his college days but he had also come to believe that religious teachers offered no practical solutions to the problems of British rule. It seemed unlikely, therefore, that Prabhupada would be captivated by the teacher's lecture. It also seemed that taking on a strict Vaishnava religious path at this particular time was an exceedingly unlikely course for Prabhupada.

This all changed, however, when Prabhupada came into the presence of Bhaktisiddhanta. As Satsvarupa dasa Goswami's official ISKCON biography of Prabhupada notes, "No sooner did Abhay and his friend respectfully bow before the saintly person and prepare to sit than he said to them, 'You are educated young men. Why don't you preach Lord Chaitanya's message throughout the whole world?'"[9] This statement, Goswami notes, purportedly struck a deep chord within Prabhupada: "Śrīla Prabhupāda would later recall that on that very night he had actually accepted Bhaktisiddhānta Sarasvatī as his spiritual master. 'Not officially,' Prabhupada said, 'but in my heart. I was thinking that I had met a very nice saintly person.'"[10]

Besides requesting, allegedly right off the bat, that Prabhupada travel the world in order to preach the message of Chaitanya, Bhaktisiddhanta is said to have also "made a deep impression on Abhay" by entering into debate with him and skillfully answering all of his questions.[11] Over the course of this initial meeting with Bhaktisiddhanta, the teacher is said to have been able to convince Prabhupada that politics was not where he ought to put his efforts, because "no man-made political system could help humanity."[12] Instead, speaking about Krishna and Chaitanya and quoting from texts such as the *Bhagavad-Gītā*, Bhaktisiddhanta argued that people should give up all affiliations and endeavors and simply surrender to Krishna.

Prabhupada's initial meeting with Bhaktisiddhanta Sarasvati is said to have been an extremely fateful one for the would-be leader of ISKCON. Following this meeting, Prabhupada spent more and more time with Bhaktisiddhanta and became more and more invested in his teachings and his mission. In 1932—ten years after they met—Prabhupada took formal initiation under

Bhaktisiddhanta and officially became his disciple. Following this initiation, Prabhupada dedicated himself fully to becoming a servant of Bhaktisiddhanta's mission. Prabhupada's life, in other words, came to be lived executing the request that Bhaktisiddhanta had made to him at their initial meeting—namely that he attempt to preach Chaitanya's message throughout the world. "The story of the next thirty years of [Prabhupada's] life in India [following this initiation] is the story of a single, growing desire to preach Kṛṣṇa consciousness worldwide, as his spiritual master had ordered him."[13]

Bhaktivinoda Thakura

The mission of Bhaktisiddhanta Sarasvati, which came to be the mission of A. C. Bhaktivedanta Swami Prabhupada, cannot be fully understood without understanding the mission of another key Vaishnava figure: Bhaktivinoda Thakura. Bhaktivinoda Thakura was Bhaktisiddhanta Sarasvati's father and was "perhaps *the* major influence in Bhakisiddhānta's life."[14]

Bhaktivinoda Thakura was born Kedarnath Datta in 1838 in the city of Ula (now Birnagar, West Bengal). Although he spent most of his youth enjoying the idyllic lifestyle that Ula afforded him, a family bout of illness, death, and other hardships forced the young Datta to move from Ula to Calcutta in 1952 in order to complete his studies.[15]

Datta thrived in Calcutta. With the help of his maternal uncle, Kashiprasad Ghosh, with whom he lived while studying,[16] Datta demonstrated a penchant for intellectualism and writing. These earned him a place in Calcutta's intelligentsia, and he eventually came to associate, study, and write among such prominent figures as Gajendranath Tagore and Keshub Chandra Sen. In Calcutta, Datta also impressed the likes of Alexander Duff, the prominent Scottish missionary figure (1806–1878) who eventually came to be his mentor.[17] While studying with Duff, he formed a close bond with Dwijendranath Tagore, with whom he "studied not only Sanskrit and religion but also Kant, Goethe, Hegel, Swedenborg, Hume, Voltaire, and Schopenhaur."[18] Finally, throughout these studies, Datta got exposed to the reformist ideology of the Brahmo Samaj, as well as with the Unitarian Universalists' theistic take on Christianity. Datta soon became a Christian and eventually joined the Unitarian Universalist Congregation of the Reverend Charles Dall.[19]

Economic hardships forced Datta to leave Calcutta to take up work as a civil servant in Dinajpur in 1868. It was in Dinajpur that he came to study Chaitanya Vaishnavism and in particular the *Bhagavata Purana* and the *Caitanya Caritāmṛta*, texts that sources say captured him in a way that no other texts had in his previous studies. "It was at this point that Vaishnava *bhakti* emerged as the all-encompassing focal point of his life."[20]

It is important to note, however, that although Bhaktivinoda became fully captivated by Chaitanya Vaishnavism, his captivation was also combined with a reformist spirit. This is not surprising, given his associations with prominent Hindu reformers and colonial and missionary figures in mid-nineteenth-century Calcutta (Kolkata). In particular, his reformist positions centered on a belief that the Chaitanya tradition needed to be "modernized" or reinterpreted through the lens of "reason" in order to be suited to the needs of contemporary intellectuals.[21] As Thomas J. Hopkins puts it, once Bhaktivinoda came to be attracted and devoted to the ideas of Chaitanya Vaishnavism, "his immediate task, as is evident from the context, was to restore the *Bhagavata Purana* and the Chaitanya tradition as a whole to respectability."[22]

Bhaktivinoda Thakura developed his Hindu reformist positions in response to colonial critiques of Hinduism, just as many of his contemporaries did. During the colonial period in the Indian subcontinent, many Hindu reformers—such as Rammohan Roy (1772–1833) and Dayananda Saraswati (1824–1883)—emerged from the Hindu traditions in order to reconfigure and reformulate aspects of Hinduism in response to the British. The reasons for these reformulations were complex and varied, but they revolved around a common perception that was operative at the time and that was largely produced and fueled by the British colonial rulers (as well as Christian missionaries). This perception was that Hinduism—though it had once been great—had changed to become, in its more contemporary iterations, "corrupt," "degraded," and "overly licentious," its conceptual textual underpinnings overshadowed by its "popular" temple practices and their concomitant praxes of "over-emotionality."[23] In actuality, what had changed about the Hindu traditions was the lens through which they had begun to be viewed—not only that of the British rulers and Christian missionaries but also their religious sensibilities.

As is often the case in colonial encounters, the colonial lens is not just used by those in power to examine the citizenry under colonial rule; it is also used by the citizenry to examine themselves. This was the case for Bhaktivinoda Thakura (who himself occupied an ambivalent space between colonizer and citizen during his own lifetime).[24] As Varuni Bhatia writes in her foundational work *Unforgetting Chaitanya*, Bhaktivinoda Thakura's "own personal engagements with English education, Enlightenment philosophy, Christianity, Theosophy, and the Brahmo Samaj had made [him] particularly aware of the disaffection toward Vaishnavism that resulted from such exchanges. In Kedarnath Datta's [Bhaktivinoda Thakura's] writings, we find an explicit mention of the scorn of the English-educated youth for Vaishnava theology. Datta candidly wrote about his own disapproval of texts such as the *Bhāgavata Purāṇa* during his days as a college student in Calcutta when he was extensively reading Enlightenment thinkers and European poets and philosophers."[25]

More than this, Bhatia explains that Bhaktivinoda Thakura's biographies show that he "saw Vaishnavism refracted through the eyes of the missionary and the colonialist . . . [and] . . . tended to agree with the largely denunciatory evaluations of Bengali Vaishnava practices and rued the low or unclean status of existing Vaishnavas in the region. [Further, he saw that] the way forward was two-pronged: purge, purify, and reform Vaishnava practices, on the one hand, and recover material cultures connected to Vaishnavism, on the other hand. Datta's endeavors resulted in the formation of a modern and reformed Gaudiya Vaishnavism."[26]

Being a Hindu reformer, in other words, did not just mean being aware of, or troubled by, colonial critiques of Hinduism; rather, it also meant reformulating Hindu religious practices and systems of thought in order to craft "new and improved" sets of them—sets that retained the "respectable" features of the Hindu traditions (i.e., those that appealed to the British rulers and Christian missionaries) while casting out those features that were "problematic" (i.e., those that did not appeal to them). And this is precisely what Bhaktivinoda Thakura did. Although his studies and government positions eventually took him to a committed position as a practitioner of Vaishnavism, his Vaishnavism was nonetheless characterized by an ever-present endeavor to restore the tradition to "respectability." As Jason Fuller notes in his foundational work on Bhaktivinoda Thakura, "In a period (late nineteenth century) when Gauḍīya Vaiṣṇavism was considered by most middle-class intellectuals to be an inferior and debased form of religion, Bhaktivinode Thakur ably utilized every means at his disposal to reclaim and retrieve Vaiṣṇavism from its taboo status . . . [and] to create a sacred and viable Vaiṣṇava cosmos for the colonial middle-class."[27] Bhaktivinoda Thakura passed this spirit of reform on to his son, Bhaktisiddhanta Sarasvati, who promoted a Chaitanyaite theism that was rooted in Vaishnava *bhakti* but that was also heavily institutionalized, ascetic, and averse to the amorous devotional emotions that characterized many of the *bhakti* traditions at the time.[28] Adding to this reform, importantly, Bhaktisiddhanta Sarasvati worked extra hard to solidify a Vaishnavism that did not rely on the Advaita Vedānta of Shankaracarya (or other such varieties of nondualism such as that of Vivekananda) in its response to the colonial critique. As Ferdinando Sardella put it,

> the content of the teachings that Bhaktisiddhānta propagated . . . stood in stark contrast to the nondualism [e.g., Shankara's Advaita] that had become so prevalent among most of his contemporaries. . . . [Instead his] teachings

> were deeply theistic, presenting the highest truth or "Supreme Godhead" as personal rather than impersonal, with form rather than formless. In this regard, he championed Vaishnavism's iconic practices as well as the ultimate reality of the form, abode, and activities of a Supreme Being. He did so, however, not on the basis of [what he saw to be] popular sentimentalism and eroticism, but on the basis of a complex philosophical understanding that posed a direct challenge to the nondualistic views of Vivekānanda and others.[29]

Like his father, Bhaktivinoda Thakura, Bhaktisiddhanta Sarasvati endeavored to restore to Chaitanya Vaishnavism what he saw to be a long-lost prestige, glory, and respect.

THE RELIGIOUS MISSION: FROM BHAKTIVINODA THAKURA TO SWAMI PRABHUPADA

Bhaktivinoda Thakura strove hard to "restore respectability" to Chaitanya Vaishnavism in India and to spread his reformed version of the tradition there. In order to do so, he fashioned and promoted his reformed Vaishnavism for a middle-class audience by utilizing various "colonial technologies" to his advantage;[30] for example, he used the printing press to publish journals and books, he wrote novels and used them with the aims of promoting his reform ideas for Chaitanya Vaishnavism, and he refashioned and reconceptualized the location of pilgrimage sites through the use of textual and archeological argumentation (along with other more organizational means).[31] More than this, he also sought to promote his Vaishnavism through the creation of a Nāma Haṭṭa (marketplace of the name) program—"a marketing program designed to rationalize, bureaucratize, systematize, and coordinate the missionary, proselytizing, and propagandistic activities of his new brand of Vaishnavism."[32] This was a program whereby Bhaktivinoda Thakura sought to spread his movement in India (and justify his efforts to do so) through the establishment of a very corporate-like institutional structure and through the language of marketing and the marketplace (for example, speaking of utilizing religious "currencies" such as faith in order to obtain or "purchase" religious "commodities," such as benefiting from chanting the holy name, etc.).[33] As Fuller argues, these moves collectively "had the consequence of relocating religious authority within Gauḍīya Vaiṣṇavism from its traditional centers into the hands of Bhaktivinode and the *bhadralok* class [middle class]. Or, put another way," they allowed Bhaktivinoda to "effectively arrogate [] the power and right of religious (Vaiṣṇava) representation unto himself and his middle-class brethren."[34] This arrogation of power subsequently allowed for his Vaishnava reform movement to spread widely and efficiently throughout India.

But Bhaktivinoda Thakura's aim was not just to restore Chaitanya Vaishnavism and its practices to prominence in India. Instead, his larger and more primary religious mission was to make Chaitanya Vaishnavism a *universal* religion—that is, one practiced *globally*, by people not just in India but in countries all over the world. As Thomas Hopkins notes, "Even in his early writing . . . the breadth of his [Bhaktivinoda Thakura's] vision went well beyond the immediate concern for intellectual acceptance. As his conclusion indicates, the ultimate *goal can be no less than a worldwide religion based on the principles of the Bhagavata:* . . . 'See how universal is the religion of the *Bhagavata.* It is not intended for a certain class of Hindus alone, but it is a great gift to man at large in whatever country he is born and in whatever society is bred.'"[35]

That Bhaktivinoda Thakura's main mission was to establish a universal, or global, religion practiced by people around the world is a feature about his theology that many scholars of his life and works discuss. For example, in his examination of Bhaktivinoda's theology, Ferdinando Sardella discusses this universalism, noting that Bhaktivinoda rooted it in the teachings of Chaitanya himself. "In [Bhaktivinoda's] view, Caitanya had come to establish a religious understanding that transcended all national boundaries and all narrow sectarian views, an understanding that had the potential to encompass the spiritual aspirations of all of humanity."[36] This, he continues, was the root of the "world vision of the sort that Bhaktivinoda had sweepingly spelled out in 1892":

> When in England, France, Russia, Prussia, and America, all fortunate persons by taking up *kholas* (drums) and *karatālas* (cymbals) will take the name of Śrī Caitanya Mahāprabhu again and again in their own countries, and raise the waves of *saṅkirtāna*, when will that day come! Oh! When will the day come when the white skinned British people will speak the glory of Śrī Śacīnandana [another name of Caitanya] on one side and on the other and with this call spread their arms to embrace devotees from other countries in brotherhood, when will that day come! The day when they will say, "Oh, Aryan Brothers! We have taken refuge at the feet of Caitanya Deva in an ocean of love, now kindly embrace us," when will that day come![37]

It is not just scholars of early Bengali Vaishnavism who point out the dreams for universalism that characterized Bhaktivinoda's theology, however; rather, discussions of it also play a prominent role in narrative accounts of the Vaishnava teacher in contemporary ISKCON circles and publications. For example, in ISKCON's many internally published texts and translations, devotees often quote Bhaktivinoda as discussing his own global Vaishnava vision and also as tracing it back to Chaitanya:

> Lord Chaitanya did not advent Himself to liberate only a few men in India. Rather, his main objective was to emancipate all living entities of all countries throughout the entire universe and preach the Eternal Religion. . . . There is no doubt that his unquestionable order will come to pass. . . . Very soon the unparalleled path of *hari-nāma-saṅkīrtana* will be propagated all over the world. . . . Oh, for that day when the fortunate English, French, Russian, German, and American people will take up banners, *mṛdaṅgas*, and *karatālas* and raise *kīrtana* through their streets and towns! When will that day come? . . . That day will witness the holy transcendental ecstasy of the Vaiṣṇava *dharma* to be the only *dharma*, and all the sects and religions will flow like rivers into the ocean of Vaiṣṇava *dharma*. When will that day come?[38]

As is evidenced in these remarks, Bhaktivinoda Thakura dreamed of a time in which his Vaishnavism would be universal, which he understood to mean practiced by people from all over the world including the English, French, Russians, Germans, and Americans. Bhaktivinoda Thakura's ideals of universalism were more than just dreams, however. Instead, for him, they were also predictions—expectations of a religious world order that he believed would certainly come to pass in the future, just as Chaitanya himself is believed to have prophesied that Krishna's "glorious names and the Hare Kṛṣṇa mahā-mantra would be broadcast in all the towns and villages of the world."[39]

Before moving ahead, it is important to pause for a moment and reflect on Bhaktivinoda Thakura's conception of universality. For starters, one cannot deny that Bhaktivinoda Thakura's desire for universalism—nor his conception of universalism as necessarily including people such as the "English, French, Russian, German, and American[s]"—was itself rooted in, and produced by, the colonial encounter. Part of what it means to acknowledge the colonial impact on religions in India is understanding that Hindu responses to the colonial critique involved Hindus not just changing their theologies and rituals in light of the critique but also trying to make their traditions appealing to (and accepted by) the British, Christian missionaries, and other European figures. It is therefore very likely that Bhaktivinoda Thakura sought to gain a globally based following *precisely because* this would have indicated to him that his reformulation of Hinduism was, in fact, acceptable to the British—and not just to them but to others like them outside of India as well. In other words, Bhaktivinoda Thakura's interest in universality—along with his sense of it to mean being appealing to a global audience of people—was *itself* a response to the colonial critique. Importantly, couching Bhaktivinoda Thakura's universality in the framework of the colonial critique allows us not only to understand the motivations that might have produced it but also to understand why Bhaktivinoda's sense of the globe outside of India was so Eurocentric: with his listing as the "globe" principally places only in Europe—England, France, Russia, and Prussia (although he also mentions America). His sense of the globe outside of India, in other words, seems to have consisted almost exclusively of places whose people he saw to be racially and ethnically similar to the British.

Establishing this globally practiced (as he understood it), universal Vaishnava religiosity was a major goal of Bhaktivinoda Thakura's life. It was also a goal that he believed was destined to come to fruition. As such, he worked hard throughout his life to lay the foundations for his vision to come to pass. Toward this end, by 1885 in Calcutta, Bhaktivinoda had created the Viśva Vaiṣṇava Rāja Sabhā (the Royal World Vaishnava Association),[40] an organization intended to serve as an opportunity for the free association of religious individuals across a variety of backgrounds and perspectives and give them a forum in which to gather for intellectual religious discussion and fraternity.[41] As Ferdinando Sardella argues, the name of this *sabhā* "had been mentioned in the *Bhakti-sandarbha* of Jīva (ca. 1517–1608), one of the 'Six Goswamis' of Vrindavan." As such, it reflected to Bhaktivinoda Thakura what he believed to be "the early universal vision of the Six Goswamis," as well as his belief that these Vrindavan Goswamis had "conceived of a religious society that could embrace all the peoples of the world, regardless of sectarian affiliations"[42]—a conception that he also traced back to Chaitanya.[43] For these reasons, the Viśva Vaiṣṇava Rāja Sabhā was both the concretization of Bhaktivinoda's universalist goals and a forum in which to develop them. It was also perfectly suited to the intellectual milieu of his historical context: "The vision of a *sabhā*—a community—that transcended religious borders fit well with the cosmopolitan world of Calcutta . . . [as well as with] Unitarians and evangelical missionaries both in India and in England [who] had already propagated a universal Christian religion, conceived as a pluralist, multiracial brotherhood."[44]

Bhaktivinoda dedicated his life to trying to get this society off the ground and to his plans of bringing Chaitanya Vaishnavism to people outside of India. However, unfortunately, "Bhaktivinoda's dream of a global Vaishnava community under the flag of Caitanya was not fulfilled in his lifetime, and he spent all his years in East India. Nonetheless, he was able to transmit his vision to his son [Bhaktisiddhanta Sarasvati], who later organized a venture to Europe to carry it out."[45]

As the son of Bhaktivinoda Thakura, Bhaktisiddhanta Sarasvati tried desperately to fulfill his father's wishes of a globally practiced, universal religiosity. His primary way of doing so was by doing his part to attract a global audience—or people outside of India—to Chaitanya Vaishnavism. Like his father, he primarily understood the globe to mean Europe and America, and so wanting to make Chaitanya Vaishnavism global mostly meant spreading it to people in those places. Importantly, people who inhabited the "globe" outside of India had, by Bhaktisiddhanta's time, come to be known as "westerners" in the lineage and circles that would later produce the ISKCON movement. Similarly, the term *the west* referred to this "globe" outside of India.

Ferdinando Sardella claims that what is "arguably Bhaktisiddhānta's most enduring legacy [is] his conviction that Westerners could seriously embrace the teachings of Chaitanya Vaishnavism, and his unprecedented attempt to spread those teachings beyond the shores of India."[46] Toward the aim of realizing his father's vision, Bhaktisiddhanta not only breathed new life into Bhaktivinoda's Viśva Vaiṣṇava Rāja Sabhā, but he also established several institutions of his own—including the Gauḍīya Maṭh—by which he hoped to officially carry out the mission. He even sent three disciples—Swami Bhakti Pradipa Tirtha, Swami Bhakti Hrdaya Bon, and Samvidananda dasa—on mission trips to England and Germany in 1933.[47] These missionaries did much to start the process of bringing Chaitanya Vaishnavism to the west and to westerners, principally by making connections with prominent figures in England and Germany and by attracting the strong affections of a small number of English and German citizens. However, they were unable to generate the widespread western interest in Chaitanya Vaishnavism for which Bhaktisiddhanta and Bhaktivinoda had hoped. It was not until 1965, when another one of Bhaktisiddhanta's disciples would take a mission trip to the United States, that the universal vision of Bhaktisiddhanta Sarasvati and Bhaktivinoda Thakura would begin to take off. This disciple was none other than Swami Prabhupada.

Swami Prabhupada and the Decision to "Go West"

In 1936, just one month before Bhaktisiddhanta's death, Swami Prabhupada wrote his elderly guru a letter asking him what more he could do to support his mission. In response to the query, Bhaktisiddhanta Sarasvati wrote Prabhupada the following response: "I am fully confident that you can explain in English our thoughts and arguments to the people who are not conversant with the languages [Bengali and Hindi]. . . . This will do much good to yourself as well as your audience. I have every hope that you can turn yourself into a very good English preacher."[48]

According to Prabhupada's ISKCON biographer, Satsvarupa dasa Goswami, this letter was a revelatory moment for Prabhupada. This is because upon receiving the letter, "Abhay at once recognized this to be the same instruction he had received at his first meeting with Śrīla Bhaktisiddhānta, in 1922. He took it as a confirmation. He now had no doubt as to the purpose of his life": he was to become an English language preacher so that he could spread Chaitanya Vaishnavism to people in the West.[49]

Becoming an English-language preacher, however, involved more than just making plans to travel outside of India; it also required the securing of paperwork and funding to do so, as well as the garnering of enough publicity to secure the paperwork and the funds. In order to attract the money and attention he needed, Prabhupada worked tirelessly as a writer, first on the publication of a Gauḍīya Maṭh periodical *Back to Godhead* and then on the translation of, and commentary on, several important Vaishnava works, including the *Bhagavad-Gītā*, and the *Bhāgavata Purāṇa*. To dedicate himself fully to these tasks, Prabhupada made the weighty decision—in 1959—to take *saṃnyāsa*. Prabhupada made this decision, ISKCON sources report, after having had a dream in which a visage of Bhaktisiddhanta Sarasvati told him to do so—a dream he interpreted to be yet another calling for him to preach to those living in the west.[50]

Having become a *saṃnyāsī* (renunciant) and renouncing society and his previous involvement in family life, Prabhupada moved to Vrindavan, the land of Krishna's mythical youth, so that he could live and work in full concentration on his guru's mission. From his quiet room in the Radha Damodar temple, Prabhupada was able to see the *samādhi* (memorial tomb) of Rupa Goswami—one of the six Vrındavan Goswamis associated with Chaitanya, as well as one of the most prolific philosopher-theologians of the Chaitanya tradition.[51] Prabhupada is said to have drawn inspiration from living in Vrindavan and from his close proximity to the *samādhi*. In fact, it was by seeing the *samādhi* on a daily basis that devotees believe Prabhupada was able to feel—with an overwhelming certainty—the weight of the call of his mission. As Satsvarūpa dāsa Goswami notes:

> Feeling Rūpa Gosvāmī's presence, he would think of his own mission for his spiritual master. Bhaktivedanta Swami's spiritual master and the previous spiritual masters in the disciplic succession had wanted the Kṛṣṇa consciousness movement to spread all over the world, and as Bhaktivedanta Swami daily gathered inspiration, sitting before Rūpa Gosvāmī's *samādhi*, he prayed to his spiritual predecessors for guidance. The intimate direction he received from them was an absolute dictation, and no government, no publisher, nor anyone else could shake or diminish it. Rūpa Gosvāmī

> wanted him to go to the West; Śrīla Bhaktisiddhānta Sarasvatī wanted him to go to the West; and Kṛṣṇa had arranged that he be brought to the Rādhā-Dāmodara temple to receive Their blessings. At the Rādhā-Dāmodara temple, he felt he had entered an eternal residence known only to pure devotees of the Lord. Yet although they were allowing him to associate intimately with them in the place of their pastimes, he felt they were ordering him to leave—to leave Rādhā-Dāmodara and Vṛindāvana and to deliver the message of the *ācāryas* [teachers] to forgetful parts of the world.[52]

Not long after arriving in Vrindavan, Prabhupada boarded the *Jaladuta.*

FROM HISTORICAL UNIVERSALISM TO THE CONTEMPORARY KRISHNA BRANDERS

It is in this context that we must understand the arrival of Swami Prabhupada in the United States, including the reasons why he traveled there to begin with and his religious vision for the society that he started there after he arrived. Scholarly works on ISKCON typically begin the movement's story in the New York Harbor in 1965, when Prabhupada first arrived in the United States. To do so, however, is to omit much that is important in understanding Prabhupada's, and therefore ISKCON's, historical context. Swami Prabhupada came to the United States on what he believed to be the express command of Bhaktisiddhanta Sarasvati: "I was ordered by my spiritual master to preach this Kṛṣṇa consciousness in the Western countries. So in 1965 I first came in New York" is something that Prabhupada said on many occasions.[53] When Prabhupada came to the United States, in other words, he did so with a history and a sense of mission that extended far beyond himself and included those figures who preceded him in his lineage. Failing to contextualize him in this light is to fail to understand not only his historical context but also the missiological motivations that it produced.

But seeing Prabhupada and his arrival in the United States in historical context does not just allow us to more deeply understand him; rather, it is also essential if one wishes to understand the contemporary ISKCON movement. This is especially the case if one wishes to understand the Krishna Branders—those devotees and gurus who are developing and administering the myriad and diverse centers, programs, and global initiatives that are explicitly aimed at attracting westerners to ISKCON. In fact, I want to argue that it is precisely the same set of motivations—and mission to universalism—that inspired Prabhupada to spread Krishna Consciousness to the West in 1965 that underscores the Krishna Branders' aims today, especially their efforts toward attracting westerners to ISKCON. What is different is only that the sense of the term *westerners* has broadened; a term that used to mean (for Prabhupada's gurus) predominantly Europeans and Americans has come to mean (for the contemporary Krishna Branders) *anyone* who is not Indian (or of Indian heritage), including people with heritage in Australia, Africa, and even countries in East Asia (such as China and Japan).

In order to see the connection between the missiological motivations of the contemporary Krishna Branders and those of Prabhupada and his own guru lineage, it is helpful to consider an important teaching within the ISKCON tradition. ISKCON devotees interpretively derive this teaching from a *śloka* (verse) in Rupa Goswami's *Padyāvalī* 74—which also appears in the *Caitanya Caritāmṛta*—that reads as follows:

> "*nāhaṁ vipro na ca nara-patir nāpi vaiśyo na śūdro*
> *nāhaṁ varṇī na ca gṛha-patir no vanastho yatir vā*
> *kintu prodyan-nikhila-paramānanda-pūrnāmṛtābdher*
> *gopī-bhartuḥ pada-kamalayor dāsa-dāsānudāsaḥ.*"[54]

As translated to English, within ISKCON this *śloka* states:

> "I am neither a priest nor a king, nor a merchant nor a worker. Neither am I a celibate, nor a householder, nor a forest dweller nor a renunciant. Rather, I am *the servant of the servant of the servant of the lotus feet of the lord of the gopīs* [e.g., Krishna] who is an ocean of nectar, full of supreme and all-encompassing bliss."[55]

Although it is short, this teaching—as ISKCON devotees interpret it—provides the framework of religiosity by which nearly all devotional action is situated within the ISKCON movement. Put simply, this framework is based on the idea that the superlative mode of religious action lies not in executing one's own independent will but rather in faithfully and earnestly executing the will of one's religious predecessors. In other words, the notion of being "the servant of the servant of the servant of Krishna" is taken prescriptively within ISKCON. Devotees argue that the paradigmatic and first—servant of Krishna was none other than Chaitanya himself, whom they believe manifested in sixteenth-century India in order to spread the *saṅkīrtan* movement and love of Krishna throughout the world. By extension, therefore, being "the servant of the servant of the servant of Krishna" means serving not just Chaitanya but importantly also serving those figures who themselves served him, and within ISKCON, these servants are interpreted to be none other than Bhaktivinoda Thakura, Bhaktisiddhanta Sarasvati, and Bhaktivedanta Prabhupada.[56]

Not all practitioners of Gauḍīya Vaishnavism interpret this *śloka* or the Chaitanya traditions more generally, in this manner. For example, many in the Gauḍīya Vaishnava traditions believe that Chaitanya was none other than Krishna himself, who descended to earth in human form in order to experience the love and bliss of life as his own devotee. Put simply, while many in the broader Gauḍīya traditions focus on the importance of *experiencing* devotional love of Krishna, devotees in ISKCON put more focus on *spreading* that love. This is not to say that experiencing love of Krishna is not important for ISKCON devotees or that ISKCON devotees do not believe that Chaitanya was also Krishna; rather, it is to say that ISKCON's theology is predominated by a highly evangelical spin on many of the texts that form its foundation. This evangelical spin is evident in ISKCON's interpretation of a number of texts and *ślokas*, not just Rupa Goswami's *Padyāvalī* 74. For example, when *Bhagavad-Gītā* 18.68 describes those who "explain Krishna's supreme secret to his devotees" as "having performed his supreme devotion" (*ya idaṁ paramaṁ guhyaṁ madbhakteṣv abhidhāsyati / bhaktiṁ mayi parāṁ kṛtvā*), ISKCON devotees take this to mean that those who give out or sell Prabhupada's books to the public are performing Krishna's most cherished devotional acts.[57]

For his part, Swami Prabhupada believed that Krishna, as Chaitanya, had descended to the world in the fifteenth century in order to spread love of Krishna far and wide. When Prabhupada came to the United States endeavoring to spread Krishna Consciousness around the world, therefore, he saw himself as part of a lineage of servants of Chaitanya enacting this mission. In other words, he saw himself not as enacting his own will but rather believed he was serving the servants of the servant of Krishna; he saw himself to be serving the mission of Bhaktisiddhanta Sarasvati, who was himself serving the mission of Bhaktivinoda Thakura. Importantly, it was in this same light that Prabhupada saw his own disciples. Upon his arrival in the United States, Prabhupada did not intend to serve the mission of his predecessors on his own. Rather, he designed a religious institution (ISKCON) whereby his own disciples would eventually plug themselves into the paradigm as well, becoming servants of the servant of the servant of Krishna themselves by becoming servants of him and his mission (which was none other than the mission of his predecessors). Consider, for example, a letter he wrote to his disciples in 1972:

> My dear beloved Children,
>
> Please accept my blessings. I am so much pleased with your kind and affectionate words on the occasion of my birthday anniversary on the Nandotsava day this year (1972). My Guru Maharaja wanted me to spread this Krishna Consciousness Movement in western world [*sic*], and you are

all helping in this great attempt. My Spiritual Master knew it that alone I could not do this great work. Therefore He has very kindly sent you all to help me in this task. I accept you therefore as representatives of my Guru Maharaja playing as my affectionate disciples. It is said that child is father of man. Kindly therefore continue your help in this great task and act as my young father and mother in my old age. I am

Your ever well-wisher,
A.C. Bhaktivedanta Swami[58]

Prabhupada came to the United States as part of his bigger mission to attract westerners to Krishna Consciousness. And as can be seen from his many letters to his disciples, he intended them to carry on his work with him as fated inheritors to a historical lineage of servants.[59] Prabhupada emphasized these wishes not only in letters but also in public lectures. For example, he expressed them in Los Angeles on December 13, 1973, on the occasion of a holiday observing the death of Bhaktisiddhanta Sarasvati:

Bhaktivinoda Ṭhākura, he desired, and, that Śrī Caitanya Mahāprabhu's message, it should be accepted by East and West equally, and both the Indians and Europeans, Americans, they should dance together in ecstasy of Śrī Caitanya Mahāprabhu's mercy. That was his desire, Bhaktivinoda Ṭhākura. He simply expressed the desire, "When I shall see this happening, that both the Eastern and Western people, they are united on the basis of Śrī Caitanya Mahāprabhu's cult and dancing together in ecstasy?" . . . That was ambition [*sic*] of Śrī Caitanya Mahāprabhu and this was the ambition of Bhaktivinoda Ṭhākura. And Śrī Bhaktisiddhānta Sarasvatī Ṭhākura [*Thākura* here is honorific] took up this affair, business, and he [also] wanted [it] first of all. So every student, any disciple, every disciple, especially those who are competent, he requested that "You take up this mission of Caitanya Mahāprabhu and preach in the Western countries."[60]

He expressed similar sentiments during a talk he gave at the Mayapur Chandrodaya Mandir in Mayapur, West Bengal, on September 27, 1974:

It was the desire of Srīla Bhaktivinoda Ṭhākura that Europeans and Americans would come here and chant Hare Kṛṣṇa mantra. That prophecy is now being fulfilled, and that is my satisfaction. I tried my little bit to fulfill the desire of Bhaktivinoda Ṭhākura. At my old age of seventy years, I just. . . . It was a gambling also. I simply thought that "This was the desire . . . " Of course, my Guru Mahārāja, Bhaktisiddhānta Sarasvatī Gosvāmī Prabhupāda, he also asked me to do this. Anyway, at least there

> is a place now . . . where these Europeans and Americans may come and live peacefully, chant Hare Kṛṣṇa mahā-mantra and advance in spiritual understanding [. . .] So at least the basic principles is being done, and I am very much thankful to you, you American, European boys and girls who are helping me in this mission. So go on cooperating in this way, and I am sure this mission of Caitanya Mahāprabhu will be successful. It must be successful, because Śrī Caitanya Mahāprabhu wanted it to be done. Simply we, the workers, the servitors, must be very sincere [. . .] So keep this mission always in view and do your best. That is my only request.[61]

As can be seen from these lectures, Prabhupada saw his mission to be the spreading of Krishna Consciousness around the world, among those in both the "East and West equally" (by which he primarily meant among Americans, Europeans, and Indians, but also to people from all continents on the globe).[62] Further, Prabhupada understood himself to be serving the mission of his predecessors by executing their mission in his own religious actions. Most importantly, however, Prabhupada intended his disciples to continue on the chain, themselves serving him and his mission and therefore the mission of his predecessors (including Chaitanya himself).

To say that Prabhupada was ever in servant mode in relation to his own gurus and lineage is not to say that he was merely a meek or quiet cog in a chain of disciple succession, although he often portrayed himself in this way. On the contrary, Prabhupada spoke boldly and confidently on his beliefs and became a guru in his own right upon migrating to the United States and amassing a large following there. Moreover, his disciples did not just unemotionally aim to execute his mission; instead, they also took delight in showering him in their devotion and did not hold back in offering it to him. For his part, Prabhupada also basked in their affections, as can be seen by even cursory glances through still and video footage of his interactions with his disciples. This relationship dynamic of disciple-to-guru reverence in the early ISKCON movement, in other words, existed alongside the movement's central raison d'être—serving the mission of Chaitanya and his servants—that Prabhupada consistently propagated in his writings, purports, and lectures.

Putting It All Together

In many ways, one could say that Swami Prabhupada came to the United States in order to start the Vaishnava equivalent of a multilevel marketing system—a system whereby he would make new disciples and whereby his new disciples, under his tutelage, would themselves become evangelists for Krishna's movement—working to spread his and his gurus' mission alongside him. In this vein, Prabhupada often included his new disciples in his language of missiological fulfillment. "Lord Caitanya Mahāprabhu," he said, "predicted that both His glorious names and the Hare Kṛṣṇa mahā-mantra would be broadcast in all the towns and villages of the world. Śrīla Bhaktivinoda Ṭhākura and Śrīla Bhaktisiddhānta Sarasvatī Prabhupāda desired to fulfill this great prediction and *we are following in their footsteps*."[63]

In Prabhupada's theological understanding and disciplic lineage, following in the footsteps of his predecessors meant executing their missiological desires, and these predecessors wanted a Krishna movement that was universal—that is, one that was global (as they understood it) in presence or one that had moved beyond the borders of India to include westerners. It was this universal movement that Prabhupada himself also wanted, although his sense of universality had a more global tinge than that of his predecessors. He passed along a desire for this universality to his own disciples, who now understand his and his gurus' project for ISKCON's universality to be centered in attracting *all* people in the world to the movement: both people from India and people from everywhere else in the world. As one disciple writes in an essay entitled "Patterns in ISKCON's Historical Self-Perception," this historical mission for a universal movement is one that has been strongly etched onto the self-understanding of Prabhupada's disciples, including his contemporary ones.

> Prabhupada's achievement in successfully propagating Caitanya's mission outside of India fulfills the prediction of Caitanya and the desire of Bhaktivinoda Thakura. Consequently, we who are his disciples in ISKCON see our institution as historically special, a part of this momentous step towards fulfilling the destiny of Caitanya's movement and Krishna's mission of salvation. Above all, Prabhupada has charged his disciples in ISKCON with the mandate to further the progress of Chaitanya's mission just as he has done, and, by so doing, work to bring about the full manifestation of 10,000 years of the golden age of Krishna Consciousness. . . . Seeing themselves in the context of this sacred history, ISKCON devotees are self-conscious historical actors, makers of history.[64]

Given Prabhupada's instructions to devotees to fulfill his and his predecessors' mission of creating a universal Vaishnavism, we are now better poised to understand why it is that many contemporary ISKCON devotees take issue with the current largely homogenous demographic makeup of ISKCON. We can also understand why a large number of them—the Krishna Branders—are actively trying to attract more westerners (now understood to mean all non-Indian converts) to ISKCON, so as to make the movement more diverse and more globally representative. In fact, the logic is quite straightforward: they believe that since their goal is a globally practiced universality, they do not have a universal movement if their base consists primarily of congregants with heritage in one country of the world. Prabhupada and his predecessors had a mission of universality for their movement, and ISKCON in its present demographic composition—according to many devotees—is failing that mission. This is why when devotees talk about the issues they have with ISKCON's current demographic homogeneity, they often do so by noting that Prabhupada came to the West because he wanted to liberate everyone in the world—and not just those of Indian heritage. As one devotee writes in an ISKCON periodical piece, "The Need for Diversity," that she penned, "The preaching to the indigenous people of the UK has more or less stopped. One can only wonder why Srila Prabhupada came to the West. To liberate the two percent of Hindus in the UK? Their Krishna Consciousness is just under their skin. But what chance do the 98% of Westerners stand if the outreach towards them has trickled to almost zero? How will they get liberated or receive Lord Nityananda's mercy?"[65]

In this statement, which echoes the sentiment of Bhaktivinoda Thakura cited earlier, it is clear that this devotee believes that a failure to preach to westerners violates Prabhupada's mission—one that she believes was intended to give salvific access to everyone, both Indians and westerners alike. And this is a viewpoint repeated often by devotees: "Maybe more effort to do something to bring the non-Indians back in is necessary. . . . I think if non-Indians become less involved it would be a great loss. It would be unfortunate because it would mean Prabhupada's intention was sidelined. Prabhupada definitely wanted that his movement would not just be for Indians."[66]

In fact, as those in the movement often point out, in "Prabhupada's praṇāma-mantra [or guru prayer], which he wrote himself . . . Prabhupada claims to be pāścātya-deśa-tāriṇe, the 'savior of the Western countries.'"[67]

As ISKCON devotees interpret it, the mission that Prabhupada was executing, which was the mission of his gurus, was to construct a movement that would not just be practiced in India (or by Indians) but would also move outside of India to be practiced globally, or be universal. Most importantly, this mission was not an idea that was simply tacked on to devotional life within ISKCON as an afterthought. Rather, it was the very raison d'être of the ISKCON movement—the very reason the movement was started, the very heart of its teachings, and the very core of what it meant to live them. Being a devotee in ISKCON means to plug oneself into the message of the messengers or to serve the mission of universalism that they served by being their servant. And this is precisely why the Krishna Branders feel it to be such a failure that their movement has become largely demographically homogenous and why they feel that if the trend goes unchanged, they are failing in their role as servants of Prabhupada. It is also why they are willing to go to such great lengths to attract westerners so as to make ISKCON once again diverse. As one Krishna Brander put it:

> If you look at the progress we're making in the Western world in the last 10–15 years, it's minimal, I mean, just to be honest. I mean, most of our temples in the West are primarily functioning with Indian devotees, and you know, I love Indian devotees, I work with them all the time, but if you go to the West and its only Indian devotees, it would be like going to India and having only Americans in your temple. . . . I mean, it's just weird, isn't it?![68] . . . And then what that means long term is that we're not going to have a worldwide movement anymore, it's just going to be one particular culture that's going to be in the movement whereas Prabhupada wanted a United Nations of the Spiritual World. He wanted everyone to work together, you know the Westerners, the Indians, the Chinese, the Russians. I mean, this is the success of our movement if we can do that.[69]

Although this desire to attract westerners is rooted in a servitude toward Prabhupada and his predecessors, it is also about placing oneself at the heart of the ISKCON story. And the heart of this story, for devotees, is not about obtaining Krishna's love and relishing in it for oneself but is rather about paying this love forward and passing it on to others so as to save what they (devotees) see to be the suffering world. This impetus to save the whole world underscores what many of the Krishna Branders do, and the Krishna Branders make it very clear that in order to save the whole world, it is crucial that they save those living in the west. Krishna Brander Hridayananda Das Goswami states, "Prabhupada"

> made very clear that his entire global strategy depended on ISKCON's success in Western countries, among Western people. Are we now to abandon that vision? Is it not instead our sacred duty to defend Prabhupada's honor by making his words come true? . . . We all know that Prabhupada sometimes said he would be satisfied if he made one pure devotee. But that one pure devotee would surely dedicate his or her life to fulfilling Prabhupada's ultimate dream and ambition: *to save this suffering planet*. Fortunately, not just one, but many great souls have joined Prabhupada's mission, and now is the time to do all we can to fulfill Prabhupada's greatest hope and dream. Our duty is not to reinterpret, scale down, compromise, or renounce Prabhupada's grand vision for his Western mission.[70] . . . Prabhupada's vision to save the world *requires, requires* that we have a *powerful* movement in the west. It's very simple.[71] . . . In his words, let us "do the needful."[72]

This "doing the needful"—for the Krishna Branders—means not only acknowledging Prabhupada's belief that having westerners in the movement is essential to having a universal ISKCON but also embracing an active and explicit outreach to westerners as one's devotional calling. As William H. Deadwyler III (Ravindra-svarupa das) notes, ISKCON devotees trace their impetus to evangelize all the way back to the story of the "enlightenment of Brahmā" or the passages in *Bhāgavata Purāṇa* 2.9, wherein Krishna explains to Brahmā the nature of his own (Krishna's) Being.[73] While many Vaishnavas read these passages as musings on the nature of divine ontology, Prabhupada interpreted them evangelically. "In his commentary on this chapter," Deadwyler notes, "Prabhupada treats Brahma's enlightenment as a paradigm for the *sampradaya* [tradition]. . . . Like Brahma [who was himself enlightened by Krishna], the devotees in his *sampradaya* ("tradition") should have a sense of mission. Having been enlightened in spiritual knowledge, they should in turn enlighten others."[74] Within ISKCON, this commitment to enlightening others is interpreted to mean that devotees should extend themselves to *everyone*, which is why the Krishna Branders are so intensely reaching out to attract westerners in particular, whom they see as being underrepresented in the movement. As one Krishna Brander put it, "When you see how little, how few people are joining in the western world, *you gotta try something radical*. Because we have very little time left. Cause another point is, the Prabhupada disciples like myself, Hridayananda Maharaj and others, I mean, *we're old*. . . . And ya know, how much time do we have left? And what have we done for Prabhupada? I mean, what are we gonna tell Prabhupada when we leave this world and go to join Prabhupada and [he asks], ya know, 'what did you do?'"[75]

In the next chapter, we begin our exploration into the work that the Krishna Branders are doing in their attempts to bring westerners back to ISKCON. This work involves not just changing the way that ISKCON is marketed for the public, but it also involves a radical revolutionizing of the contemporary ISKCON worship-scape around the world. It is to a discussion of the programs and centers that the Krishna Branders are founding and administering that I now turn, beginning with the initiatives of Devamrita Swami and his global network of disciples.

NOTES

1. Abhay Charan De received the name Abhay Caranaravinda Bhaktivedanta Swami in 1959 at the ceremony by which he became a *saṃnyāsī* (renunciant) within his religious lineage. See Satsvarūpa Dāsa Goswami. 1983. *Prabhupāda: Messenger of the Supreme Lord*. Mumbai: The Bhaktivedanta Book Trust, xxxiii.

He is known within ISKCON as A. C. Bhaktivedanta Swami Prabhupada, and devotees typically shorten his name to just *Prabhupada*, an affectionate honorific. *Srila* (or *Śrīla*) is another affectionate honorific often used in place of *Swami*. I use his various names interchangeably throughout this chapter. I do the same with the given and religious names of Bhaktisiddhanta Sarasvati and Bhaktivinoda Thakura. I also refer to all three figures by their shortened names throughout: Prabhupada, Bhaktisiddhanta, and Bhaktivinoda, respectively.

2. Ferdinando Sardella. 2013. *Modern Hindu Personalism: The History, Life, and Thought of Bhaktisiddhānta Saravatiī*. Oxford and New York: Oxford University Press, 102. Sardella's book is a well-documented historical account of the life and influence of Bhaktisiddhanta Sarasvati.

3. Goswami 1983, xiv.

4. Sardella 2013, 64. Kurma is the second incarnation of Vishnu (or Krishna, within ISKCON) and is said to have descended to earth in the form of a tortoise.

5. Ibid., 66.

6. Ibid., 90.

7. Ibid., 90.

8. Ibid., 102.

9. Goswami 1983, xv.

10. Ibid., xvi.

11. Ibid., xvi.

12. Ibid., xv.

13. Ibid., xviii.

14. Sardella 2013, 55. Italics in original.

15. Shukavak Dasa. 1999. *Hindu Encounter with Modernity: Kedarnath Datta Bhaktivinoda Vaiṣṇava Theologian*. Los Angeles: Sanskrit Religions Institute, 33–46. Dasa's book is an excellent reference on the life and theology of Bhaktivinoda Thakura. Excellent academic works on Bhaktivinoda Thakura include Varuni Bhatia. 2017. *Unforgetting Chaitanya: Vaishnavism and Cultures of Devotion in Colonial Bengal*. New Delhi: Oxford University Press; and Jason Dale Fuller. 2005. *Religion, Class, and Power: Bhaktivinode Thakur and the Transformation of Religious Authority Among the Gauḍīya Vaiṣṇavas in Nineteenth-Century Bengal*. PhD Dissertation: University of Pennsylvania.

16. Ibid., 46–47.

17. Sardella 2013, 58–59.

18. Ibid., 59–60.

19. Ibid., 60. For comprehensive biographical details on Bhaktivinoda Thakura, see Fuller 2005.

20. Ibid., 61.

21. Readers are encouraged to read Bhatia 2017 and Fuller 2005 for a full discussion of Bhaktivinoda's reinterpretive framework. See also Dasa 1999

and Thomas J. Hopkins. 1989. "The Social and Religious Background for Transmission of Gaudiya Vaishnavism to the West." In *Krishna Consciousness in the West*. David G. Bromley and Larry D. Shinn, eds. Lewisburg: Bucknell University Press and Associated University Presses.

22. Hopkins 1989, 46.

23. See Bhatia 2017; Fuller 2005; Jason Dale Fuller. 2009. "Modern Hinduism and the Middle Class: Beyond *Reform* and *Revival* in the Historiography of Colonial India." *The Journal of Hindu Studies* 2: 160–178. Jason Dale Fuller. 2003. "Re-membering the Tradition: Bhaktivinoda Ṭhākura's *Sajjanaṭosanī* and the Construction of a Middle-Class Vaiṣṇava Sampradāya in Nineteenth-Century Bengal." In *Hinduism in Public and Private: Reform, Hindutva, Gender, and Sampraday*. Antony Copley, ed. New Delhi: Oxford University Press; David L. Haberman. 1994. "Divine Betrayal: Krishna Gopal of Braj in the Eyes of Outsiders." *Journal of Vaishnava Studies* 3, no. 1: 83–111; David L. Haberman. 1999. "First Annual Robert C. Lester Lecture on the Study of Religion." University of Colorado. Delivered February 11, 1999; David L. Haberman. 1993. "On Trial: The Love of the Sixteen Thousand Gopees." *History of Religions* 33, no. 1: 44–70; and Sardella 2013.

24. Fuller 2005. Fuller complicates the strict dichotomy between the British colonial rulers and the Indian citizenry (including the position of Bhaktivinoda Thakura) in his 2005 work.

25. Bhatia 2017, 58–59.

26. Ibid., 59.

27. Fuller 2005, 5–6.

28. Sardella 2013.

29. Ibid., 10–11. Ferdinando Sardella (2013) skillfully argues this point detailing the "personalist" position of Bhaktisiddhanta Sarasvati, and the reader is encouraged to consult his work on the topic. For a more general discussion of the Advaita Vedanta based reformulations of Hinduism that Hindu reformers devised in response to British colonial—as well as Orientalist, missionary, and other—critiques, the reader is advised to consult to work of David L. Haberman, who discusses the context for and shape of these reformulations more generally. Haberman's work will also help provide further context on several of the British figures with whom Bhakivinoda and Bhaktisiddhanta had close association. See Haberman 1994; Haberman 1999; and Haberman 1993.

30. Fuller, 2005.

31. Ibid. Apropos of the pilgrimage sites whose locations were refashioned and reconceptualized, Sukanya Sarbadhikary has written an excellent book chronicling the different ways in which diverse groups of Bengal Vaishnavas experience the pilgrimage locations of Navadvip-Mayapur. See Sukanya Sarbadhikary. 2015. *The Place of Devotion: Siting and Experiencing Divinity in Bengal-Vaishnavism*. Oakland: University of California Press.

32. Ibid., 288.
33. Ibid.
34. Ibid., 6.
35. Hopkins 1989, 46. Italics added for emphasis.
36. Sardella 2013, 95.
37. Ibid., 96. Bracketed text in original. Citing *Sajjanatoṣaṇī* 4, no. 3 (1892): 42. *Sajjanatoṣaṇī* was a monthly periodical first published by Bhaktivinoda and later published by his son, Bhaktisiddhanta (Sardella 2013, 309).
38. Subhananda Dasa, ed. *Śrī Nāmāmṛta—The Nectar of the Holy Name.* Accessed May 9, 2017. https://docs.google.com/file/d/0BzR876u4ZuxEYmEoY Tg1NWEtZTI1YS00NTYyLThkYmYtMTQ4MzJhMGJmMzFk/view. Ellipses in original. Citing *Sajjanatoṣaṇī* 1885.
39. A. C. Bhaktivedanta Swami Prabhupada. 1974. *Śrīmad-Bhāgavatam: With the Original Sanskrit Text, Its Roman Transliteration, Synonyms, Translation and Elaborate Purports by His Divine Grace A.C. Bhaktivedanta Swami Prabhupada Founder-Acarya of the International Society for Krishna Consciousness.* Fourth Canto, "The Creation of the Fourth Order" (part 4, chapters 25–31). Los Angeles: Bhaktivedanta Book Trust, 4.29.55. Official ISKCON digital book. Accessed May 10, 2017. http://vanisource.org/wiki/Srimad-Bhagavatam.
40. Sardella 2013, 65.
41. Ibid., 94.
42. Ibid., 93.
43. Ibid., 94.
44. Ibid., 94.
45. Ibid., 79. See also Hopkins 1989, 48–49.
46. Sardella 2013, 134.
47. Ibid., 146.
48. Goswami 1983, xxi. Bracketed text and ellipses in original.
49. Ibid., xxi.
50. Ibid., xxxii.
51. Ibid., xxvi.
52. Ibid., xxxvi–xxxvii.
53. A. C. Bhaktivedanta Swami Prabhupada. 1975. "Lecture Festival Ratha-Yatra—Philadelphia," July 12. Accessed May 10, 2017. http://vanisource.org/wiki /Ratha-yatra_--_Philadelphia,_July_12,_1975.
54. This *śloka* is taken from Prabhupada's version of the *Chaitanya Caritāmṛta* in *Madhya-Līlā*, text 13:80. A. C. Bhaktivedanta Swami Prabhupada. 1975. *Sri Caitanya-caritamrta, Madhya-lila: The Pastimes of Lord Caitanya Mahaprabhu.* Los Angeles: Bhaktivedanta Book Trust. It also appears as text 74 of Rupa Goswami's *Padyāvalī*. This text is archived in full text on a number of sites, including KrishnaPath.Org. *Śrī Padyavali*. Accessed May 10, 2017. http://

www.krishnapath.org/Library/Goswami-books/Rupa/Rupa_Goswami_Sri_Padyavali.pdf. This *śloka* also appears as *Śloka* 5 of *Madhya Līlā* 13.75 of the *Caitanya Caritāmṛta of Kṛṣṇadāsa Kavirāja*. See Edward C. Dimock Jr. 1999. *Caitanya Caritāmṛta of Kṛṣṇadāsa Kavirāja: A Translation and Commentary*. Tony K. Stewart, ed. Cambridge: Harvard University Press. This edition is, overall, an excellent resource for those interested in reading the *Caitanya Caritāmṛta*.

55. Italics added for emphasis.

56. This verse is also important within ISKCON because it articulates what devotees believe to be the true identity and role of the *jīva* (individual self). Put simply, rather than having its role or identity based in societal occupations (such as being a priest, warrior, etc.) or in any "bodily designation" whatsoever (nationality, race, sex, gender, etc.), devotees say that the true identity of the *jīva* is a "spirit soul" that is utterly distinct from the body.

57. Ramananda Prasad. 1995. *The Bhagavad-Gītā*. Delhi and Fremont: Motilal Banarsidass and The American Gita Society, 18.68. ISKCON Mayapur head *pujārī* (priest). Interview by Nicole Karapanagiotis. In person, Mayapur, West Bengal, India, December 24, 2015.

Another question one might be interested in asking is whether or not ISKCON devotees—or the ISKCON tradition more broadly—would include the *mañjarī sādhana* of Rupa Goswami as an example of what they might count as servitude. *Mañjarī sādhana* refers to a type of devotional practice within some Gauḍīya Vaishnava Hindu traditions wherein devotees engage in imitative action of the close associates of Krishna. More specifically, in this form of practice, devotees engage in a type of religious role-playing; they imaginatively visualize themselves in the role of the adolescent girlfriends of Krishna's divine consort Radha. The point of this practice, from the perspective of those who engage in it, is to generate the same emotions of love for Krishna and Radha that Radha's mythological adolescent girlfriends had for them. Importantly, this imaginative visualization includes meditatively role-playing oneself as a witness to, and servant of, the needs of the divine couple (Radha-Krishna) in their divine lovemaking (imaginatively offering the couple a fan to cool them down, offering flowers for their bed, etc.). Devotees who practice this form of meditative imagining believe that their visualizations put them into the mythological stories themselves, allowing them to feel the intense love for the couple that Radha's girlfriends themselves felt. *Mañjarī sādhana* is part of a broader set of practices, known as *rāgānugā bhakti sādhana,* in which devotees imitate the actions and moods of a broader set of characters from Krishna's mythological associations, not just the adolescent girlfriends of Radha. All of these practices have been written about in several books, such as David Haberman's classic text, *Acting as a Way of Salvation*. See David L. Haberman. 1988. *Acting as a Way of Salvation: A Study of Rāgānugā Bhakti Sādhana*. Delhi: Motilal Banarsidass Publishers.

From a certain perspective, *mañjarī sādhana* can be read as a form of servitude. However, *mañjarī sādhana* is a very different path from that of the ISKCON tradition or the servitude that ISKCON devotees practice. In fact, many in the ISKCON tradition have outright rejected *mañjarī sādhana* altogether (as well as *rāgānugā bhakti sādhana* more broadly), believing it to be too contrary to their ascetic endeavors and conservative devotions. Instead, they practice *vaidhī bhakti sādhana*, which literally translates to the *devotional path of rules*.

58. A. C. Bhaktivedanta Swami Prabhupada. 1972. "Letter to Devotees Written from Los Angeles," August 26. Accessed May 10, 2017. http://vanisource.org/wiki/Letter_to_Devotees_--_Los_Angeles_26_August,_1972.

59. William H. Deadwyler III (Ravindra Svarupa Dasa). 1989. "Patterns in ISKCON's Historical Self-Perception." In Bromley and Shinn 1989.

60. A. C. Bhaktivedanta Swami Prabhupada. 1973. "Lecture Festival Disappearance Day, Bhaktisiddhana Sarasvati—Los Angeles," December 13. Accessed May 10, 2017. http://vanisource.org/wiki/His_Divine_Grace_Srila_Bhaktisiddhanta_Sarasvati_Gosvami_Prabhupada%27s_Disappearance_Day,_Lecture_--_Los_Angeles,_December_13,_1973.

61. A. C. Bhaktivedanta Swami Prabhupada. 1974. "Lecture Arrival—Mayapur," September 27. Accessed May 10, 2017. http://vanisource.org/wiki/Arrival_Lecture_--_Mayapur,_September_27,_1974. Non-bracketed ellipses in original. Bhaktivedanta uses *Prabhupāda* as an affectionate honorific for his own guru, Bhaktisiddhanta Sarasvati.

62. Prabhupada sent ISKCON devotees to spread ISKCON in Zambia, Kenya, Nigeria, and China, for example.

63. Prabhupada 1974, 4:22:42, Purport. Italics added for emphasis. Here, A. C. Bhaktivedanta uses *Prabhupāda* as an affectionate honorific for his own guru, Bhaktisiddhanta Sarasvati.

64. Deadwyler 1989, 73.

65. Urvashi Patel. 2006. "The Need for Diversity." *Jagannatha's Chakra: Discussions*. Accessed May 10, 2017. http://www.chakra.org/discussions/IntJun08_06.html. In ISKCON literature, *Hindu* is often conflated with *Indian*.

66. Dr. Kenneth R. Valpey. 2013. "Interview with Dr. Kenneth R. Valpey." In *Hare Krishna in the Modern World: Reflections by Distinguished Academics and Scholarly Devotees*. Graham Dwyer and Richard J. Cole, eds. London: Arktos Media, 88.

67. Hridayananda Das Goswami. 2015. "Reply to a Senior Leader." Unpublished essay. Posted on Hridayananda das Goswami—Friends and Disciples Facebook page (public), October 24. Accessed May 11, 2017. https://www.facebook.com/groups/acharyadeva/permalink/10153917775293646/.

68. Bir Krishna Dasa Goswami. 2014. "Krishna West Overview by Bir Krishna Dasa Goswami, Part 2." YouTube video, April 15. 2:07–2:34. Accessed May 11, 2017. https://www.youtube.com/watch?v=TBYnL9rTfgc.

69. Ibid., 3:43–4:05.

70. Goswami 2015. Italics added for emphasis. Versions of this essay are posted publicly on a number of other websites. Hridayananda Das Goswami also shared drafts of this essay with me via email.

71. Hridayananda Das Goswami. 2014. "KRISHNA WEST— The Interview, Vol. 2." GourTube YouTube channel, November 20. 1:12:40–1:12:50. Accessed May 11, 2017. https://www.youtube.com/watch?v=X3q7l5L_E5w&t=3360s. Emphases in original.

72. Goswami 2015.

73. For a full account of this story, see C. L. Goswami and M. A. Shastri. 2003. *Śrīmad Bhāgavata Mahāpurāṇa* (with Sanskrit text and English translation), Part 1 (book 1 to 8). Gorakhpur: Gita Press.

74. Deadwyler 1989, 61.

75. Bir Krishna Dasa Goswami. 2014. "Krishna West Overview by Bir Krishna Dasa Goswami, Part 3." YouTube video, April 16. 11:01–11:34. Accessed May 11, 2017. https://www.youtube.com/watch?v=4PrVXbMyNI8. Emphases in original.

THREE

KRISHNA GETS A NEW PR TEAM

Branding ISKCON as a Meditative Social Club

On the weekend of May 1–3, 2015, ISKCON Chicago hosted a conference entitled Reaching the Hearts and Minds of the Western Public (Effective Models of Western Outreach).[1] The conference was attended by hundreds of ISKCON devotees from all over the world—temple presidents, program leaders, and lay devotees alike—all interested in learning methods and strategies they could employ to become more effective at attracting westerners to ISKCON. The conference drew devotees of all nationalities and cultures and included a number of sessions and seminars, such as "Core Spiritual Marketing," "Srila Prabhupada's Global Strategy of Focusing on Reaching the Westerner Audience," "Internet Outreach," and "Effective Models of Western Outreach for North America Today."[2]

Although there were many speakers at the conference, the weekend primarily revolved around the ideas and programs of one main figure: Devamrita Swami, the Krishna Brander at the heart of this chapter. Speaking on several occasions at the conference, Devamrita Swami sought to teach the gathered attendees methods by which they might revolutionize their outreach efforts to westerners. Most importantly, he sought to invigorate their enthusiasm about attracting westerners to ISKCON, hoping to inspire them to make greater efforts in this regard. In ISKCON he said, "We've been very successful with persons from a fortunate background that understand something about the importance of the Vedas, the importance of Krishna." "We've been very successful," in other words, with "those from a fortunate Indian background."[3] But pleading with the crowd, he noted that success with those of an Indian background is not enough to fulfill Prabhupada's true mission of global success. Instead, he urged attendees to endeavor more into the difficult task of reaching those who are currently being left behind by ISKCON and to whom Prabhupada himself compassionately reached out. Those from an Indian background, he said, are "the juicy low-hanging fruit. And, yes, that fruit is sweet. But it's now time—and that's why you gathered here this weekend—to go to branches of the tree that seem less accessible."[4] It's time, in other words, to engage in deliberate and pointed outreach to westerners by actively developing programs and strategically rebranding the movement so as to attract them.

Devamrita Swami has been rebranding the ISKCON movement for twenty-four years, having started highly successful programs in New Zealand, Australia, Canada, and the United States. A Yale graduate who refers to himself as the "razzle-dazzle Ivy League" ISKCON guru, Devamrita Swami is an original Prabhupada disciple who now serves both as guru to a number of worldwide disciples and as an administrator on ISKCON's Governing Body Commission (GBC). Born in 1950, Devamrita Swami received a scholarship to attend Yale when he was just seventeen years old.[5] As he tells his own story, soon after starting at Yale, he began to feel dissatisfied with the education he was receiving. He wanted to find a "solution to all human problems" but found it difficult to do so through his studies.[6] After "search[ing] the university high and low for anything that would make a lasting cure for humanity's ills," he notes, "upon graduating I came to the conclusion that no material solution would suffice."[7]

After graduating, Devamrita Swami received a copy of the *Bhagavad-Gītā*, and everything in his life changed. As he told me one day, "After I graduated, I read Prabhupada's books four hours a day for six months straight without going to any center or gathering or anything."[8] It was only after such intense study that he decided to visit an ISKCON center—the Brooklyn center in 1972—to meet devotees and check out the ISKCON movement. He tells me that once he visited the center, he was drawn to the movement immediately because he "could see the books in action."[9] Following his first visit, it didn't take long for the young Devamrita Swami to become confident that he had found the solution to his many questions, and he soon came to believe that it was only through the path of *bhakti yoga* that the world could be rescued from its various ills. Just two years after visiting the Brooklyn center, at the age of twenty-four, Devamrita Swami became an initiated disciple of Swami Prabhupada, and after having been in the movement for just eight years, Devamrita Swami took *saṃnyāsa*, or formal renunciation, to live a life of devotion, preaching, and celibacy.

It took a lot for Devamrita Swami to become a monk. His parents had lived in the United States during the era of segregation, and they worked hard to ensure that their son grew up to have the opportunities and privileges that they themselves never had. As a young Black man in the late 1960s, Devamrita

Figure 3.1 Devamrita Swami (pictured above) delivering a lecture to a group in Fishtown, Philadelphia. Photo courtesy of Mantra Lounge, Philadelphia (Facebook).[10]

Swami had become a model of success: he was prep-school educated and had already been on scholarship at prep school for two years prior to receiving a scholarship to attend Yale at just seventeen. Leaving all of this behind took a lot of bravery, as he told me one early spring evening in 2016. "[But] I knew the only way [to do this] was to open the door in the airplane as it's in flight and just jump."[11]

Devamrita Swami has continued blazing bold trails since he made the decision to enter the movement in 1974. Most especially, Devamrita Swami is known within ISKCON for his bold and trailblazing approaches to marketing and for his groundbreaking efforts to reenvision and re-create the public face of the movement in an attempt to draw the attention and interest of westerners. Just as he believed in college that his old ways of knowing and living would not suffice if he wanted to truly find "a lasting cure for humanity's ills," so too did he come to realize twenty-four years ago—long before other ISKCON gurus did—that something fresh and new needed to be done if ISKCON was to fulfill Prabhupada's dream of attracting westerners and becoming a globally representative and universal religious movement. Over the past twenty-four years, Devamrita Swami has studied business extensively and has visited various institutions, centers, and businesses worldwide in order to get a sense of how successful groups of different kinds market themselves to wide publics. Applying what he has learned, Devamrita Swami has made it the focus of his devotional work in ISKCON to engineer a practical solution to the following question: "Without changing our stripes, how can we make *bhakti* accessible for those who are not from a fortunate Indian background, who don't have the culture, don't have the inclination, yet are curious, or sometimes desperate?"[12]

It is to this practical solution—Devamrita Swami's rebranding of the ISKCON movement—that this chapter now turns.

THE MARKETING NEED AND DEVAMRITA SWAMI'S "LOFT MODEL"

Central to understanding Devamrita Swami's lifelong efforts to rebrand the ISKCON movement is first understanding the need that he perceives for doing so. This need stems from the simple observation that the demographics of the ISKCON movement have shifted in such a way that today the movement is primarily comprised of Indian Hindus. "While the movement is flourishing with Indians," Devamrita Swami notes frequently, he is often left wondering "what happened to our non-immigrant [westerner] base?"[13] His disciples—especially those who work alongside him in his "western marketing" endeavors—make similar remarks, noting that attending ISKCON centers and programs today "is like living in little India."[14] "If you look around . . . at the Sunday Feast, or look around in your temples and congregations," one disciple notes, and "you see that the demographic in the room doesn't match the demographic in the country that you live in, then you may come to the conclusion that there *is* a need" for new western marketing methods.[15]

Devamrita Swami believes that there are two central reasons why there are so few westerners in ISKCON today, and these reasons form the central building blocks in the design of his initiatives to rebrand the movement. The first reason has to do with the fact that the ISKCON movement is currently centered in temples, and "most non-immigrants [westerners] don't have an immediate—shall we say—attraction to all that."[16] What Devamrita Swami means by "all that" primarily has to do with the ritual worship of *mūrtis* (embodied forms) of Krishna that devotees perform multiple times a day in ISKCON temples. *Mūrtis* (known in ISKCON as *deities*) are typically physically cast three-dimensional forms of the divine that are made of tangible material (stone, wood, granite, etc.). Within ISKCON, as in Vaishnavism and Hinduism more generally, devotees believe that *mūrtis* are physical embodiments of the divine—not symbols of the divine, but the divine itself, present before them. As Prabhupada himself said in a letter he wrote to his disciples in 1975, "Never think of the Deity as made of stone or wood. Every worshiper must remember that Kṛṣṇa is personally present [as the deity]. He is simply kindly presenting Himself before us in a way so that we can handle Him. That is His mercy, otherwise, He is unapproachable."[17]

Scholars of Hinduism have written much about the bias that many have had (and often continue to have) against the worship of embodied forms of God in Hinduism. These biases are often rooted in problematic understandings of embodied divinity and are bound up in the idea that the worship of images is reserved only for "uneducated worshiper[s] incapable of abstract thought."[18] Moreover, these biases are often located in the belief that embodied forms of God are "expression[s] of idolatry, and hence misplaced devotion."[19] Sometimes, these "idol anxieties" are even located in theories of religion themselves, especially those of religious studies' earliest thinkers.[20,21] For his part, Devamrita Swami says that he recognizes these biases still today and believes they are stumbling blocks to westerners' initial attraction to the ISKCON movement. "The fortunate souls will be satisfied coming to the temple immediately and seeing the deities and saying, 'I want to surrender.' You get a few like those every year.... But that's not the extent of what's available out there."[22] Instead, he says that most non-Indians are "challenged by the deities" when they first visit the temple and that seeing the deities is often a "shock" for them.[23]

But it's not just the deities themselves with which westerners struggle, Devamrita Swami notes. Rather, they struggle with the whole setup of the ISKCON temple, which has the deities at its center. Within ISKCON temples, the whole of devotional life revolves around the deities. Most noticeably, the centrality of the deities can be read in the arrangement of the temple space itself. At the front of the main room of most, if not all, ISKCON temples is a large, platform-like altar where different embodied forms of Krishna are hosted for the act of *darshan* (a ritual whereby visitors and devotees can see and be seen by them). Sometimes on the altar are Krishna and his beloved consort, Radha; sometimes, it is Krishna as Jagannath, standing upon the altar with his brother, Balarama, and his sister, Subhadra; at other times, it is Sri Sri Gaur-Nitai, the centrally important ISKCON deities believed to be the embodied forms of Chaitanya and his close associate Nityananda, respectively. Most often, however, ISKCON temple altars host several of these deities in some combination, along with pictures of Chaitanya and his associates and the gurus in the ISKCON lineage—including Bhaktisiddhanta Sarasvati, Bhaktivinoda Thakura, and, of course, Swami Prabhupada.

More than just governing the spatial arrangement of the temple, however, the deities also drive all of the temple's daily ritual activities. "The presence of the deity," writes William H. Deadwyler III:

> makes the temple quite literally the house of God, and the devotees dwell with the Lord in his house as a staff of servants wholly dedicated to the pleasure of their resident master. The devotees worship and serve the deity in the same way that retainers, ministers, and domestics used to serve and pay homage to the king in his palace. The deity is regarded as the factual owner and proprietor of the temple. . . . The life of the temple revolves around the deity, and the day is regulated according to the service of the deity.[24]

What this servitude to the deities translates to liturgically is that at multiple times throughout the day and evening, devotees engage in the worship of Krishna's deity forms on the altar. Most prominently, this worship involves the act of *darshan,* whereby devotees and guests visit the temple in order to "see and be seen by" Krishna. These rituals also include the act of *puja,* rituals during which the deities enshrined in the temple are treated to a royal ceremony; they are offered food, water, a fan, incense, and so on. These ceremonies form the central rituals of the ISKCON movement today. As such, it is these rituals that often serve as newcomers' introduction to the movement when they visit for the first time. This is the case whether they come for one of the regular ceremony times or for a "Sunday Feast"—the weekly, several-hour Sunday openhouse program wherein devotees and visitors alike gather for an afternoon *kīrtan* (devotional singing) performed in front of the deities, a lecture on the *Bhagavad-Gītā,* a second *kīrtan,* and finally *prasādam* or *prasād,* a communal vegetarian meal of sanctified food that has been offered to the deities. For his part, however, Devamrita Swami does not think that this ritual model appeals

Facing top, Figure 3.2 ISKCON Juhu Temple Room (Mumbai, India). Note the deities and altar front and center in the room. Tuesday, January 12, 2016. Photo taken by author. Mumbai, Maharashtra, India.

Facing bottom, Figure 3.3 ISKCON Mayapur Temple Room. ISKCON Mayapur is the world headquarters for the ISKCON movement. Although they vary in size, all ISKCON temples worldwide share a similar interior temple room setup, where the deities on the altar are at the front and center of the interior space. Wednesday, December 23, 2015. Photo taken by author. Mayapur, West Bengal, India.

Above, Figure 3.4 Evening *kīrtan* and *āratī* in temple room of ISKCON Philadelphia. Sunday, February 12, 2017. Photo taken by Ernest Michael Nelson. Philadelphia, Pennsylvania, United States.

Facing top, Figure 3.5 ISKCON Delhi deities. Sri Sri Gaur-Nitai. Also featured on the altar are Swami Prabhupada (photo left) and Bhaktisiddhanta Sarasvati (photo right). Monday, December 28, 2015. Photo taken by author. Delhi, India.

Facing bottom, Figure 3.6 ISKCON of Philadelphia deities. Photo left to right: Sri Sri Sri Balarama, Subhadra, and Jagannath. Thursday, August 25, 2016. Photo taken by author. Philadelphia, Pennsylvania, United States.

to westerners; instead he believes they find it too foreign, overly theistic, and too focused on material forms of divinity that they do not understand. The centrality of this model, therefore, is one reason—he believes—that westerners are not drawn to the ISKCON movement.[25]

The second reason why Devamrita Swami believes there are currently relatively few westerners within ISKCON is that (he believes) westerners do not feel that they fit into the culture that dominates the movement; they do not feel that they can relate to the Indian congregants who make up ISKCON's present majority. Devamrita Swami is not the only person to make this observation about westerners' lack of comfort in associating with Indians within ISKCON. Nurit Zaidman suggests it in her analysis of the ISKCON temple community in Philadelphia, noting that during worship services there, the two groups of congregants (westerners and Indians) do not interact (much) at all.[26] E. Burke Rochford Jr. makes this point much more overtly in his *Hare Krishna Transformed*, noting that "apart from the limited interaction between Western devotees and Indian Hindus, there are also fewer Westerners choosing to attend the Sunday temple program because of the large Indian presence. At a 2005 community meeting of a dozen longtime Western devotees," Rochford notes, "each [attendee] said that they only infrequently attended the Sunday feast" because of the Indian presence.[27] More than this, Rochford argues that for many devotees, "the number of Indians present on Sundays has made the temple an unattractive place to bring Westerners interested in Krishna Consciousness."[28] Rochford documents much evidence of devotees who hold this position, noting that at the aforementioned 2005 meeting of western devotees, "when one of them acknowledged that he 'would never bring a new [Western] person to the temple because they would be put off' by the overwhelming number of Indians, others quickly nodded their heads in agreement."[29] (Rochford also notes that Indians, too, feel estranged at ISKCON services, and that—like westerners—Indians are also embarrassed to bring their friends to the temple. In particular, Indians are embarrassed about the westerners' loud singing and pronounced dancing.)[30] For these reasons, some temples have toyed with innovative methods to attract westerners to the temple, such as "hold[ing] separate feasts and worship services at different times on Sunday for Indians and Westerners."[31]

These statements and suggestions about having separate worship times are not surprising (although they are troubling and jarring); as scholars have long pointed out, religious congregations—from Christian churches to Hindu guru movements—tend to be divided along ethnic, cultural, and racial lines. It was not for nothing, after all, that Dr. Martin Luther King, Jr., called eleven o'clock on Sunday morning "the most segregated hour in America."[32] However, what is important for the present purposes is the question of why it is, within ISKCON, that westerners do not feel comfortable joining a congregation with a predominantly Indian base. Devamrita Swami eschews the more obvious answers to this question—that westerners perceive differences in language, customs, clothing choices, and even food preferences between themselves and Indian congregants—and instead argues that westerners are uncomfortable sharing a devotional community with Indians because they perceive differences between their own familial, social, and psychological well-being and that of the Indian congregants. Put simply, the westerners feel out of place in ISKCON communities, Devamrita Swami says, because the Indian community members are too well-adjusted, stable, and straitlaced for them.

> In terms of how to live, in terms of stability, these Indians have it really together. They've got it together. They're married, their family life is stable, divorce is like, "Oh my God, who could ever think of it?!" Their kids get educated, they study, ya know, no one's on drugs, random relationships, all that is taboo for them.... And so, they're not looking for an alternative lifestyle so to speak. They're looking for how to add God to the center of their *stable life*. Their life already makes sense, materially. Their family life makes sense.... [On the other hand] you have the non-immigrant [westerners], their family life is *just shattered* most of the time. Their lifestyles are chaotic.... They have random affairs, various kinds of intoxicants.... So, you see they're just kind of two different worlds, you know? ... And so these two different groups have completely different needs.[33]

Indian congregants are too straitlaced and "put together" for western would-be converts to successfully relate to them when they visit ISKCON communities, Devamrita Swami argues. As a result, westerners feel unable to form meaningful community ties within ISKCON. And this—combined with the fact that they feel bewildered by the temple itself, the temple ritual, and the worship of embodied forms of Krishna—leads them to believe that the ISKCON movement cannot possibly be for them. Their first time at an ISKCON center, if they visit at all, is often their last.

What, then, does Devamrita Swami think can be done to successfully attract westerners to ISKCON today? As Devamrita Swami says, "A devotee doesn't just rest on his or her laurels [and say], 'Well, I presented it to them, they didn't take it, so [my duty is done].'"[34] Instead, devotees should always try to be innovative in their preaching methods, especially if what they are doing is not working. Devotees should always "try to improve [their] presentation," because "that's what outreach requires—that we have to put ourselves out on the limb and trust that Krishna will back us up, [that] Krishna will instruct us, [and that] Krishna will empower us with the ways and means [of] how to reach out."[35] In other words, "it's very wonderful for a devotee to think, 'I'm going to keep trying. . . . I'm going to be the servant of the servant.'"[36]

In order to solve the western outreach problem, Devamrita Swami has created a marketing model called *loft preaching.* Put simply, loft preaching is a marketing model designed to "meet westerners where they are," to present ISKCON to them in a way that they like and in a way that makes them feel both comfortable with and interested in it. The loft model operates on the logic that since westerners are not attracted to ISKCON as it is, it is better to attract them to the movement through programs, activities, physical spaces, and social scenes that they find easily appealing. These programs, activities, spaces, and social scenes are intentionally designed to obscure their ties to ISKCON and its temple center so that they can be religiously and socially comfortable spaces for westerners. And it is precisely through these religiously and socially comfortable spaces that Devamrita Swami and his disciples aim to subtly introduce westerners to ISKCON's teachings and rituals and to gradually entice them into a movement that they believe they would never otherwise consider joining. If, as Sita-pati das puts it, "the ISKCON temple functions to provide Vaisnava brahminical culture, [then] the Loft [model] functions to bring people to the point where they can recognise, appreciate, and take advantage of that culture."[37]

Although the loft model is a conceptual marketing framework, it rests on the creation and promotion of physical spaces (lofts and lounges) that are designed to function as *bridges*—or the centers through which Devamrita Swami and his disciples try to gradually and subtly introduce westerners to ISKCON. (In fact, the loft model is often referred to by the terms *bridge model, bridge program,* and so on.) In order for the model to be effective, these spaces themselves need to be appealing to westerners. Therefore, Devamrita Swami has devised a brand that he and his global disciples are currently promoting and administering around the world. This brand presents ISKCON—through these lofts and lounges—as an edgy, urban meditation-based social club: one that provides visitors and regulars alike a space in which to practice a variety of meditation forms and gather for broad-based philosophical discussion and healthy vegan meals in a fellowship environment. This brand is designed to attract to ISKCON the "twenty-year-old to thirty-five-year-old age group—kind of the cool, savvy, educated, young person who cares about the world and how the world is . . . the young urban hipster [who is] . . . looking for a higher way of life."[38] And it presents ISKCON to them in a way that is both removed from the temple and temple ritual and situated in a social environment in which they can associate with like-minded peers.

Devamrita Swami and his disciples currently run this brand in lofts and lounges in New Zealand, Australia, Canada, and the United States. The rest of this chapter takes the reader through a focused look at one of these lounges—the Mantra Lounge in Fishtown, Philadelphia—to see up close and in detail the ways in which Devamrita Swami and his disciples orchestrate this complicated and multilayered branding enterprise as they attempt to diversify the ISKCON movement for Swami Prabhupada. The orchestration of this brand begins online.

ESTABLISHING THE MANTRA LOUNGE AS A MEDITATION-BASED SOCIAL CLUB: ONLINE

A quick Google search of "meditation in Fishtown" pulls up the Mantra Lounge as the first search result. The descriptor under the result reads that the Mantra Lounge is a "meditation center" that "seeks to spread knowledge of yoga around the city, giving people a place to truly be themselves and understand the world around them." If one does a little further digging through the search results, one also finds several online magazine articles about the Mantra Lounge, as well as a number of local online calendars that advertise it on their "things to do" list. These various articles and online calendars advertise the Mantra Lounge as "one of the best kept secrets in Philly,"[39] a "meditation studio" aimed "to help you free your mind,"[40] where "10 bucks [will] get you a yoga or meditation class followed by a vegan dinner."[41] They also describe the lounge as "a volunteer-led non-profit yoga and meditation-focused center," where "mindfulness goes into everything,"[42] a place where patrons can "feel part of a community, and . . . [eat] plates of healthy vegan grub like pad Thai and apple pie."[43] Additionally, the Mantra Lounge is a place where patrons can learn the "spiritual side of yoga and mantra meditation," with the latter being defined as "a sound-based meditation that . . . is recommended for urban environments."[44] As David Ogilvy has famously stated, a brand is "the intangible sum of a product's attributes: its name, packaging, and price, its history, its reputation, and the way it is advertised."[45] When potential patrons read about the Mantra Lounge through these various online sources, they get the chance to build up in their minds a sense about the place—its identity, its vibe, and its story. And these online descriptors, articles, and calendar sites do much to contribute to the Mantra Lounge's brand as a meditation-based social club—one where patrons can not only learn meditation and reduce stress but also can plug into a lifestyle that includes healthy vegan eating.

If a brand is "the intangible sum of a product's attributes" or the story and meaning that consumers can infer about a product,[46] then branding is the process of creating and sustaining these brands. Branding "is about meaning making—taking the individual aspects of a product and turning them into more than the sum of their parts. It is about giving consumers something to think and feel about a product or service beyond its physical attributes."[47] Branding, in other words, is a process of storytelling that aims to generate particular thoughts, emotions, and ideas about a product and/or an organization in the minds of consumers through the intentional use of imagery, text, presentation, and so on. Branding asks not who we are but who do we want people to we think are and, most importantly, how do we go about creating that impression.

As Mia Lövheim, Alf. G. Linderman, and others have noted, "The Internet greatly increases the possibility for an individual seeker to find information about established as well as alternative religious organizations."[48] Knowing that the public browses the web for information on religion, religious groups quite frequently use the internet for branding purposes, as well as for proselytization and evangelism.[49] Further, religious groups spend a significant amount of time designing and maintaining these websites, thoughtfully crafting their design in ways that they believe will both attract and hold the attention of newcomers. This website design can range anywhere from the deliberate choice of images, words, colors, and texts to the explicit choice of keywords and search terms, and even to the use of more direct audience-drawing tactics, such as search-engine optimization.[50,51]

The website for the Mantra Lounge is http://Mantraphilly.com.[52] The Mantra Lounge's website actively promotes the branding of the lounge as a meditation-based social club, and Mantra Lounge staff deliberately design the site to draw newcomers to the lounge as a place where they can relax, unwind, de-stress, and find respite from the city through the practice of meditation and the sharing of healthy food with like-minded peers. Clicking on the lounge website, one immediately sees a scrolling banner at the top of the page that features four images on a rotating set. The first of these images, which advertises an event titled "Retreat!," is an image of a woman in a hooded sweatshirt petting a cow. Clicking on the image, one finds an advertisement noting that "city living can be stressful. From catching trains to making rent, everybody needs some down time to recharge and rejuvenate. But in a place that's all about getting ahead as fast as you can, where do you go to slow down? A perfect place to take a break from the rat race is Gita Nagari Eco Farm."[53] What the advertisement doesn't mention, of course, is that the Gita Nagari Eco Farm is an ISKCON community—complete with a fully functioning ISKCON temple—that happens to be located on a farm. Instead, it simply informs patrons that "Gita Nagari is a place like no other," telling them that whether they "are interested in farming, sustainability or just getting

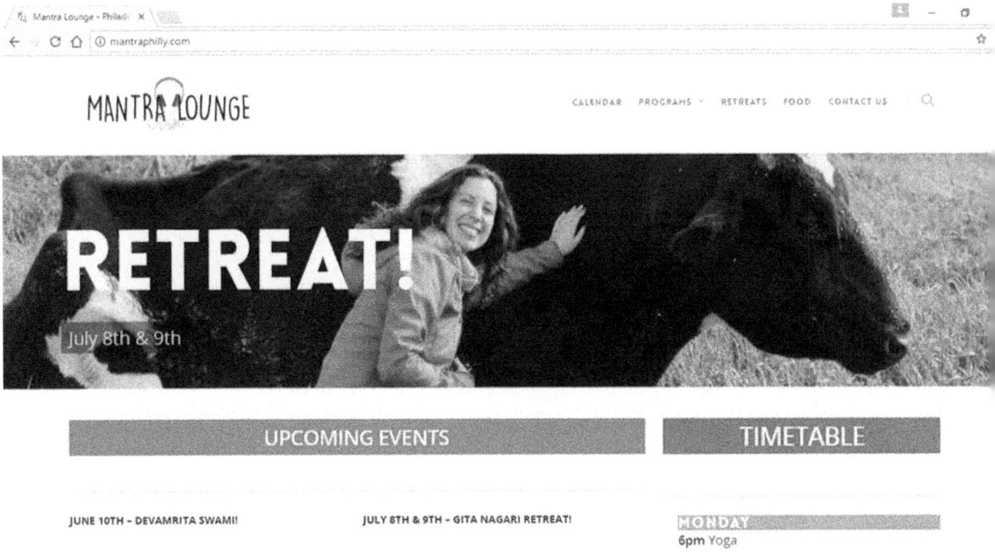

Figure 3.7 Mantra Lounge website (main page) banner image. Screenshot by author.

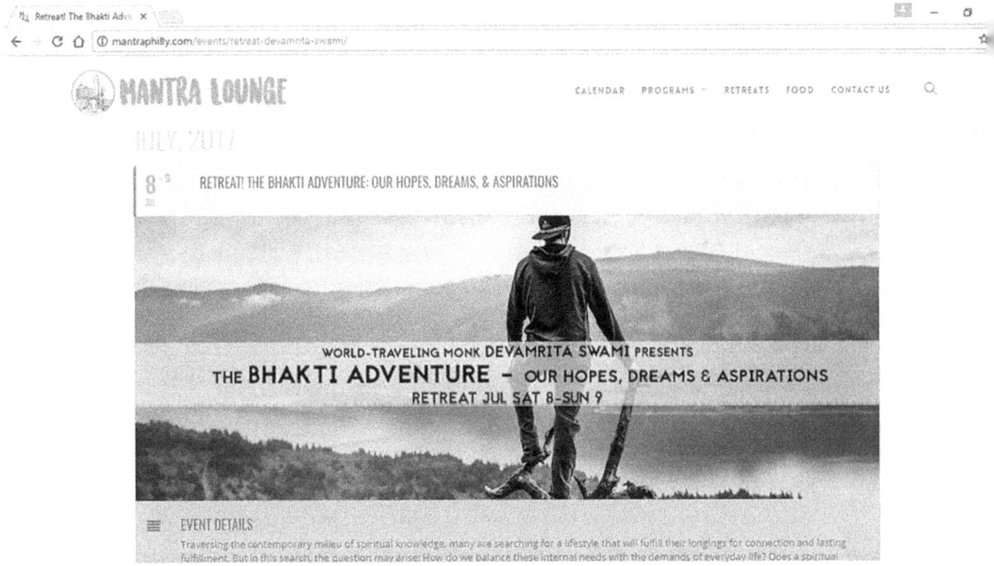

Figure 3.8 Mantra Lounge website retreat program advertisement. Screenshot by author.

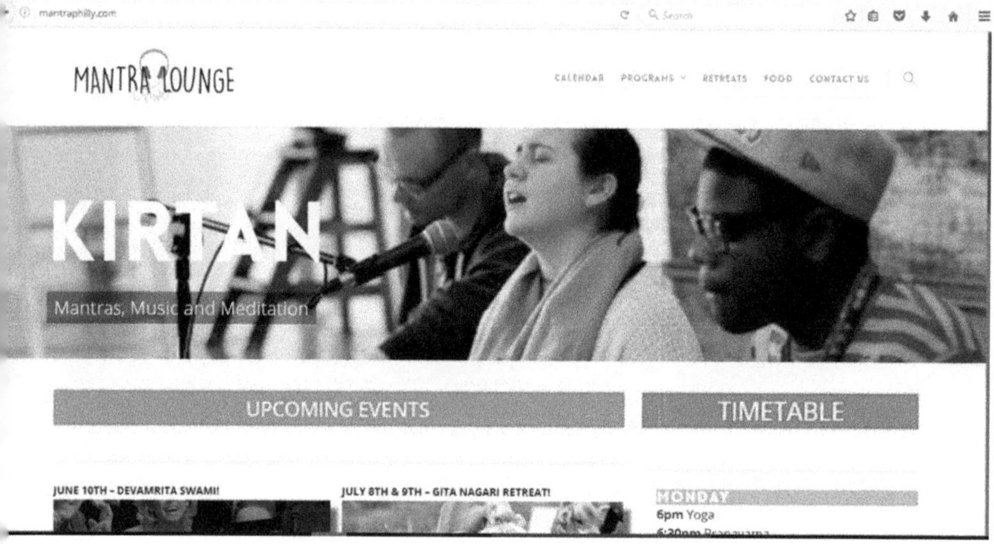

Figure 3.9 Mantra Lounge website (main page) banner image. Screenshot by author.

away from the city," they can "join us for our next retreat with Devamrita Swami [for] an opportunity to get away from the stress of everyday life and immerse in meditation and stimulating discussion."[54,55]

Newcomers to the Mantra Lounge website will also find other events designed to attract them to the lounge for an evening of stress reduction and meditation. For example, a second image on the rotating banner of the site's main page showcases a *kīrtan* being sung by three young performers: two men and a woman. Clicking on this *kīrtan* banner brings one to a description of a weekly event at the Mantra Lounge called "Kirtan Connection: Music Meditation and Dance": "Many people use yoga to relax, strengthen and tone the body," it says,

> but few people have a such a healthy activity for their mind. Fortunately, there is a very simple way of calming the mind and freeing it from anxiety in the same way that yoga is used for the body. In a form of musical meditation known as "Kirtan," ancient mantras (literally "that which frees the mind") are used to bring the mind to rest. Kirtan is a live music meditation, a collective call and response that incorporates these mantras, our voices, and a variety of instruments. All are welcomed, as anyone can experience the clarity and exquisite happiness that come from Kirtan, regardless of musical talent! Participants can sit back and relax, or get up and dance. At the

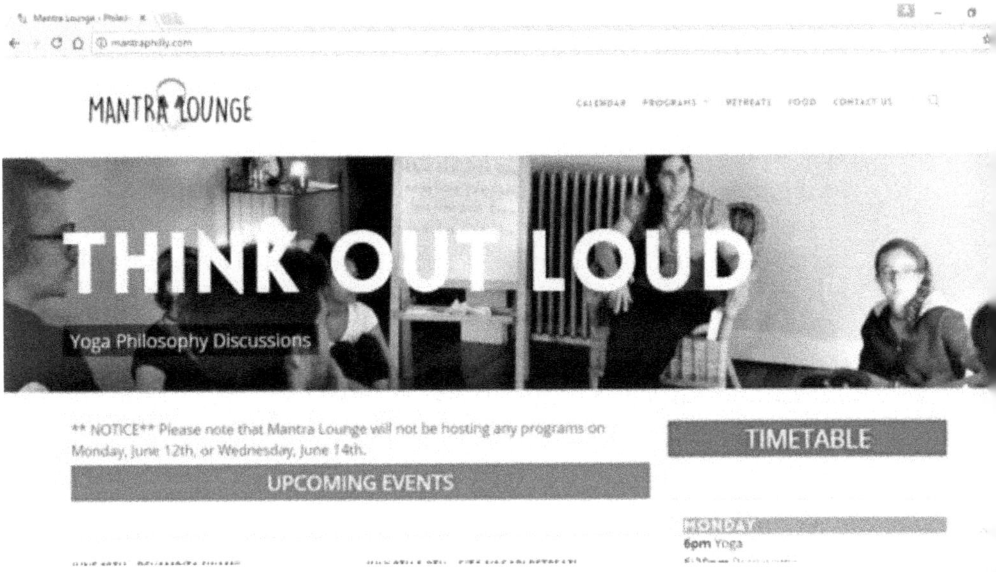

Figure 3.10 Mantra Lounge website advertisement for Friday Soulfeast program.

> end of the Kirtan, a delicious vegan meal will be served, leaving everyone invigorated in body and peaceful at heart.[56]

This same event is described elsewhere on the site, as well as on the Facebook page, as follows: "Mantra is a sanskrit [*sic*] word which means 'that which delivers the mind.' Our mind is full of all sorts of ideas all wrapped up into a big mess. If you're one of those people who want to unwind, or enter into your inner self, or just explore a cool way to meditate, come out for our Tuesday kirtan groups. Kirtan is a powerful expression of the self to unite and balance all the facets of our life. Specifically, when performed with the association of other enthusiastic spiritualists, mantra yoga connects one with sweetly surcharged happiness like no other."[57]

Browsing around the Mantra Lounge website as well as its Facebook page (which posts what are mostly duplicate texts and image sets from the website), one finds a number of these such events designed to attract patrons to the lounge by promoting it as a space in which they can find calm, joy, and meditative peace in the midst of a chaotic life. But the Mantra Lounge is promoted as more than just a meditation studio; it is also marketed as a meditation-based social club and as a place in which patrons can convene with like-minded others. Central to the social club aspect of the brand is the fact that the Mantra Lounge offers a communal vegan dinner after each nightly program (programs that also include discussion groups on topics like sustainability, happiness, etc.). All nightly programs, the website notes, are followed by an "enlivening vegan feast, amongst like-minded souls!"[58] This "wonderful vegan meal" is one of the main selling points of the lounge on the website; it is included after the description of each of the lounge's events on the banner and calendar and also on the lounge's "Time Table" displayed on the main page.[59]

Last but not least, the online branding of the Mantra Lounge as a meditation-based studio (and social club) is, incidentally, supported by the advertising of its yoga classes—which themselves are pitched as exercises into meditation. "Beyond stretching our limbs and relaxing our mind," the site notes, yoga "has the potency to stimulate a meditative state and connect us to a higher consciousness."[60] And like nearly all of the practices advertised on the Mantra Lounge website, this yoga meditation does not just help one reach a higher consciousness; it also provides stress relief for the fast-paced, modern life.

> Our minds get filled with all kinds of ideas, thoughts, emotions, etc. all jumbled up in a big mess. This is what many of us may refer to as stress, and it gets fuelled by our absorption in the constant stream of things to do, bills to pay, people to please—to name only a few. How do we break free of this anxiety-brewing cycle?
>
> Ancient methods of meditation allow us to navigate the hefty loads we tend to carry with a bit more of a spiritualized intelligence. On Monday nights we dive into some of these techniques. The first way that we explore these methods is the art of yoga, using physical movements to relax the body in order to calm the mind. Afterwards, we go deeper into a meditative state with pranayama ("breath-control"), which one can practice everywhere, and end with calming the mind itself by meditation using mantras ("that which frees the mind"). Join us for a night of relaxation and a soothing dive into breathing meditation, as well as some ancient bead meditation and a wonderful vegan meal.[61]

These ancient mantras that "calm" and "free the mind" are none other than ISKCON devotional hymns. And the "ancient bead meditation" that concludes the yoga class is a round of *japa*—chanting the Hare Krishna *mahā mantra* ("Hare Krishna, Hare Krishna, Krishna Krishna, Hare Hare, Hare Rama, Hare Rama, Rama Rama, Hare Hare") on the *tulasī* (holy basil) beads that devotees use each day to call out in prayer to Krishna. Put simply, religious practices that are performed within ISKCON as prayer to the god Krishna are being rebranded on the Mantra Lounge website as meditation tools for the reduction of stress in the overcharged lives of modern-day city dwellers. And it is the hope

Figure 3.11 Mantra Lounge website advertisement for yoga program. Screenshot by author.

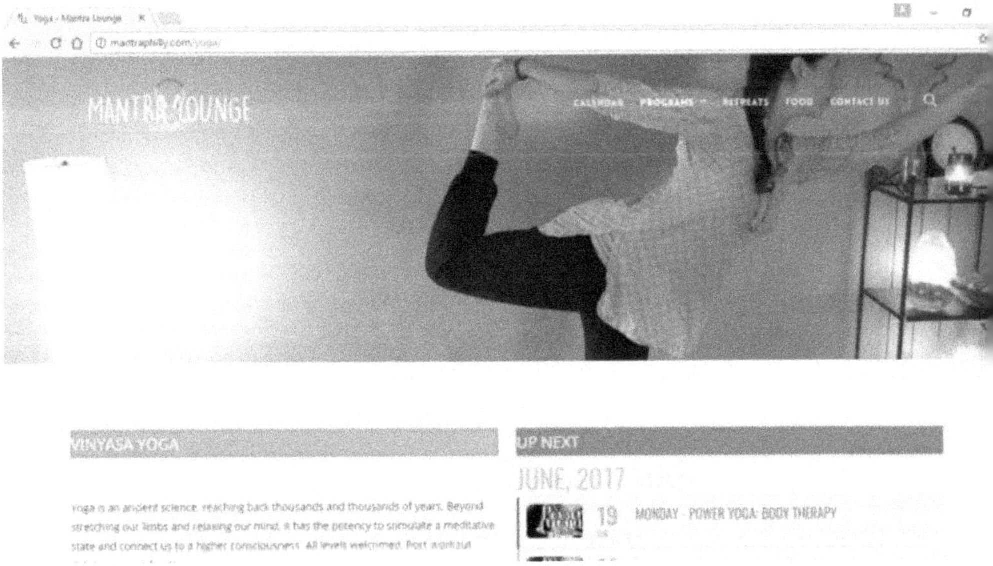

Figure 3.12 Mantra Lounge website advertisement for yoga program. Screenshot by author.

of Mantra Lounge staff that the millennial and Gen Z residents of Philadelphia who have seen the Mantra Lounge online will be so enticed by its branding as a meditation-based social club that they will decide to pay the lounge a visit, where they will find the online brand supported by a brick-and-mortar location: an edgy meditation studio that hosts meditation, yoga, discussions, and vegan meals on a nightly basis.

ESTABLISHING THE MEDITATION-BASED SOCIAL CLUB: THE BRICK-AND-MORTAR LOUNGE

Visiting the Mantra Lounge, Philadelphia, for the first time, one would never know that the lounge is an ISKCON-run center. Instead, one would expect oneself to be happening upon a meditation studio: one whose members discuss their various paths, practices, and lifestyles of meditation in a hip, vegan-friendly environment.

Situated in the up-and-coming hipster-trendy neighborhood of Fishtown, Philadelphia, the Mantra Lounge is located on the popular Girard Avenue, a busy thoroughfare lined with old trolley car lines, vintage and used clothing stores, bars, secondhand stores that sell items like Sk8t lamps, and even a sanctuary restaurant. Nicely wedged between a vintage clothing store and a community design studio, the Mantra Lounge looks (from the street) like a trendy coffee shop, complete with cushioned couches visible from the window and an inviting reading nook. On some days, passersby can see directly through the lounge's large exterior window all the way to the inside of the space. On other days, the lounge's exterior window is covered with posters and fliers advertising its various upcoming programs. On any given day, these advertisements include those for the center's upcoming events: meditation classes, mindfulness days, sustainability talks, yoga, music meditation sessions, and vegan meals. They also display advertisements for upcoming lectures by a "traveling monk, author, and speaker." This traveling monk is none other than Devamrita Swami, who visits the lounge frequently to host programs and give talks.

Just inside the Mantra Lounge, the center opens up to a small sitting area that has a window nook with a cushioned bench where patrons can read, wait for a program to begin, or comfortably remove or put on their shoes before and after programs. In this small sitting area, one also finds a large bookshelf with devotional items for sale: Prabhupada's books, prayer beads (*japa mālā*), and so on. There is also a cubby closet space for patrons to store their shoes, coats, and other belongings.

When Devamrita Swami visualized what he wanted his lounges to look like, he told his disciples that "the décor should be inviting, like [patrons'] own

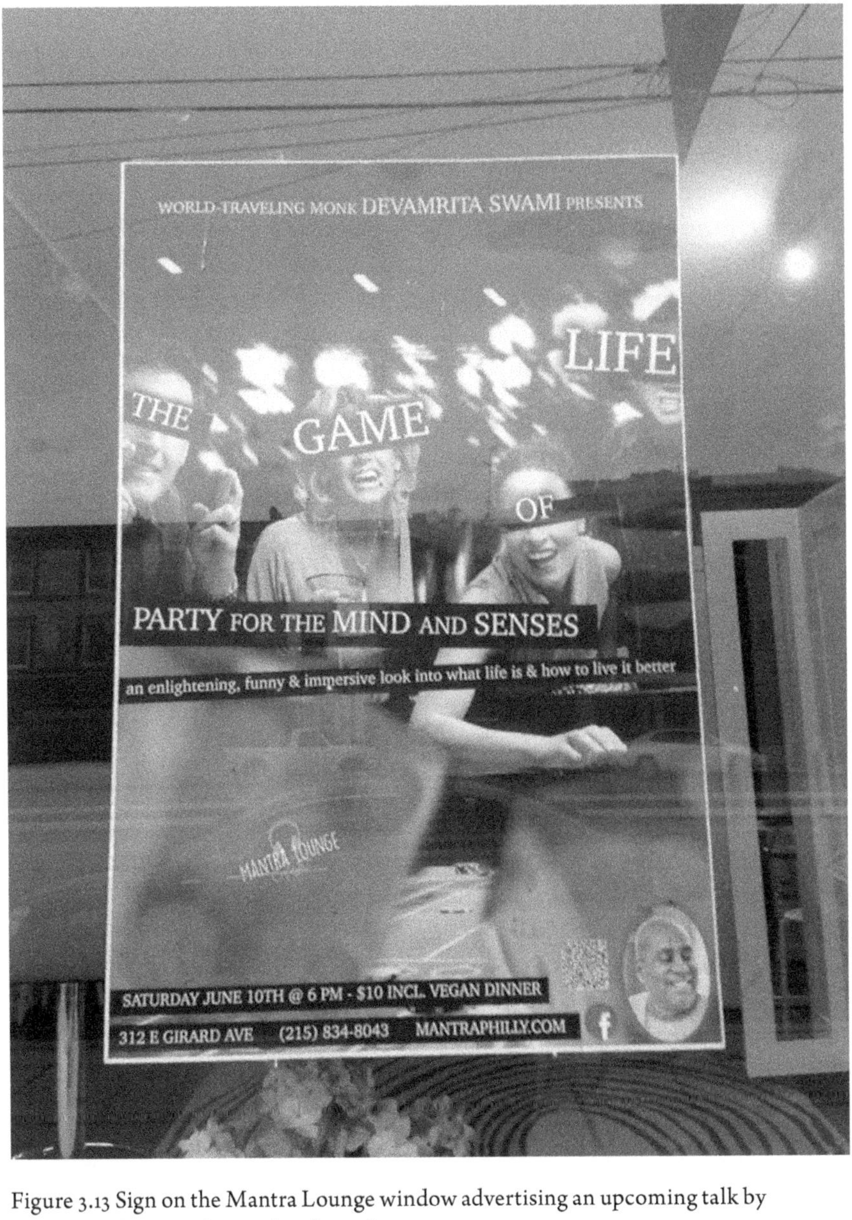

Figure 3.13 Sign on the Mantra Lounge window advertising an upcoming talk by Devamrita Swami. Photo taken by author.

living room."[62] He said that "when they walk in the door," you should "show them into a room where there are couches" that are "seated close enough for discussion," as well as "a rug on the floor."[63] Further, he said, "connected to that... [should be] a *prasād* taking room, [with] tables and chairs."[64] More than this, he repeatedly stressed, "You don't want an atmosphere which knocks the person over with things that are *exotic*. You want it to look like a place where someone coming for the first time will *relax*. You're not trying to be a temple, in other words. This is a very important point to understand. You're NOT trying to be a TEMPLE. You're trying to be a CLUB, a LOUNGE, that means relaxation."[65]

But what it also means, besides relaxation, is the absence of anything that westerners might find "off-putting" or "exotic":

> Don't make so many cultural barriers for them to cross. So many things they're not acquainted with. Deities are wonderful of course—Hare Krishna—in the temple. But you don't want to have to deal with that at your urban center [another name for lounge]. *Vyāsāsanas* [elevated chairs for gurus], and you know, people ya know, *daṇḍavats* [prostrations], and obeisances and all these kind of things. There'll be a time for that. But you don't want to place so many barriers in front of them.... [Instead] you want them to be able to let their hair down so to speak, and relate... I mean it's nervous [*sic*] enough for them to be coming to *your* place [for the] first time.[66,67]

It is clear that the staff set up the Mantra Lounge space using Devamrita Swami's instructions as a road map. Immediately in front of the sitting area at the center's front window, the room opens up to the lounge's main space: a moderately sized living room, adorned tastefully yet simply with IKEA furniture and decorations. The living room is arranged just as Devamrita Swami envisioned it. There are no deities in the room, nor does it look anything like a temple. Instead, the room is simply a sitting area, with couches arranged in a circular fashion around several decorative rugs, along with some high-top retro chairs, a reclined wicker chair, and a bean bag. Besides the chairs, couches, and decorative carpets, the only pieces adorning the room are a few salt lamps, candles, faux brick and teal (paisley) wallpaper, and a decorative, woven wall hanging of Radha-Krishna. There is also a picture of Krishna painted on the main wall of the room, but it looks more like an image one might see on the exterior of a new age storefront than an image one would see in a temple or on an altar.

Facing top, Figure 3.14 Mantra Lounge main room. The room opens into a communal dining area. Photo taken by author.

Facing bottom, Figure 3.15 Mantra Lounge main room. Photo taken by author.

Figure 3.16 Mantra Lounge communal dining room. Photo taken by author.

Finally, leading out of the main sitting area of the Mantra Lounge is—just as Devamrita Swami envisioned it—a *prasād*-eating area: a cozy nook that has two long, low-level tables at which patrons sit and enjoy their food and the company of each other.

It is within this "club" or "lounge" atmosphere that patrons enjoy the meditation, yoga, and other such classes that the Mantra Lounge offers.

Mantra Lounge Programs

The first program that I attended at the Mantra Lounge was on its opening night, when the lines to get in the door were so long that people were standing around the bend just to get in. I had heard about the Mantra Lounge through a devotee contact I had at ISKCON of Philadelphia. Serendipitously, I was at the Philadelphia temple one night talking to a devotee, and as I explained to her that my book project was about ISKCON's western-focused marketing, she suddenly gasped in delight: "I'm a disciple of Devamrita Maharaj!" As luck would have it, she turned out to be the head disciple in charge of Devamrita Swami's Bhakti Lounge in Toronto, a lounge designed to be a copycat version of his highly successful lounge programs in New Zealand and Australia. And as further luck would have it, this devotee had just been sent to Philadelphia with a team of three other women from Toronto (all four of whom are discussed below) to head up a new lounge in Philadelphia—one that would mirror those down under and in Toronto. This lounge was to be the Mantra Lounge.

Since its opening night, attendance at the Mantra Lounge has thinned out some, but it still fills its main room to near capacity for many of its nightly programs. Each night of the week, from 6:00 to 8:00 p.m., Philadelphia-area residents pile into the space for programs on conscious yoga or meditation or for thought-provoking, open-ended conversation with like-minded peers on topics such as sustainable living, happiness, and the ills of modern-day city life.

The Mantra Lounge is run almost exclusively by three women disciples of Devamrita Swami, as well as two relative newcomers to the movement, a young woman from Canada and a young man from Philadelphia. Together, these four women make up the team that was sent from Toronto to start the Mantra Lounge; the man is a newcomer they recruited in Philadelphia once they arrived. Demographically, all five staff members are roughly between the ages of twenty and forty, and only one of them is married. Of the five staff members, four are westerners (according to ISKCON's use of the term)—in particular, westerners of European heritage. The main staff member, however, is from New Delhi, India. She is also the devotee I serendipitously met at the Philadelphia temple, and she is the one in charge of the majority of the lounge's operations and preaching programs. Having visited one of Devamrita Swami's lounge programs in Toronto while she was living there for work, she quickly joined ISKCON and has since become one of Devamrita Swami's most prominent western outreach preachers. Finally, for a short while, there was also a sixth member of the Mantra Lounge staff: a middle-aged Indian woman disciple of Devamrita Swami. She traveled to Philadelphia from a lounge program in New Zealand to help get the Mantra Lounge on its feet and has since returned to New Zealand.

Unlike traditional ISKCON temples, which are open from the early morning hours until the late evening, Devamrita Swami's lounges are only open in the evenings. The Mantra Lounge in Philadelphia is open to the public Monday through Friday from 6:00 to 8:00 p.m. There are several reasons for this, visitor traffic on Girard Avenue being only one of them. Primarily, these hours have to do with staffing concerns. The devotees who run the Mantra Lounge (whom Devamrita Swami refers to as the "staff") are full-time ISKCON devotees, and as such, they follow a strict and time-consuming daily devotional program of which running the Mantra Lounge is just a part. Their day begins at 5:00 a.m., with the traditional ISKCON morning program consisting of *maṅgal āratī* (early morning worship), a discussion on ISKCON theology, and two hours of chanting the "Hare Krishna" mantra on a *japa mālā* (prayer beads). Following this, they typically go out on *saṅkīrtan*: selling Prabhupada's books in locations throughout Philadelphia (such as Rittenhouse Square) and/or on Philadelphia's various college campuses. They also host *bhakti* clubs on several college campuses in the area—programs whereby they "collaborate with several universities in the Philadelphia area to bring meditation, yoga and and [*sic*] much more onto campus."[68] Running these daytime *saṅkīrtan* and *bhakti* club programs is essential for the functioning of the Mantra Lounge because it is through these programs that the staff recruit newcomers—typically students and young professionals—to attend the various programs that they host at the lounge in the evenings.

Although the Mantra Lounge is only open in the evenings, it nonetheless boasts a full schedule of events for visitors' differing needs. All programs begin at 6:00 p.m. and rotate depending on the day. On Mondays and Thursdays, there is vinyasa yoga, which is described variously on the lounge's media sites and advertisements as "pranayama yoga," "vinyasa yoga," and "power yoga." The yoga classes are taught by one of the lounge staff members who is both an ISKCON devotee and a professionally trained yoga instructor—a dual training that is becoming increasingly popular within the ISKCON movement (as we will see in chap. 4).

While Mondays and Thursdays are both yoga nights, other nights of the week each host different programs. On Wednesdays, there is a "sustainability circle," described as an evening during which attendees spend time "delving into the issue [of sustainability] through a variety of lenses and seeking, at its core, the essence of this [sustainability] movement and what it could mean for humanity at large."[69] Tuesdays at the lounge are dedicated to the "Kirtan Connection," which is also advertised as "music meditation." Staff at the Mantra Lounge tout this program as being a meditation seminar that engages the whole body—not only the mind and the faculties of speech and hearing but also all of the limbs as well, as patrons are encouraged to participate in "dancing meditation" while they sing. Last but not least, Fridays are reserved for the Soulfeast: an evening workshop designed to bring "the philosophy of yoga into contemporary discourse" by allowing attendees to "engage in discussion with a diverse group of people" and doing so through "reference to classic yoga texts such as Bhagavad-gita."[70] (Calling the *Bhagavad-Gītā* a yoga text, of course, somewhat misrepresents the purpose and language of the text.)[71]

Building the Brand

Just as the Mantra Lounge is branded online as a meditation-based social club, Mantra Lounge staff also promote this brand in the brick-and-mortar location. To some extent, this branding is done through the layout of the lounge itself, which is designed to promote the vibe of a "club" or "lounge." Mantra Lounge also staff promote this brand through the lounge's evening programs, each of which presents some ritual or theological dimension of ISKCON to patrons through a spin of meditation, yoga, mindfulness, and the like.

In the yoga classes, for example, although the instructor guides the patrons through various yoga moves, such as downward-facing dog, up-dog, and so on, she does so set to *kīrtan* recordings of the "Hare Krishna" mantra that play as backdrop music for the duration of the class. Moreover, as she presents the yoga moves, she tells patrons that yoga is part of a holistic meditation system: one wherein the "spiritual and meditative side" of the practice helps guide and contextualize the physical dimension (e.g., the postures). In order to give the patrons a chance to see for themselves the ways in which yoga is part of a bigger meditation system, at the conclusion of class, she guides the patrons through a meditation herself. For this meditation, she hands out to each patron a *japa mālā*—a stringed prayer necklace made of *tulasī* (holy basil) beads. She then guides them through a round of *japa*, a chanting of the Hare Krishna *mahā mantra*—"Hare Krishna, Hare Krishna, Krishna Krishna, Hare Hare, Hare Rama, Hare Rama, Rama Rama, Hare Hare"—for up to a total of 108 times, or once per bead, on the stringed prayer necklace. This meditation, she says, is aimed at helping them relieve stress and connect to their inner selves. But it also produces the zenith—and goal—of yoga, she says: a higher state of mind in which their "inner self" is connected to a "higher consciousness." In this way, Krishna consciousness itself—that is, the devotional consciousness that is one-pointedly focused on Krishna—is being branded as the culmination of yoga. And meditation, or chanting the "Hare Krishna" mantra, is positioned as the way to get there.

The Kirtan Connection night works in the same way, where the practice of *kīrtan* (or singing the names of Krishna) is branded as a meditation and as an opportunity for patrons to alleviate the anxieties that have been weighing on them.[72] The Kirtan Connection is run by two members of the Mantra Lounge staff. At the outset of the program, these staff members usually ask the gathered crowd about their favorite forms of meditation. In what then becomes a rather free-flowing conversation, the different patrons typically discuss the various meditations that they enjoy doing; some talk of mindfulness, others about focusing on the senses, and still others about using various crystals for concentration. Along the way, the two staff members deftly guide the discussion toward "the most potent form of meditation of all." This form of meditation, they say, is "singing mantra meditation," and the most powerful mantra, they explain, is the *mahā mantra*. After piquing the interest of the gathered patrons—some of whom are regulars but many of whom are new to the lounge (although not new to meditation)—the two staff members lead the group in what is, for all intents and purposes, an ISKCON *kīrtan*: the "Hare Krishna" mantra sung in call-and-response style, accompanied by *mṛdaṅga* drums, *karatālas* (cymbals), a harmonium, and sometimes dancing. Rather than being presented to the group as a singing prayer to a Hindu god, however, *kīrtan* is presented to them as a stress-relieving meditation—one that is useful for clearing their cluttered minds as well as connecting them to a "higher purpose and consciousness." And for their part, the patrons are usually thrilled, with many of them noting in the discussion that follows that they never knew one could sing and dance as a meditation.

The other two weekly programs hosted at the Mantra Lounge also rebrand dimensions of ISKCON as meditation. However, these two programs are more focused on rebranding the conceptual (or theological) dimensions of ISKCON rather than the performative (or ritual) ones. The Sustainability Circle, held every Wednesday evening, is an example of one such program. The Sustainability Circle at the Mantra Lounge is run by a disciple of Devamrita Swami's who began teaching the class on his request. It is the newest of all of the programs at the lounge and was started in recognition of "people's interest in environmentalism and their concern about our current environmental crisis." The devotee who runs the Sustainability Circle is a highly qualified host; she spent several years doing development work across the continent of Africa prior to joining the ISKCON movement in New Zealand (at a lounge program), and she is one of the women who moved to Philadelphia from Toronto to head up the Mantra Lounge.

During a typical evening in the Sustainability Circle, the devotee host asks the gathered patrons to reflect on and discuss a challenging question related to sustainability. For example, during one evening that I attended, she presented the group with a dilemma often faced by aid workers: namely, that after struggling to find long-term solutions to help those in the greatest need, workers in developing countries almost always grow cynical, believing themselves incapable of contributing to others' welfare in what are often complicated and corrupt systems. She then asked the class: "How can we solve a dilemma like this? What are some solutions that can actually work long-term to help those in developing countries?" On other occasions, the Sustainability Circle host leads the group through a series of discussions that not only present the environmental problems that we currently face—melting ice caps, polluted rivers, global warming, and so on—but that also ask attendees to reflect on the ways that their own actions might be contributing to these problems. In these cases, she asks questions like, "What are *you* doing that might be causing the problems?"

While the messages differ each week, the primary aim of the Sustainability Circle is always the same: to convince gathered attendees that materialism and low consciousness are to blame for the environmental crisis and that a meditation-based lifestyle can solve it. This lifestyle includes an attachment not to material pleasures but to a "higher pleasure." It also includes a regular practice of vegetarianism, high thinking and simple living, and a study of "ancient yoga texts," by which devotees ordinarily mean the *Bhagavad-Gītā* (again, despite the fact that the label of "yoga text" somewhat misrepresents the purpose and language of the *Gītā*). Most important, at the heart of this lifestyle is the cultivation of a meditative consciousness accomplished through the chanting of the "the most powerful mantra of all," the Hare Krishna *mahā mantra*. In this way, ISKCON ideas about detachment to material desires, attachment to Krishna, vegetarianism, and chanting of Krishna's names are rebranded not only as meditative tools but as meditative tools that can solve the eco crisis.

Like the Sustainability Circle, the Friday evening Soulfeast is also a program that rebrands ISKCON theology through a lens of meditation (and yoga). The Soulfeast is advertised to patrons as an evening during which they can "explore the answers to life's big questions" and "stimulate [their] mind, challenge [their] perceptions, and engage in discussion with a diverse group of people."[73] The Soulfeast, in other words, is an evening promoted as one of intellectual conversation and camaraderie.

Each Friday during the Soulfeast, lounge staff guide patrons through intellectual conversation on a wide range of philosophical topics. Examples of topics that staff have focused on include *What is true happiness?*, *What is desire?*, *Does satisfying desire lead to happiness?*, and *Is there more to life than just working to live for the weekends?*, to name just a few. Although these topics vary, they tend to focus on a common theme: the idea that the pursuit of material desire does not bring lasting contentment but instead brings stress, emptiness, and the various other emotional ills that characterize modern city life. And just as they do in all of the other nightly classes, during the Soulfeast, Mantra Lounge staff present the chanting of the Hare Krishna *mahā mantra* as the "meditation solution" (or "yoga answer") par excellence to all of these ills and as the best way to address the myriad of big questions raised during Soulfeast discussions. During the Soulfeast, in other words, ISKCON theology—couched though it is in vague ideas such as "spiritual living," "yoga consciousness," "meditation," and "a life centered in 'the Absolute'"—is presented as the best answer to all of life's biggest and most enduring questions. More than this, it is at the Soulfeast where patrons are most actively encouraged to "perform a lab experiment with the meditation system" that goes along with these "ancient yoga" ideas. This means that the Mantra Lounge staff encourage patrons to give meditation a try by taking a *japa mālā* home, trying the meditation (chanting) out on their own, and waiting and watching to see how their life becomes more peaceful, relaxed, and centered. In the meantime, patrons are encouraged to not only keep attending programs at the lounge but also to participate in its social dimension: the communal meal.

The Communal Meal

While the Mantra Lounge is advertised (and functions) as a meditation-based center, central to its brand is that it is more than this. Instead, Devamrita Swami wants the Mantra Lounge—like all of his lofts and lounges worldwide—to be a meditation-based *social club*: a "Krishna Conscious café [or] nightclub," as he puts it.[74]

Central to the establishment of the Mantra Lounge as a social club is the nightly communal meal that is served to attending patrons following each program. At the Mantra Lounge, this meal is served sit-down style, and patrons gather together along two long tables in a small dining-room area to eat. The meal's fee schedule is set up in such a way that when patrons pay for each nightly program—be it yoga, a sustainability class, or the Soulfeast—they also get an all-you-can-eat, several-course vegan dinner. The combined program and dinner fee is ten dollars. Clearly, this is an attractive opportunity for visitors, who are often shocked that they get such an elaborate home-cooked dinner included in the minimal program fee.

The aim of the communal meal is to give patrons a chance to make friends and associate with like-minded others in a community setting. Since the communal meal immediately follows the nightly programs, there is much buzz and excitement that transfers from the classes over to the meal. As I have seen, the classes tend to raise great interest in the patrons, many of whom—by their own admission—have never before thought so deeply about the topics raised therein. For example, the notion that their own pursuit of desire and "identification with the body" might be causing their unhappiness is something that many patrons find surprising. Similarly, the idea that their own views on desire and happiness might be causing the eco crisis (as well as the suggestion that the chanting of a mantra might help solve it) is something that they find equally thought-provoking, if not troubling. As such, when the classes are over, there is a great residual buzz that bleeds into the communal meal, and patrons are eager to sit down and not only enjoy the food but also engage in a discussion about the ideas and practices raised in the evening's program.

Being that the classes are interesting to the patrons, patrons have an easy entryway into conversation with each other: they discuss what they thought about the meditation, the music, and so on. And these conversations often segue into more social ones. From what I have seen, for example, patrons often talk about their "meditation journeys" at the communal meal and how they have been dabbling with different forms of meditation in recent years of their lives. Moreover, as they sit and converse over pasta, vegan cake, potato pancakes, and other delicacies, they often talk about their personal hardships, stresses, and "journeys"—journeys to wellness, peace of mind, and/or a life free from social media, stress, and distractions. More than this, they sometimes share their passions and their life goals, which often include doing social good, being mindful, pursuing meaningful careers, and cultivating themselves. These conversations tend to have real depth and are occasions for otherwise strangers to meet and commune on a level beyond mere small talk. As a newcomer at my table on one visit told me, "I will definitely be coming back here. . . . I don't know, I just feel like I found my people. Like I found my clique, ya know?" Others express similar sentiments: "I can be real with people here, unlike at other times."

When Devamrita Swami came up with the idea for rebranding ISKCON twenty-four years ago, this is exactly the kind of plugging in to a social environment that he thought was needed in order to bring westerners back to the movement. It is the dimension of his brand that he often refers to as the *creation of a scene*. As he told me during one of my sit-down conversations with him, "What I found is they [westerners] need a constructive social scene where they can support one another and plug in [so] . . . that's what I try to do," create a place that has "good food, good ambience, and good people to rub shoulders with."[75] Central to creating this social ambience and community is providing a space that patrons think is their own—one that is a "hangout space" in which they can assemble freely and meaningfully share and cultivate their "spiritual lifestyles" with each other. As Devamrita Swami says, "We want some things for Krishna, so you have to give them what *they* want."[76] And according to Devamrita Swami, a big part of what they want is a place to hang out and meet others like themselves—a place to gather that resonates with their own cultural tastes, preferences, lifestyles, interests, and place in life. This is why, as Devamrita Swami explains,

> a veeeeeeeerrrry important concept to understand [is that] you want the people to think it's *their* place, not the Hares' place. Then you're successful. As long as they think it's *their* place, they're gonna feel comfortable and bring other people there. "Ya know, this is *our* club, this is *our* scene here," they're gonna feel proud about that, ya know. Just like some people have a

> bar or a pub they hang out with, or a particular café or restaurant.... So, you want the people to think that this is [their] scene.... You want them to think "it's *our* place"... then you know you've set up your *saṅkīrtan* scene very properly, to catch them off guard. That's the name of the game, let them relax.[77]

By creating a "scene" that lets patrons relax and feel a degree of social comfort, Devamrita Swami hopes that patrons will be more inclined to "bring their friends" to the lounge. More than this, however, he believes that if patrons find the lounge to be a socially comfortable and enjoyable place, then they are more likely to attend themselves multiple times per week. And if they visit several times a week, enjoy the company of the people who attend the programs (as well as the staff who run them), and take even a small interest in the teachings presented to them during the classes, then, Devamrita Swami says, "they've joined the club. They may not even think they've joined the Hare Krishna movement. They just think, 'I've joined the club,' you know, I'm in on this place, you know.'"[78] And this, he thinks, is the start of success.

CONCLUSION

In response to the fact that westerners are no longer joining ISKCON, Devamrita Swami has rebranded the ISKCON movement as a meditation-based social club. In this environment, patrons can learn about the fundamentals of ISKCON devotional life—such as chanting, detachment from materialism, and attachment to "the Absolute"—through a spin of meditation, mindfulness, and a meditative lifestyle.

In the broadest sense, Devamrita Swami is rebranding ISKCON by creating centers that he believes are comfortable spaces for westerners. This rebranding has two dimensions, which correspond to the two reasons why Devamrita Swami believes that westerners are no longer attracted to ISKCON. The first dimension entails establishing spaces that change the *social culture* of ISKCON. As discussed earlier in this chapter, Devamrita Swami argues that westerners are uncomfortable in traditional ISKCON communities, in part, because they cannot relate to the congregants there; they find the Indian congregants who make up the communities' majorities to be too straitlaced, too well-adjusted, and too financially well-off to be relatable to them. Patrons who frequent Devamrita Swami's lounges, on the other hand, are typically twenty- or thirty-somethings working in their first career stage who have not yet established full financial comfort for themselves. They also tend to be unmarried and can be characterized as "seeker" types. Moreover, as Devamrita Swami describes them, lounge patrons tend to be individuals who favor "alternative lifestyles."

(Incidentally, they also tend to be predominantly non-Indian, although there are on occasion second-generation Indian Americans, Indian Kiwis, etc.) As such, westerners who visit Devamrita Swami's lounges for the first time have the chance to find a social comfort with other patrons there that they don't find with congregants at many ISKCON temples. And for Devamrita Swami, this is the first step to creating an ISKCON that westerners will join: if westerners can find in ISKCON lounge centers a community of people to whom they can relate and with whom they can be comfortable—others whose lives and social positions are similar to their own—then he believes their interest in joining ISKCON will increase exponentially.

Equal in importance to creating a *social space* that resonates with westerners, however, is the second dimension of Devamrita Swami's rebranding of ISKCON. This dimension involves the creation of a *worship space* that resonates with them. As the reader will recall, Devamrita Swami believes that besides their discomfort with the social culture of ISKCON, westerners are also uncomfortable with ISKCON temples themselves, complete with the *mūrtis* (embodied forms) of Krishna that they host and the ritual worship of them that they offer. In response to this discomfort, Devamrita Swami's lounges are designed to be centers in which westerners can participate in the ISKCON movement *without being in a temple.* Within Devamrita Swami's Mantra Lounge, for example, all of the dimensions of ISKCON are present in some (albeit rebranded) form—the texts, the teachings, the food, the chanting, and even the association of other devotees (i.e., the staff). The only dimension of ISKCON missing completely from the lounge is the temple setup with the deities (as well as the ritual worship of them).

This setup of the space is by design, and all of Devamrita Swami's lounges follow this same format. As Devamrita Swami explains in one of his talks, the point of building a lounge "is to produce an atmosphere where people [westerners] can feel comfortable to relax and talk."[79] This means a space in which "there's not too much exotic things to overwhelm them" and "they're not challenged by the deities right away."[80] If the goal is to get westerners to relax and talk, then the presumption is that they cannot do this in an atmosphere in which there are "exotic things" like the deities to "overwhelm them." Although the deities play a central role in ISKCON, Devamrita Swami consistently maintains that they are "not for the customers, [but] for the staff," which is why none of his lounges have deities or an altar.[81] All of this is to say that in trying to create a worship space that resonates with westerners, Devamrita Swami actively downplays the religious and ritual dimensions of ISKCON in order to garner wider appeal.

Many gurus employ similar tactics when trying to universalize their movements beyond a single marketing segment. In fact, scholars have argued that when religious groups aim to "go global," or universalize their messages so as to reach and attract a worldwide base of followers, they often downplay their religiosity and ties to ritual and instead reinvent themselves as more general, and often therefore more generic, forms of "spirituality." For example, Joanne Punzo Waghorne has studied this phenomenon with respect to Hindu guru movements in Singapore,[82] and Amanda J. Lucia has examined it in her theoretical analysis of innovative Hindu gurus.[83] Both scholars have argued that when Hindu gurus aim to "transmit their messages to global audiences," they often do so by "attempt[ing] to insert distance between their movements and traditional Hinduism."[84] Some of the ways that they create this distance is by "speaking[ing] in universalistic language, embrac[ing] generalized theologies of 'spirituality,' and plac[ing] minimal requirements on their followers."[85] Another way that they do so is by downplaying the role of ritual within their centers and theologies because, as Waghorne has aptly argued, "de-ethnization requires de-ritualization."[86]

It is not just Hindu gurus who engage in such practices in order to garner widespread appeal, however. Jeff Wilson has also studied this phenomenon in reference to the promotion of Buddhist mindfulness in the United States, arguing that "obscuring how mindfulness operated in historic Buddhist practice, or even going so far as to hide mindfulness's origins and Buddhist connections makes it (allegedly) available to everyone, increasing the sellers who can appropriate it and the buyers who can consume it."[87] Christian preachers distance themselves from what might be seen as overly sectarian or religious theologies (and overly ritualized practices) as well, especially those whose aim is to reach an exceptionally wide audience of people (for example, televangelists). As Mara Einstein argues, "In order to draw in the masses, [these] preachers must include what will attract the largest number of people—ideas about how their lives will be better, more prosperous, more fulfilling—and exclude those things that will lead viewers to reach for the remote control—mentions of Jesus, requests for contributions, suggestions that they are going to hell."[88]

In many ways, Devamrita Swami's rebranding moves are similar to those described by Waghorne, Lucia, Wilson, Einstein, and others. However, what makes Devamrita Swami's paradigm different from those of many other gurus and religious figures who de-ritualize and de-theologize their traditions in order to broaden their audience is the fact that for Devamrita Swami, these strategies are just a stepping stone (recall his loft model paradigm) or an "on ramp to the transcendental highway."[89] That is, the de-ritualized and de-theologized

ISKCON that Devamrita Swami presents to lounge patrons is just a temporary resting place for them to stop until he and other lounge staff believe they are ready to be introduced to and participate in temple ISKCON—complete with its theologies of embodied divinity and the ritual worship of *mūrtis* (embodied forms). In other words, participating in the lounges' variety of religiosity—meditating, doing yoga, chanting the *mahā mantra* for stress reduction, discussing mindfulness, and so on—is not where Devamrita Swami wants his lounge patrons to stop. Instead, he wants them to become fully committed practitioners of, and initiated members in, Swami Prabhupada's movement. And for him, this means—among other things—participating in ISKCON's temple culture and worshipping the deities. It also means having a personal relationship with Krishna in his visible, tangible (embodied) forms. As Devamrita Swami himself told me, you cannot have ISKCON without the deities: "You wouldn't want to . . . everything we do in ISKCON is done for the deities."[90]

So how, then, does Devamrita Swami introduce and endeavor to move lounge patrons to the ISKCON movement, complete with its temple culture and ritual worship of the deities? Admittedly, his plan for helping them achieve this introduction is not as well-formed as his plan for bringing them to the lounge in the first place. Instead, his strategy essentially rests on the hope that *if* patrons take an interest in the de-ritualized ISKCON that is presented and practiced in his lounges—including the teachings, the meditations, and so on—then they will not mind once they come to learn that ISKCON is actually a devotionally based religious movement complete with elaborate Vaishnava ritual and a predominantly temple-based set of worship spaces. This is especially the case if they have formed friendships with lounge staff over the course of their visits to the lounge. As Devamrita Swami explained to a group of devotees who gathered to hear him speak about his loft preaching model in January of 2012:

> If they can get to be friends with you in a way that you've caught them off guard, then the poison so to speak has already entered their system . . . then they can't reject you because you're their friend. And gradually you can introduce them to the whole world of devotion, at which point it's too late because you're their friend. . . . In that way it becomes natural for them because you've established a relationship. The hardest thing in sales is to change a cold contact into a warm contact. But if you've got warm contacts, then anything can go.[91]

Through his use of the sales metaphor of cold versus warm contacts, Devamrita Swami is saying that once patrons have established a bond with the staff members at his loft and lounge centers, then they are happy to accept the more devotional, religious, and ritualistic dimensions of the ISKCON movement (the temple, the deities, etc.) because the bond itself breaks down any barriers they might initially have to these dimensions. This is especially the case if patrons have already also taken a liking to the philosophical ideas and meditation practices promoted at the lounge, such as reading Prabhupada's books and chanting the "Hare Krishna" mantra. A conversation that I had with Devamrita Swami evidences this viewpoint quite well:

> DEVAMRITA SWAMI: We do not parade the institution [ISKCON] or institutional membership before our clientele . . . only later down the road, when they've got some kind of a taste and a passion, do we lightly mention that this [lounge] is part of an institution.
>
> ME: How does that go?
>
> DEVAMRITA SWAMI: By that time, they are so in love with the place and the people there that they don't mind.
>
> ME: Are there deities there [at your lounges]?
>
> DEVAMRITA SWAMI: No, no we don't have deities there.
>
> ME: So is that a hard transition for people [once they get to the temples]—
>
> DEVAMRITA SWAMI: Surprisingly not. Once they get into the chanting and read the books, then it's not a hard transition for them. Straight out? Yes.
>
> ME: How do they get introduced to the deities? Do they, so, I'm trying to think, I'm trying to imagine this scene which—
>
> DEVAMRITA SWAMI: After some time, after you're attending the scene, if there's a temple with deities in the area, then someone like Krishna Devi Dasi will say, "Well, let's go out there on a Sunday."
>
> ME: OK . . . I see—
>
> DEVAMRITA SWAMI: When the staff feel the person is ready—[they take them there]. But by that time, they've [the patron] already had some preparation, education, nurturing. So it's not just like a cold shower, it's not such a *shock*.[92]

Devamrita Swami believes that once patrons have developed a taste for the chanting of the "Hare Krishna" mantra and for basic conceptual ideas that underscore the ISKCON tradition (that they learn in a "de-theologized" form at the lounges), then transitioning to a deity-centric, devotional religious path is ostensibly not difficult for them. This is also the view taken by Mantra Lounge staff themselves, several of whom told me that although patrons who are invited to the temple are initially "creeped out" by the deities, eventually "they don't really mind them." Instead, once they are introduced to the temple, patrons are able to continue on in their ISKCON path, seeing the deities and the temple itself as but one dimension of the movement—a dimension that staff claim becomes less and less "exotic" to them over time.

Religious Marketing or Religious Deception?

When he journeyed to the United States in 1965 to found and spread the ISKCON movement, A. C. Bhaktivedanta Swami Prabhupada instructed his disciples to spread Krishna Consciousness as far and wide as possible. In order to equip them to do so, Prabhupada encouraged his disciples toward creative preaching. That is, rather than simply instructing them to recapitulate traditional Vaishnava models of evangelism, Prabhupada instead gave his disciples the flexibility to spread his movement in innovative and inventive ways and in manners that suited their particular interests and natural talents. Most importantly, he encouraged them to preach in ways that were appropriate to the "time, place, and circumstance" and in ways that they believed would best draw people to the movement. In so doing, Prabhupada was following the example of the innovative preachers in his lineage before him—Bhaktivinoda Thakura and Bhaktisiddhanta Sarasvati.

Central to understanding this innovative preaching spirit and the way that Prabhupada instructed his disciples to employ it in their lives is understanding the concept of *yukta vairāgya* as it is interpreted in ISKCON. Literally translated as *joined* or *attached asceticism* (*yukta* comes from √*yuj*, meaning *to link*, and *vairāgya* means *asceticism*), the principle of *yukta vairāgya* is based in the *Bhaktirasāmṛtasindhu* of Rupa Goswami. As depicted in this text, *yukta vairāgya* reflects a complex position with respect to the idea of renunciation. Rather than "ordinary" renunciation, which is marked by a rejection of the world and objects in it, Rupa Goswami identifies *yukta vairāgya* as a state of renunciation wherein the individual is not attached to material objects but instead uses them in a relationship with Krishna (*anāsaktasya viṣayān yathārhamupayuñjataḥ; nirbandhaḥ Kṛṣṇasambandhe yuktaṁ vairāgyamucyate*).[93] Typically within the Gauḍīya traditions, this idea is interpreted to mean that the individual can live a religious life in the world—and can even enjoy objects in the world—as long as she does so with the right perspective. This perspective is one in which the practitioner sees the world's existence as both part of Krishna and as a playground for his *līlā* (divine sport).[94]

Within the ISKCON movement, however, devotees take the notion of *yukta vairāgya* and add an evangelical twist (as is typical in the movement), claiming that the best way to achieve this ideal renunciation is to "use the world in the service of Krishna." That is, rather than rejecting the world or being attached to it, the *yukta vairāgī* (or practitioner of *yukta vairāgya*) is interpreted in ISKCON as one who "acts in Krishna Consciousness" (9.28), engaging in actions in which "the fruits are given to Kṛṣṇa" (9.28) or are "dovetailed in His Service" (8.27).[95] In practical terms, this is interpreted to mean that the *yukta vairāgī* ought to use whatever materials exist in the world not only to worship Krishna *but also to evangelize*: to spread the Hare Krishna movement, and Krishna Consciousness, to people near and far. As Prabhupada himself remarked, "One should not be attached to material opulence, but material opulence may be accepted in the Kṛṣṇa consciousness movement to facilitate the propagation of the movement. In other words, material opulence may be accepted as *yukta-vairāgya*, that is, for renunciation."[96]

As devotees tell me, "Prabhupada used all of the technology available to him" so that he could best spread the ISKCON movement "according to time, place, and circumstance" to various groups of people all around the world. And just like Prabhupada, contemporary devotees—as *yukta vairāgīs*—have the opportunity to do the same, meaning to find their own unique ways to spread love of Krishna far and wide. In fact, one of the central tasks for ISKCON devotees living a life based in *yukta vairāgya* becomes trying to find ever-new and creative ways to utilize the world in the service of Krishna—that is, to find fresh and innovative ways to present, or market, Krishna and Krishna Consciousness to various publics so that they may have the chance to develop their love for him.

While there are a variety of ways that *yukta vairāgya* is understood in contemporary ISKCON, many devotees today equate the idea with an ends-justify-the-means approach to preaching and marketing. On many occasions, I've heard devotees say that as long as a program, advertisement, or marketing strategy brings people to Krishna (and as long as it is in the "mode of goodness"), it can be used as a preaching device, regardless of the degree to which it is actually connected to the ISKCON movement.[97] For example, I have been told that some devotees respond affirmatively when asked to speak at events as Buddhists, knowing full well that they are not Buddhists, but nonetheless accepting the invitations simply because they are "doing it for Krishna." Even Devamrita Swami, at times, seems to take this ends-justify-the-means approach; this is why, for example, he notes that there can be a number of different activities offered at lounge programs, not just yoga and meditation. "Yoga," he says, is "just one thing." But you can also do

> martial arts . . . whatever, qi gong, this healing, that healing, ya know, whatever it is, devotees shouldn't take it too seriously, it's just something you use to get people in the door, you know. Āyurveda, this, that, the other, astrology, whatever, you know, just put it on the signboard. Cooking, anything to get them in the door. . . . The whole New Age theology thing is, it's a has-been now . . . [so] better do some martial arts, or some yoga, or, ya know, sometimes . . . aliens, UFOs and aliens . . . whatever, just get them in the door. Give them some alternative activities so they don't think we're just simply wanting to preach to them, which we are.[98]

At times, Devamrita Swami even refers to the programs that staff offer at his lounges as "loss leaders"—equating them to the free items that stores give away because they want customers to come into the store and buy the expensive goods once they are there.[99]

To ask a simple set of questions, at what point does innovative religious marketing become a deceitful tactic, like a bait and switch? What are the limits of *yukta vairāgya*, and when does an ends-justifies-the-means approach to it become religious deception? Do Devamrita Swami's lounge programs cross the thin line between marketing and deception? Finally, and more pointedly, are Devamrita Swami's lounge-preaching programs a bait and switch? Is he simply enticing patrons into his lounge centers under the auspices of programs they like—yoga and meditation, for example—only to try to sneakily preach ISKCON to them when they arrive?

These questions are difficult to navigate for many reasons, not the least of which because their answer depends on who one asks and also how one defines *deception*. Shlomo Sher, scholar of applied ethics, has written an article, "A Framework for Assessing Immorally Manipulative Marketing Tactics," in which he tries to tease out the characteristics that make something an "immortally manipulative tactic."[100] Although his framework is about manipulation more broadly, of which deception is only a part, it is nonetheless useful for the present purposes. Sher defines *manipulation* as a tactic or set of tactics "intended to motivate [an audience] by undermining what the marketer believes is his/her audience's normal decision-making process either by deception or by playing on a vulnerability that the marketer believes exists in his/her audience's normal decision-making process."[101] Playing on a vulnerability involves playing to an audience's emotions, like guilt (such as when a salesperson spends a lot of time with a customer in order to make a sale) or admiration (through the use of celebrity endorsements, for example). Sher argues that deception rests on the marketer's intentional and knowing use of false claims, important omissions, and/or misrepresentations of facts. False claims are deliberate mistruths (such as a fried chicken franchise's description of its breaded chicken as "part of a low-carb diet"). Important omissions consist of leaving out information that would likely inform an audience's decision (such as failing to mention that people promoting products or services are paid actors). Finally, misrepresentations of facts involve presenting information in such a way that skews how data appear to an audience—for example, when inconclusive studies are presented as fact, when survey data are based on only one participant (such as a company's CEO), or when marketers deliberately choose words that will mislead a public's understanding (e.g., choosing the word *capable* for a computer program on the presumption that the audience will think it means *compatible*).[102]

If we go by Sher's analysis, then to some extent, we can say that the answer to the above questions is *yes*, as Devamrita Swami's own statements sometimes seem to indicate. For example, one might argue that Devamrita Swami and his team are, in fact, omitting information—failing to mention that the Mantra Lounge is a part of ISKCON, for example, or that it is tied to a theistic Vaishnava religious tradition. One might also make the case that Devamrita Swami and his team are misrepresenting facts—for example, by claiming that *kīrtan* is dancing meditation and that chanting Hare Krishna is a practice in mindfulness, or by presenting themselves as a group of "spiritual volunteers" who run a meditation, mindfulness, and yoga center.[103]

It is important to note, however, that Devamrita Swami—along with his many disciples—vehemently objects to this characterization of them (I know because I asked them these questions many times). Instead, they unanimously claim that what they are doing in the Mantra Lounge and other similar programs is different from deception. Instead, they say that their methods are strategies designed not to trick but to "meet customers where they are" and "to present Krishna in ways that people can relate to and understand." More than this, they insist their programs are not deceitful because they do, in fact, offer patrons what they advertise. In other words, deceptive marketing such as bait-and-switch schemes, they say, advertise programs that they fail to deliver. But as Mantra Lounge staff repeatedly told me in answer to my questions about deception, "We *do* offer yoga—these are real yoga classes—so we are not deceiving people."

Finally, it also bears mentioning in this discussion that many of the staff at Devamrita Swami's lounges around the world themselves came to ISKCON through his loft preaching model, complete with the marketing strategies discussed in this chapter. And these staffers note having felt *graced* by loft preaching, not deceived. As one Mantra Lounge staff member told me, "I feel so lucky, you know, to have encountered ISKCON through the lounge program.... I just know that I would have never joined ISKCON if I had first been introduced to it in the temple." When I asked her about this and about what it is, in particular, about the temple that would have prevented her from joining the movement, she responded immediately: "It's too ritualistic, all of it. The ritual, the deities. And I would have been freaked out by the big Prabhupada in the room too. It's definitely much easier to get a softer introduction to it." The loft model, she said, allowed her to appreciate the ISKCON movement, which she otherwise would have been unable to do. "Even though it's there," she said, "it's hard to see the philosophy through the temple. It's there, but it's just hard to see it. It's kind of like, imagine if you have a coconut. What you really want in the coconut is the juice and fruit that are on the inside. But if that's what you want, if that's the good stuff, then why would you give people that essence inside of a coconut, ya know? Like inside a hard shell that's hard to actually get in and crack?"

This Mantra Lounge staff member believes that rather than being deceptive, Devamrita Swami's lounge model was actually merciful, allowing her to bypass what would have been her reservations about ISKCON—the exterior shell of the coconut, so to speak. And this exterior shell includes all of the dimensions of the movement that might have seemed too "foreign" and "exotic," too "religious" and "ritualistic" to her at the outset. And because of this mercy, she said, she found Krishna.

It is worth noting that this calculation—a sort of consequentialist approach—is also how Shlomo Sher evaluates whether a marketing strategy is immorally manipulative or not. For Sher, not all manipulative tactics (even deceptive ones) are immoral. "If the tactic is manipulative," he writes, "but sufficient redemptive moral considerations do bear on it, it is not immorally manipulative."[104] For many of the Krishna Branders, the redemptive moral value of attracting people to Krishna *is* sufficient to justify these marketing strategies—more than sufficient to justify them, in fact. But there is much debate about this question, especially from those who might have visited a loft-type center in the past, only to feel burned that it turned out to be different from what they expected. I met such people in my research, including a young college student who saved up her money and traveled far outside of her home in the United States to spend a few weeks at what she thought was a spiritual volunteer camp. To say that she felt deceived and hurt upon arriving at the remote location, only to find a residential ISKCON temple and farm community, is an understatement.

As we will see, there is also debate about this question within the ISKCON tradition itself and even within the Krishna Brander community, in particular. We will have a chance to explore this side of the debate when we examine Hridayananda Das Goswami's Krishna West sub-movement in chapter 5. But before doing so, let's first turn our attention to our next Krishna Brander, Radhanath Swami, who is ISKCON's most popular and renowned guru. Like Devamrita Swami, Radhanath Swami has also orchestrated a marketing approach for attracting westerners to ISKCON. As we will see, however, Radhanath Swami's model differs greatly from that of Devamrita Swami. Far from the gritty, hipster neighborhoods of Devamrita Swami's lounges, Radhanath Swami's brand takes us all the way from the high-end yoga markets of Manhattan and DC to the luxury yoga retreats of India and The Bahamas. It is to a discussion of this brand that I now turn.

NOTES

1. Sachin Mittal. 2015. "Seminar on Reaching the Hearts and the Minds of the Western Public." *Dandavats*. Accessed July 2, 2017. http://www.dandavats.com/?p=17198.
2. Ibid. Videos of these lectures can be found at Kishorekishori YouTube channel. Accessed June 30, 2017. https://www.youtube.com/user/kishorekishori/videos.
3. Devamrita Swami. 2015. "Devamrita Swami, Reaching the Hearts Day 2 Session 3." ISKCON Online YouTube channel, May 27. 11:43–12:00. Accessed June 30, 2017. https://www.youtube.com/watch?v=pnXkLkVasfI.
4. Ibid.
5. Throughout this chapter, I refer to Devamrita Swami by his devotional name, rather than his given name. I do the same for all of the Krishna Branders discussed in this book.
6. Devamrita Swami. "Introduction to Devamrita Swami." 0:50–0:54. DevamritaSwami.Com. Accessed July 2, 2017. http://devamritaswami.com/.
7. Ibid.
8. Devamrita Swami. Interview by Nicole Karapanagiotis. In person, Potomac, Maryland, March 28, 2016.
9. Ibid.
10. Mantra Lounge Philadelphia Facebook page. July 31, 2018. Accessed June 4, 2019. https://www.facebook.com/mantraloungephiladelphia/photos/a.657394061001739/2175448702529593/?type=3&theater.
11. Ibid.
12. Swami 2015, "Reaching the Hearts Day 2."
13. Swami 2016, Interview.

14. M. Devi Dasi. 2015. "Reaching the Hearts Day 2 Session 4." Kishorekishori YouTube channel, May 2. 3:00–3:45. Accessed July 2, 2017. https://www.youtube.com/watch?v=xL7_bQT1etc.

15. Ibid. Emphasis in original. The devotee speaking in this video is a disciple of Devamrita Swami and is the devotee he has chosen to start and run a number of his centers and programs in different parts of the world. For example, she started his Bhakti Lounge in Toronto, Canada, and also started up—and currently runs—his Mantra Lounge in Philadelphia, United States. Originally from India, she is described in ISKCON periodicals as being "one of the foremost preachers in Western settings." Sikhi Mahiti Das. 2015. "Message from the Temple President—Sikhi Mahiti das." *ISKCON Philadelphia Newsletter*, October 15. Accessed July 2, 2017. http://iskconphiladelphia.com/wp-content/uploads/2015/10/Newsletter-101615.pdf. I discuss my first meeting with her at the ISKCON of Philadelphia temple later in this chapter.

16. Swami 2016, Interview.

17. William H. Deadwyler III (Ravindra Svarupa Dasa). 1985. "The Devotee and the Deity: Living a Personalistic Theology." In *Gods of Flesh, Gods of Stone*. Joanne Punzo Waghorne and Norman Cutler, eds. New York: Columbia University Press.

18. Peter Bennett. 1993. "Krishna's Own Form: Image Worship and Puṣṭi Mārga." *Journal of Vaishnava Studies* 1, no. 4: 109–134.

19. Ibid., 109.

20. Josh Ellenbogen and Aaron Tugendhaft, eds. 2011. *Idol Anxiety*. Stanford: Stanford University Press.

21. Joanne Punzo Waghorne. 1985. "Introduction." In Waghorne and Cutler 1985.

22. Devamrita Swami. 2012. "Devamrita Swami Seminar—Urban Preaching 2." 33:59–34:10. Accessed June 1, 2017. http://iskconleaders.com/seminar-on-urban-preaching-audio-lecture-by-devamrita-swami/#sthash.ZUVANtLP.dpuf.

23. Swami 2016, Interview.

24. Deadwyler 1985, 83.

25. There is debate within ISKCON about how much centrality the deities and their ritual worship had during the time of Prabhupada. Prominent American ISKCON guru, Krishna Brander, and founder of ISKCON sub-movement Krishna West, Hridayananda Das Goswami, argues that the deities did not have such a prominent place in the movement historically and that their present prominence is a result of the movement's large Indian Hindu demographic. Hridayananda Das Goswami. Interview by Nicole Karapanagiotis. Conducted via Skype, Wilmington, Delaware, June 15, 2015. E. Burke Rochford Jr. argues a similar point in *Hare Krishna Transformed* (2007), noting that many ISKCON temples in the United States would have failed if not for the financial

contributions of the Indian Hindu community. This financial need, he suggests, drives temple practices (such as focus on the deities), as devotees want to ensure that the wishes of their largest donors are satisfied. There are many devotees in the movement, however, who maintain that the deities have always had this central a place in ISKCON, even during Prabhupada's time.

26. Nurit Zaidman. 2000. "The Integration of Indian Immigrants to Temples Run by North Americans." *Social Compass* 47, no. 2: 205–219.

27. E. Burke Rochford Jr. 2007. *Hare Krishna Transformed*. New York: New York University Press, 192.

28. Ibid., 197.

29. Ibid., 192. Bracketed text in original.

30. Ibid., 192.

31. Ibid., 198.

32. This statement has become proverbially commonplace in the United States now but is typically traced to Dr. Martin Luther King's sermon "Remaining Awake Through a Great Revolution," which he most famously delivered at the National Cathedral in Washington, DC, on March 31, 1968. Kathleen Garces-Foley. 2007a. *Crossing the Ethnic Divide: The Multiethnic Church on a Mission*. New York: Oxford University Press, 79, 167.

33. Swami 2016, Interview. Emphases in original.

34. Devamrita Swami. 2015. "Nrshima Caturdasi & Reaching the Hearts Day 2." Kishorekishori YouTube channel, May 2. 1:01:55–1:02:03. Accessed July 21, 2017. https://www.youtube.com/watch?v=YZC6ewjG2bE.

35. Ibid., 1:02:27–1:06:48.

36. Ibid., 1:08:03–1:08:12.

37. Sita-pati Das. 2006. "Loft Preaching Article." *Dandavats*. Accessed July 21, 2017. http://www.dandavats.com/?p=1840. *Brahminical* means *priestly* but also refers to the ritual dimensions of Hinduism more generally.

38. Swami 2016, Interview.

39. Adjua Fisher. 2016. "These $10 Yoga-and-Dinner Classes Are One of Philly's Best Kept Secrets." *Philadelphia Magazine: Be Well Philly*, November 15. Accessed July 21, 2017. http://www.phillymag.com/be-well-philly/2016/11/15/mantra-lounge/.

40. Amy Strauss. 2016. "Listen to My Mantra: New Fishtown Studio Fueled by Mantra Meditation and Travelling Monks." *Spirit News*, August 25. Accessed July 21, 2017. https://spiritnews.org/articles/listen-to-my-mantra-new-fishtown-studio-fueled-by-mantra-meditation-and-travelling-monks/.

41. Fisher 2016.

42. Ibid.

43. Ibid.

44. Ibid.

45. Mara Einstein quoting David Ogilvy, founder of Ogilvy and Mather. Mara Einstein. 2008. *Brands of Faith: Marketing Religion in a Commercial Age*. New York: Routledge, 70.

46. Brian Sternthal and Angela Y. Lee argue that customers are inferential processors when exposed to advertisements. Brian Sternthal and Angela Y. Lee. 2005. "Building Brands Through Effective Advertising." In *Kellogg on Branding: The Marketing Faculty of the Kellogg School of Marketing*. Alice M. Tybout and Tim Calkins, eds. Hoboken: John Wiley & Sons, 133.

47. Einstein 2008, 70.

48. Mia Lövheim and Alf G. Linderman. 2005. "Constructing Religious Identity on the Internet." In *Religion and Cyberspace*. Morten T. Højsgaard and Margit Warburg, eds. 2005. London and New York: Routledge, 126.

49. Lorne L. Dawson and Douglas E. Cowan. 2004. "Introduction." In *Religion Online: Finding Faith on the Internet*. Lorne L. Dawson and Douglas E. Cowan, eds. New York: Routledge, 7.

ISKCON communities very much use the internet—their websites, social media pages, and so on—for the sake of proselytizing. See Nicole Karapanagiotis. 2018. "Of Digital Images and Digital Media: Approaches to Marketing in American ISKCON." *Nova Religio: The Journal of Alternative and Emergent Religion*. 21, no. 3: 74–102. Scholars, however, have long suggested that people join NRMs (New Religious Movements) through social networking, not through proselytizing efforts.

50. Einstein 2008; Bobby J. Calder. 2005. "Designing Brands." In Tybout and Calkins 2005.

51. Chiung Hwang Chen. 2011. "Marketing Religion Online: The LDS Church's SEO Efforts." *Journal of Media and Religion* 10: 185–205.

52. Mantra Lounge Philadelphia website. Accessed July 20, 2017. http://mantraphilly.com/.

53. Mantra Lounge Philadelphia website. "Retreat." Accessed July 22, 2017. http://mantraphilly.com/retreat/.

54. Ibid.

55. Mantra Lounge Philadelphia Facebook page. "Yoga Revolution Retreat—Being for Real in Bhakti." Retreat April 14–16, 2017. Accessed July 22, 2017. https://www.facebook.com/events/392039644490790/.

56. Mantra Lounge Philadelphia website. "Kirtan." Accessed July 22, 2017. http://mantraphilly.com/mantrameditation/.

57. Mantra Lounge Philadelphia website. Calendar Event page. "Kirtan Connection: Music Meditation & Dance." Accessed July 22, 2017. http://mantraphilly.com/events/mantra-meditation-mindfulness-5/. This event is advertised on the Mantra Lounge Facebook page on a repeating basis.

58. Mantra Lounge Philadelphia website. Calendar Event page.

"Tuesday—Kirtan Connection: Music Meditation & Dance." Accessed July 22, 2017. http://mantraphilly.com/events/mantra-meditation-mindfulness-5/.

59. Mantra Lounge Philadelphia website. Calendar Event page. "Monday—Power Yoga: Body Therapy." Accessed July 22, 2017. http://mantraphilly.com/events/mindful-mondays-breathe-stretch-mantra/.

60. Mantra Lounge Philadelphia website. "Yoga Classes." Accessed July 22, 2017. http://mantraphilly.com/yoga/.

61. Mantra Lounge, "Monday—Power Yoga."

62. Swami 2012, "Urban Preaching 2," 05:44–05:48.

63. Swami, Devamrita. 2012. "Devamrita Swami Seminar—Urban Preaching 1." 49:29–49:49. Accessed June 1, 2017. http://iskconleaders.com/seminar-on-urban-preaching-audio-lecture-by-devamrita-swami/#sthash.ZUVANtLP.dpuf.

64. Ibid., 51:04–51:12.

65. Ibid., 50:11–50:38. Emphases in original.

66. Swami 2012, "Urban Preaching 2," 05:56–06:24.

67. Swami 2012, "Urban Preaching 1," 49:10–49:27. Emphasis in original.

68. Mantra Lounge Philadelphia website. "Find Us on Campus." Accessed June 1, 2017. http://mantraphilly.com/find-us-on-campus/.

69. Mantra Lounge Philadelphia website. "Sustainability Circle." Accessed July 23, 2017. http://mantraphilly.com/sustainability/.

70. Mantra Lounge Philadelphia website. "Workshops." Accessed July 23, 2017. http://mantraphilly.com/workshops/. The Soulfeast goes by various names (Soulfeast, Wisdom Series, Yoga Philosophy Discussion, Workshop, etc.).

71. When ISKCON devotees refer to the *Bhagavad-Gītā* as a "yoga text," they are banking on the fact that most in their western audiences will associate the word *yoga* with the sets of postural practices that characterize the yoga practiced today in yoga studios and high-end gyms, rather than with *bhakti yoga* (path of devotion) or *karma yoga* (path of ethical action)—the two "yogas" that are at the center of the *Bhagavad-Gītā*. Through this labeling, in other words, devotees aim to generate more credence for their ideas by predisposing their audiences to think in a particular way about the *Bhagavad-Gītā's* purpose and spirit.

72. I omit diacritics here to follow the lounge's spelling of the event.

73. Mantra Lounge, "Workshops."

74. Swami 2016, Interview.

75. Swami 2016, Interview.

76. Swami 2012, "Urban Preaching 2," 56:42–56:46. Italics in original.

77. Ibid., 32:22–33:40. Italics in original.

78. Ibid., 48:38–48:46.

79. Swami 2012, "Urban Preaching 1," 51:13–51:18.

80. Swami 2012, "Urban Preaching 1," 51:31–51:40.

81. Swami 2016, Interview.

82. Joanne Punzo Waghorne. 2014b. "From Diaspora to (Global) Civil Society: Global Gurus and the Processes of De-ritualization and De-ethnization in Singapore." In *Hindu Ritual at the Margins: Innovations, Transformations, Reconsiderations*. Linda Penkower and Tracy Pintchman, eds. Columbia: University of South Carolina Press, 186–207.

83. Amanda J. Lucia. 2014a. "Innovative Gurus: Tradition and Change in Contemporary Hinduism." *International Journal of Hindu Studies* 18, no. 2: 221–263.

84. Ibid., 234. Lucia notes that, as per Jacob Copeman and Aya Ikegame, gurus who transmit their messages to global audiences can be called "headline-stealing hyper gurus." Jacob Copeman and Aya Ikegame. 2012. "The Multifarious Guru: An Introduction." In *The Guru in South Asia: New Interdisciplinary Perspectives*. Jacob Copeman and Aya Ikegame, eds. New York: Routledge, 1–45.

85. Lucia 2014a, 234. Here, Lucia mentions a number of other works, including: Srinivas Arvamudan. 2006. *Guru English: South Asian Religion in a Cosmopolitan Language*. Princeton: Princeton University Press; Amanda J. Huffer (Lucia). 2011. "Backdoor Hinduism: A Recoding in the Language of Spirituality." *Nidān: International Journal for the Study of Hinduism* 23: 53–71; Smriti Srinivas. 2008. *In the Presence of Sai Baba: Body, City, and Memory in a Global Religious Movement*. Leiden: Brill; Tulasi Srinivas. 2010. *Winged Faith: Rethinking Globalization and Religious Pluralism through the Sathya Sai Movement*. New York: Columbia University Press; Hugh B. Urban. 2003. "Avatar for Our Age: Sathya Sai Baba and the Cultural Contradictions of Late Capitalism." *Religion* 33, no. 1: 73–93; Hugh B. Urban. 2005. "Osho, from Sex Guru to Guru of the Rich: The Spiritual Logical of Late Capitalism." In *Gurus in America*. Thomas A. Forsthoefel and Cynthia Ann Humes, eds. Albany: State University of New York Press, 169–192; and Maya Warrier. 2005. *Hindu Selves in a Modern World: Guru Faith in the Mata Amritanandamayi Mission*. London: RoutledgeCurzon.

86. Waghorne 2014b, 205.

87. Jeff Wilson. 2014. *Mindful America: The Mutual Transformation of Buddhist Meditation and American Culture*. Oxford and New York: Oxford University Press, 73.

88. Einstein 2008, 121.

89. Das 2006.

90. Swami 2016, Interview.

91. Swami 2012, "Urban Preaching 2," 36:05–41:24.

92. Swami 2016, Interview. Emphasis in original. Devotee's name changed for anonymity.

93. Rūpagosvāmī. *Bhaktirasāmṛtasindhu*. *The Bhaktirasāmṛtasindhu of Rūpa Gosvāmin*. Translated with Introduction and Notes by David L. Haberman.

2003. New Delhi and Delhi: Indira Gandhi National Centre for the Arts and Motilal Banarsidass Publishers, 75. A. C. Bhaktivedanta Swami Prabhupada also translated and edited an abridged summary of the *Bhaktirasāmṛtasindhu* called *The Nectar of Devotion: The Complete Science of Bhakti Yoga*. This edition serves as the primary version of the text for ISKCON devotees. A. C. Bhaktivedanta Swami Prabhupada. 1970. *The Nectar of Devotion: The Complete Science of Bhakti Yoga*. New York: The Bhaktivedanta Book Trust.

94. For an anthology on the topic of *līlā*, see William S. Sax, ed. 1995. *The Gods at Play: Lila in South Asia*. Oxford and New York: Oxford University Press. For a detailed analysis of the Gauḍīya traditions' philosophical underpinnings—especially with regard to the Acintya Bhedābheda school of Vedānta, which posits that the world of plurality is simultaneously different from and identical to Brahman—see Sudhindra Chandra Chakravarti. 1969. *Philosophical Foundations of Bengal Vaisnavism (A Critical Exposition)*. Calcutta: Academic Publishers.

95. These quotes are from Prabhupada's *Bhagavad-Gītā* purports for the verses indicated. Prabhupada composed his purports in English; these quotes, therefore, are direct citations, not translations. A. C. Bhaktivedanta Swami Prabhupada. 1986. *Bhagavad-Gītā As It Is: Complete Edition Revised and Enlarged with Original Sanskrit Text, Roman Transliteration, English Equivalents, Translation, and Elaborate Purports*. Los Angeles: The Bhaktivedanta Book Trust.

96. A. C. Bhaktivedanta Swami Prabhupada. 1974. *Śrīmad-Bhāgavatam: With the Original Sanskrit Text, Its Roman Transliteration, Synonyms, Translation and Elaborate Purports by His Divine Grace A.C. Bhaktivedanta Swami Prabhupada Founder-Acarya of the International Society for Krishna Consciousness*. Fourth Canto, "The Creation of the Fourth Order" (part 4, chaps. 25–31). Los Angeles: Bhaktivedanta Book Trust, 4.29.55. Official ISKCON digital book. Accessed May 10, 2017. http://vanisource.org/wiki/Srimad-Bhagavatam. For a discussion of the usage of *yukta vairāgya* within the ISKCON lineage prior to Prabhupada, see Ferdinando Sardella. 2013. *Modern Hindu Personalism: The History, Life, and Thought of Bhaktisiddhānta Saravatiī*. Oxford and New York: Oxford University Press.

97. Devotees are careful to note that only materials and activities that are in the "mode of goodness" are permissible to be used in *yukta vairāgya*. Weapons, illicit materials, and the like are therefore excluded. Also excluded are materials and activities that violate one of ISKCON's regulative principles (such as strict vegetarianism, etc.).

98. Swami, Devamrita. 2012. "Devamrita Swami Seminar—Urban Preaching 5." 1:16:30–1:17:44. Accessed June 1, 2017. http://iskconleaders.com/seminar-on-urban-preaching-audio-lecture-by-devamrita-swami/#sthash.ZUVANtLP.dpuf.

99. Swami 2012, "Urban Preaching 1," 54:35–56:08.

100. Shlomo Sher. 2011. "A Framework for Assessing Immorally Manipulative Marketing Tactics." *Journal of Business Ethics* 102: 97–118. Ram N. Aditya has also written a thoughtful piece on deception in marketing, and Chiung Hwang Chen raises important questions at the intersection of marketing and ethics, as well. See Ram N. Aditya. 2001. "The Psychology of Deception in Marketing: A Conceptual Framework for Research and Practice." *Psychology & Marketing* 18, no. 7: 735–737; and Chen 2011.

101. Ibid., 97.

102. Ibid.

103. It does not seem, however, that he and his team ever make false claims.

104. Ibid., 113. He notes, however, that although a tactic is not *immorally manipulative*, it might be immoral for other reasons.

FOUR

BRANDING ISKCON AS THE HEART OF YOGA

I was at an Indian grocery store near my home in Wilmington, Delaware, stocking up on *namkeen* (spiced trail mixes) and other such savory snacks one day. After I had put my items in my bags and headed through the checkout line, I noticed on the wall by the door a flyer. The flyer was an advertisement for the Delaware Yoga Society. Curious, I took note of the website given on the flyer and came home and looked it up.

At first, what I saw on the website for the Delaware Yoga Society was pretty "standard fare" for a yoga studio. For example, on the list of tabs at the top of the page were links for "hatha yoga," as well as for "philosophical discussions." More than this, the haṭha yoga offered by the Delaware Yoga Society included "yoga sessions consisting of yogasanas (Pathanjali yoga) and Pranayama," as well as a "plan [] to introduce 15 core exercises which are bare basic [*sic*] of the Pathanjali yoga system or the Ashtanga [eight-limbed] yoga system."[1] Curiously, however, there were also on the website a number of tabs and links for activities that seemed notably *atypical* for a yoga studio—activities such as "japa meditation," "karma free cooking," and conversations about the *Bhagavad-Gītā*. More than this, the Delaware Yoga Society listed its inspiration as being none other than A. C. Bhaktivedanta Swami Prabhupada. The more I browsed the website, the more I began to suspect that the Delaware Yoga Society was an ISKCON project. So, as any curious ethnographer would do, I decided to attend a session at the address listed on the website to see what the Delaware Yoga Society was all about.

It was a Sunday afternoon when I first visited. Located off of a suburban road in a small town just outside the city of Wilmington, the Delaware Yoga Society was a converted private home. As I pulled into the unpaved driveway, parked my car, and entered the main area of the house, my suspicion that the Delaware Yoga Society was an ISKCON project was immediately confirmed; in fact, the Delaware Yoga Society was a full-fledged ISKCON temple. As in all ISKCON temples, in the front of the main space was an altar with three-dimensional *mūrtis* (embodied forms) of Krishna, along with pictures of the gurus in the ISKCON lineage. Along the sides of the room were the ISKCON-stylized poster prints that one typically finds in ISKCON temples—those that depict scenes from Krishna's *līlā* (divine play). In fact, the only dimension missing from the room was the large, life-sized form of Swami Prabhupada that one typically finds in ISKCON temples, and its absence likely had to do with the temple's relative newness.[2] Besides the appearance of the space itself, however, the ritual activities at the Delaware Yoga Society were also aligned with those of ISKCON's temples. The ritual I attended started with an ISKCON *kīrtan* (collective devotional singing) and an *āratī* ceremony (fire lamp offering), was followed by a lecture from Prabhupada's *Bhagavad-Gītā As It Is,* and was concluded with a second *kīrtan* and *prasādam* (sanctified food).

Over the course of my research, I came to encounter a number of centers similar to the Delaware Yoga Society—that is, centers that were either advertised or designed as yoga studios but that were, in fact, ISKCON-based centers or temples. For example, I encountered a number of ISKCON centers across the East Coast of the United States (in Florida, in New York, in Washington, DC), as well as in India (Maharashtra) that were yoga studios offering *prāṇāyāma, haṭha,* and *vinyāsa* yoga but that were built around, or connected with, a traditional ISKCON temple with ritual worship of Krishna at the center. I also encountered a number of yoga retreat centers—in The Bahamas, in India, and in the United States—that were designed for facilitating love of Krishna through ISKCON programming but that were promoted to patrons as vacations to develop their *āsana* yoga practice.

Although these centers and programs varied, all of them can be ideologically traced to a larger ISKCON rebranding enterprise developed by internationally noted ISKCON guru Radhanath Swami, our next Krishna Brander. As I will argue in this chapter, this ISKCON rebranding enterprise consists in the efforts of Radhanath Swami and his disciples to attract westerners to the movement by rebranding ISKCON as the theological heart of postural yoga. As I will show, this is a complex and widespread brand and is one that Radhanath Swami promotes and maintains through a fascinating interplay of the conceptual and the material: by developing intricate theologies of *bhakti* as interpreted through Patañjali's *Yoga Sūtras* (what I call the conceptual arm of the brand) and by building and administering a number of ISKCON temples that are housed inside yoga studios and yoga retreat centers (what I call the material arm of the brand). Through these two arms—the philosophical and interpretive moves that make up the conceptual arm of the brand and the structural and architectural ones that make up the material arm—Radhanath Swami has developed one of ISKCON's most successful westerner-focused branding projects.[3] This chapter will explore this brand in detail, first by examining the theological argument that Radhanath Swami develops in order to facilitate it and then by exploring two of the brand's most prominent centers: the Bhakti Center in New York City and the Govardhan Eco Village in Maharashtra, India. However, let us first turn to the story of Radhanath Swami himself, the Krishna Brander behind the brand.

THE STORY OF RADHANATH SWAMI

Radhanath Swami was born in 1950 and grew up in Highland Park, Illinois, a suburb located about twenty-five miles outside of Chicago. Raised in a middle-class Jewish family, Radhanath Swami was a successful and well-liked youth. In fact, he describes his early life in a memoir that he penned, *The Journey Home*, as one that had all the trappings of material success and comfort; his family's economic needs were met, he was a successful wrestler at his high school, and he had many friends.[4] Yet, despite "having it all," Radhanath Swami characterizes his early life as one that was nonetheless nagged by a persistent dissatisfaction and restlessness, especially regarding the injustices that were befalling various communities around him in nearby Chicago and across the United States. As Radhanath Swami recounts:

> As a freshman, I was promoted to the varsity wrestling team. . . . The coach and teammates had great hope that in the coming years I could be a champion. At first I loved the challenge. Scholarships were mine if I pursued them. But something strange was happening to me. I had begun to crave a purpose in life beyond wealth, prestige, and the fads of society. How could I be content in the idyllic land of Highland Park when I knew that African Americans were imprisoned like slaves in the ghettos just miles away? How could I be satisfied with a wrestling medal when my older friends were being forced into the horrors of the Vietnam War? Haunted by such questions, I, along with my friends, questioned the very fabric of the life we knew.[5]

Prompted by an anger at the social and political injustices of his day, Radhanath Swami felt a profound sense of emptiness throughout his youth and young adulthood, an existential yearning to find a deeper meaning and purpose to life than the goals, paths, and plans laid out before him by society. These feelings prompted him during his college days to leave life as he knew it behind him and to set out on an exploratory trip to Europe with his friends. Little did he know, however, that the trip would turn out to be more than just a brief visit across the pond. Rather, it was a trip that would take him on a hitchhiking journey not only across Europe but also across Turkey into Iran, through Afghanistan and Pakistan, and eventually into India. It was also the trip that would lead him to the "home" for which he had spent his whole life searching.

This "home" for Radhanath Swami (as referenced in the title of his memoir) was not a geographical place, however, or even an eventual arriving in India. Instead, it was a symbolic home: the religious home he found in meeting his guru, Swami Prabhupada. As Radhanath Swami himself describes it, meeting Swami Prabhupada after hitchhiking all over the world in search of a meaningful life path was the one event that gave his life the personal fulfillment and purpose that he feels it has today. "I felt that all of the events of my life thus far had been conspiring to bring me to this point," he writes in his memoir.[6] "For this treasure, my whole journey had been taken.[7] . . . My quest, which had begun half a planet away in Highland Park, Illinois, had finally delivered me to the feet of my guru. In that moment, I realized that there could be no greater goal in my life than helping Srila Prabhupada to spread God's love to the world. How I longed to be even the smallest instrument in that compassionate mission."[8]

As discussed in previous chapters, the main objective of Prabhupada's mission was to bring the chance for unremitting love of Krishna—what he called Krishna Consciousness—to people all over the world, from all ethnic, racial, and national backgrounds. As Radhanath Swami himself told me, "This was the mission of Srila Prabhupada—this compassion for *everyone* in the world. And it was the mission of Lord Chaitanya."[9] Yet, as Radhanath Swami sees it—just like his Krishna Brander peers—this mission is not being reflected in the current demographics of the ISKCON movement. "There are *so many people*," he told me one day from a small cavernous room of ISKCON Chowpatty, "who are suffering in this world and who could benefit from the message of love and compassion that Prabhupada brought, yet who don't have access to that message."[10] The people he is referring to who do not have access to Prabhupada's message are, in particular, westerners, and he is referencing his view that the ISKCON movement is currently not doing well in the west. "It is not that ISKCON is dying in the west," he said, "but there is a difference between surviving and flourishing, and we want to see ISKCON flourish."[11]

Because ISKCON is not flourishing in the west in the way that he thinks Prabhupada wanted, Radhanath Swami sees it as his responsibility to "bring

[Prabhupada's] message to people out of compassion to them" and "to help them in the way that Prabhupada would. Just like Lord Chaitanya did."[12] In order to accomplish this, Radhanath Swami says that Krishna Consciousness must be presented to westerners in a way that they "can relate to" and "find relevant" and "accessible."[13] Put simply, Radhanath Swami believes that if ISKCON is to be attractive to westerners—the population of people currently missing from Swami Prabhupada's vision of an all-inclusive global movement—then it must be rebranded: "If we care, if we really care about others and have mercy on them and their suffering, [then] we try to give them that. If we really care, then we try to give them the essence of what we have—love of God. And we need to present it to them in an accessible way. If we really care, then we need to give them something they can connect and relate to."[14]

This rebranding of ISKCON to make it something that westerners can connect with and relate to is often called *western outreach* in ISKCON, and it is a set of efforts for which Radhanath Swami is particularly well-known throughout the movement. It is also a set of efforts about which Radhanath Swami's disciples speak frequently. As one of his head disciples told me in India:

> Radhanath Swami has been into this whole ISKCON preaching movement for well over a decade—since '82 he took *saṃnyāsa*. But, now, most of the world knows him for his western outreach. He is coming to limelight only like in say the past ten years or so, because mainly, ya know . . . when he came to India, he started this whole ISKCON Chowpatty ashram. . . . But then, within his heart he saw that Srila Prabhupada he [*sic*] had a very strong desire of western outreach . . . [but that despite this desire] all the temples which Prabhupada himself established in the west, due to whatever reasons, were sadly closing down. And that really pained him [Radhanath Swami] a lot. And he really wanted to see that people appreciate this movement of *bhakti*, appreciate Prabhupada's contribution. . . . So, all the western outreach that he is now taking up . . . [is] because he clearly told us that "I don't know how many years I have more, but I want to do something for my spiritual master."[15]

As this disciple notes, despite the facts that the ISKCON Chowpatty project "is one of the role model projects in [the] entire ISKCON" and that Radhanath Swami spent years heading up the Chowpatty community and turning it into one's of ISKCON's greatest success stories, Radhanath Swami felt that more needed to be done for his guru, Swami Prabhupada. More specifically, he felt that in the time that he had left on this earth he needed to do more to try and fulfill Prabhupada's mission for ISKCON's universal and global

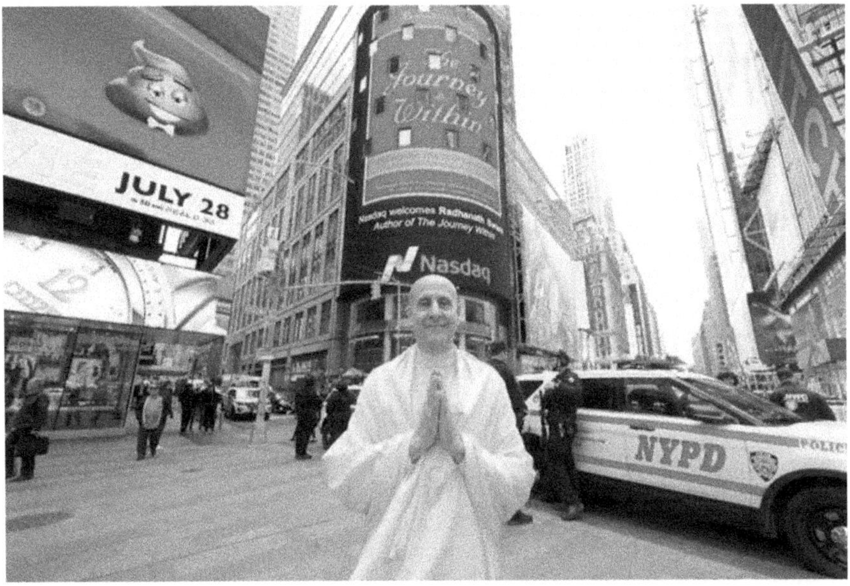

Figure 4.1 Radhanath Swami (pictured above) has come a long way since his youthful days of hitchhiking around the world to find his religious path. Having taken *saṃnyāsa* in 1982, he is now a successful global ISKCON guru. Above, he is seen standing in front of the Nasdaq Tower in New York City's Times Square on May 8, 2017, where the sequel to his memoir, *The Journey Home*—entitled *The Journey Within*—was featured on the iconic tower. Photo courtesy of RadhanathSwami.com.[17]

success. As such, Radhanath Swami set out to rebrand the ISKCON movement in order to attract more westerners and to make ISKCON once again more diverse and globally representative. However, unlike Devamrita Swami (the Krishna Brander from the previous chapter), who is rebranding ISKCON as a meditation-based social club in order to attract westerners to ISKCON, Radhanath Swami has given his brand a completely different spin: a yoga spin. Let us now turn to his brand, beginning with its conceptual arm, the part of his yoga brand developed by means of intricate philosophical interpretations of Krishna *bhakti* as interpreted through Patañjali's *Yoga Sūtras*.[16]

THE CONCEPTUAL BRAND

Yoga has a long history in the United States, and Radhanath Swami is not the first guru to develop, pitch, or promote a yoga brand to westerners. In fact, many gurus have done so before him, beginning with the first guru to step on the American yoga stage (and in some sense create that very stage himself): Vivekananda.[18] Other gurus to have done so were T. Krishnamacharya, Sri K. Pattabhi Jois, B. K. S. Iyengar, Muktananda, and more recently, Sri Sri Ravi Shankar.[19] As Andrea R. Jain has argued, in coming to the United States, these gurus faced the task of designing a yoga system that would "concede to consumer cultural trends"[20] so that it could be successful on the American spiritual marketplace.[21] In other words, when gurus brought their yoga systems to the United States, they did not merely transplant an intact product from India to the United States but rather designed and shaped an amorphous rhetorical "product" into a package that consumers would like (and would like as yoga).[22]

Take, for example, Swami Muktananda, the Indian guru who brought Siddha Yoga to the United States beginning in 1970. Muktananda was successful because he managed to associate his Siddha Yoga movement with "spiritual wares that were attractive to large target audiences of late twentieth-century spiritual seekers."[23] Some of the ways he accomplished this were by building European/American style retreat centers that would appeal to practitioners,[24] making his primary ritual of *śaktipāt* (awakening of "spiritual energy") easily available to the masses,[25] and "carefully selecting from tantra and *vedānta* as well as contemporary dominant ethical standards" the teachings he thought would be best "for marketability."[26] Similarly, Sri Sri Ravi Shankar—founder and guru of the worldwide Art of Living (AOL) movement—has earned similar success around the world by developing a religious product that "reinvents *yoga* for [a] rising middle class" by "incorporat[ing] scientific language, academic registers, and business and media savvy into the development of a new kind of religious association and a new kind of religiosity."[27]

Like Swami Muktananda, Sri Sri Ravi Shankar, and others, Radhanath Swami, too, is "selling"—that is crafting or creating—a yoga brand for western yoga audiences, explicitly designing his product to suit the needs and tastes of the community that he seeks to attract. To use the language of "selling" might incline the reader to think of profiteering, especially given the widespread commodification of postural yoga and the many for-profit yoga schools that have proliferated in recent years. However, it is important to note that Radhanath Swami is not developing a yoga brand for money. Rather, his rebranding of ISKCON as the theological heart of postural yoga is intended to pave a road for westerners to be easily and conveniently drawn to love of Krishna (and to ISKCON) through the path of postural yoga. Toward this end, he speaks at a number of yoga events around the world and lectures frequently at high-end yoga studios in the United States (the Jivamukti Yoga School in Manhattan, for example). He has even been noticed by several public news outlets for these efforts, including *New York Magazine*, which identified him in a feature piece as the "Hare Krishna Leader Who's Bringing the Movement into the Age of Lululemon."[28]

Although Radhanath Swami shares similarities with figures like Muktananda, Sri Sri Ravi Shankar, and others, there is an important way in which the branding enterprise of Radhanath Swami differs from those of many of his yoga branding predecessors and contemporaries. This main difference has to do with the product with which he starts. Put simply, since ISKCON is a devotional tradition, complete not only with a Gauḍīya Vaishnava theology but also with a Gauḍīya Vaishnava set of rituals and practices, the task at hand for Radhanath Swami's branding efforts is to establish a connection between ISKCON's interpretation of Gauḍīya theology on the one hand, and the practices and viewpoints that make up what might be called the postural yoga "movement," on the other.[29] Therefore, unlike many other gurus who try to craft and sell a yoga brand to westerners, Radhanath Swami faces a task that is far more difficult: he must first brand ISKCON as yoga and then pitch *this* yoga product to westerners. This is, indeed, a tricky task. So how does he accomplish it?

Building the Conceptual Brand

In order to rebrand ISKCON as the heart of postural yoga, Radhanath Swami has systematized a complex theology that places Krishna as the philosophical heart of one of yoga's most central texts: Patañjali's *Yoga Sūtras*. More than this, he advances the theological idea that devotion (or surrender) to Krishna is the highest goal of the *Yoga Sūtras*. This interpretation of the *Yoga Sūtras* is one that Radhanath Swami develops and promotes in a sophisticated manner over the course of his books, yoga events, and seminars. He also develops and promotes it at the numerous lectures that he delivers at yoga locations and events around the world—such as at various yoga studios, retreats, and festivals.

Generally speaking, scholars of the *Yoga Sūtras* have understood the text as embedded within a Sāṃkhya interpretive context.[30] Read in a Sāṃkhya light, Patañjali's yoga is a system of practices meant to reduce the fluctuations of the mind stuff (*yogaś citta vṛitti nirodhaḥ* being the famous *Yoga Sūtras* adage).[31] In Patañjali's yoga, this reduction or cessation in the fluctuations of the mind stuff or, more colloquially, the reduction of our "mental chatter," is aimed toward the larger goal of achieving a state of objectless and contentless awareness—or the standing of pure consciousness alone. This goal is known in yoga as *samādhi*. As Christopher Key Chapple puts it, "Patañjali defines *samādhi* as the collapse of distinctions between grasper, grasping, and grasped, wherein the person or witness becomes like a clear jewel (YS I:41). All separation between subject and object disappears."[32] More specifically, this objectless state of *samādhi* is known as *asamprajñāta samādhi* or *nirvīja samādhi,* and it is by most interpretations the highest goal of the *Yoga Sūtras.*[33]

On most accounts, interpreters of the *Yoga Sūtras* note that in order to achieve this goal of *samādhi,* the yogi must engage in one-pointed meditation. For example, Edwin Bryant notes that "in order to attain the complete cessation of thought," the *Yoga Sūtras* explain that "the yogi has to first focus the mind on an object without deviation, with increasingly penetrative intensity, and Patañjali lists various options in this regard."[34] One of these options, Bryant explains, is a focused concentration on, or submission to, *īśvara.* "In verse 23, Patañjali states: *īśvara praṇidhānad va* 'or [the previously mentioned state of *nirbija samadhi* is attainable] by submission to the Lord.'"[35] What this means, is that in their endeavor to reach the state of objectless awareness, the yogi can focus on (or submit to) *īśvara* as a meditative means for doing so.

While there is much room for interpretation, *īśvara* is typically understood by scholars of yoga as an idealized being, one "who never becomes muddied by karma."[36] This means that rather than being a god per se—a being who is recognized as an ontological ground for existence or prayed to for favors, for example—*īśvara* of the *Yoga Sūtras* is instead usually understood as more of an ideal figure or a concept upon which to meditate in striving to achieve *samādhi.* As Christopher Key Chapple notes, "Īśvara as portrayed in the *Yoga Sūtra* functions in a manner similar to how a Tirthaṇkara functions in the Jain tradition: as an exemplar and model, but not a reciprocator."[37] By a single-focused meditation on *īśvara* as an exemplar or model, one can achieve the *Yoga Sūtras'* goal of objectless *samādhi.*

Although most accounts of the *Yoga Sūtras* follow this interpretation, Radhanath Swami's conceptual brand of ISKCON rests on a different understanding of the text. In particular, Radhanath Swami holds that rather than meditation on or submission to *īśvara* being a tool by which to achieve *samādhi,* submission to *īśvara is itself samādhi.* More than this, Radhanath Swami teaches that rather than (just) being an idealized exemplar on which to concentrate, *īśvara* from Patañjali's *Yoga Sūtras* is none other than Krishna himself, whom he sees as the source and lord of the universe: the same God from the *Bhagavad-Gītā,* the *Bhāgavata Purāṇa,* and other Vaishnava texts. As he said in a lecture he delivered on October 15, 2012:

> The explanation is given in the yoga scriptures that the different types of yoga are like steps on one ladder—it's one path, but different steps. And *aṣṭāṅga* [eight-limbed] yoga, Patañjali—who's the founder of it—he writes

> *samādhi siddhir īśvara praṇidhānāt*—that the perfection of *samādhi*—and *samādhi* is the perfection of *aṣṭāṅga* yoga—the perfection of *samādhi* is surrendering our heart with love to *īśvara* or to the supreme God. Īśvara is a name of—*īśvara parama Krishna*—*īśvara* is a name of Krishna, it's a name of the One God of all religions, actually. So *bhakti* is a culmination [of yoga].[38]

In this lecture, which he delivered at the Cambridge Union Society, Radhanath Swami equates *samādhi*—which he calls the perfection of yoga—with devotion to *īśvara*. And *īśvara*, he says—using *Brahma Saṃhitā* 5.1—is Krishna.[39]

This placing of Krishna (and devotion to him) at the heart of Patañjali's *Yoga Sūtras* is a careful move and is one that Radhanath Swami makes not only in his public lectures but also across a number of different fora. For example, he promotes this idea in his book *The Journey Within*, which is the highly publicized sequel to his *Journey Home*. When discussing yoga therein, Radhanath Swami notes that "yoga is the science of cleansing the heart and experiencing the joy of living in spiritual harmony with God, nature, and others."[40] Then, after discussing the various *yamas* and *niyamas* (rules) of Patañjali's yoga, he turns to what he sees to be yoga's final culmination. "Finally," he writes, "there is *ishvara pranidhana*, or 'surrender to the Supreme.' This means to dedicate one's actions, words, and thoughts and ultimately, one's *prana* or essence, to the will of the Divine. . . . As the sage Patanjali states, '*Samadhi siddhi isvara pranidhanat* (the perfection of samadhi is to surrender to the Supreme).' . . . By sincerely and honestly offering one's heart to the Supreme Beloved, the ultimate goal of all religions, all yoga processes, and all life—is received."[41]

Last but not least, Radhanath Swami preaches this conceptual brand in the more intimate lectures that he delivers at yoga studios and yoga retreat centers in both the United States and India (as well as in The Bahamas and elsewhere). For example, at a three-day yoga immersion retreat in Lanexa, Virginia, he remarked to the crowd:

> *Samādhi siddhir īśvara praṇidhānāt*. Patañjali has explained in the *Yoga Sūtras* that the perfection of *samādhi* is this *śaraṇāgati*, this surrender, this taking shelter of *īśvara*, of the root of all existence, of the source of all who exists, the ultimate mother and father of all of us. And what is that *samādhi*, that absorption? It means our consciousness is naturally flowing in its natural direction . . . where we learn, we learn the art of allowing the river of our natural desire for pleasure, for happiness, for love, to flow toward its source, toward its true destination: *karuṇā sindhu*, the sea of God's love. . . . The nature of the soul is to love Krishna, to love the supreme, to be an instrument of that love. But the ego, the *ahaṁkāra*, the false ego . . . blocks the flow of

> grace [and] love . . . [Thankfully, however] yoga is to reunite with the true nature of our true self. . . . If we can somehow direct that current of that flow of the river towards the higher power of God's grace, *Samādhi siddhir īśvara praṇidhānāt* . . . it becomes our perfection of yoga.[42]

Through a set of subtle interpretive moves such as these—which he roots in variants of the phrase *samādhi siddhir īśvara praṇidhānāt*—Radhanath Swami promotes a conceptual brand wherein the heart of Patañjali's yoga looks a lot like ISKCON's variety of Gauḍīya Vaishnavism. More specifically, through his lectures and discourses and through his reading of the *Yoga Sūtras* with a lens of Vaishnava texts and ideas, Radhanath Swami transforms the concept of *īśvara* into Vaishnavism's celebrated Lord Krishna. Moreover, he transforms the *Yoga Sūtras'* goal of objectless *samādhi* into a full-fledged state of *bhakti*—one wherein the soul enters into a loving and surrendered relationship with Krishna. These interpretive moves are not only conceptually sophisticated but they are also crucial for Radhanath Swami's branding of ISKCON as yoga. If ISKCON and yoga seemed far apart on first glance, they seem much less so following this conceptual branding; in fact, through these interpretive moves, Radhanath Swami has made devotion to Krishna the very heart of yoga. These interpretive moves, therefore, set the stage for his further preaching and developing of the brand across a variety of venues and audiences. More than anything else, however, they set the stage for the building and promotion of the physical centers that operationalize Radhanath Swami's rebranding of ISKCON as the heart of yoga: ISKCON temples that are housed inside—or at the heart of—yoga studios and yoga retreat spaces. It is to a discussion of these centers that we now turn.

OPERATIONALIZING THE BRAND: YOGA TRAINING CENTERS AND YOGA STUDIOS

There are many ways in which Radhanath Swami promotes his rebranding of ISKCON as the heart of postural yoga. Chief among them, as discussed in the previous section, is through the promotion of the brand conceptually, which he accomplishes not only in his writings and books but also in the lectures he delivers at places ranging from high-end yoga studios in Manhattan to rustic yoga retreats in Virginia, The Bahamas, and India. However, equal in importance to Radhanath Swami's conceptual branding of devotion to Krishna as the heart of yoga is the second, material arm of his rebranding enterprise. This arm is the construction and maintenance of ISKCON centers that physically operationalize his brand: ISKCON-run yoga studios and retreat centers—complete with a variety of postural yoga classes, seminars, and retreat opportunities—that have at their center full-service ISKCON temples. Let's turn to two such centers that Radhanath Swami and his disciples administer: the Bhakti Center in New York City and the Govardhan Eco Village in rural Maharashtra, India.

The Bhakti Center

The Bhakti Center is a popular yoga studio located in Manhattan's East Village.[43] Although the street it's on is crowded and somewhat gritty, the Bhakti Center manages to transcend it, looking clean and sparse—almost ethereal—from the outside, with an all-glass exterior facade and a brightly illuminated marquee advertising upcoming yoga events, classes, and seminars, as well as a selection of vegan food and fresh juice. Through the windowed exterior, passersby can see a set of tables topped with flyers and advertisements for a number of the center's yoga events—classes, inversion seminars, teacher trainings, and other such programs—as well as copies of Radhanath Swami's books, including most prominently *The Journey Home*.

Physically speaking, the Bhakti Center is a six-story building located directly on Second Avenue. The first floor of the building is a brightly lit, immaculately designed space that has a vegan restaurant and juice bar, dining tables, chairs, a sectioned-off space with couches for drinking tea and juice, and a rather large India-inspired gift shop, complete with a variety of brightly colored cloths, tapestries, books, jewelry, and a number of other trinkets for sale.

Above the first floor, which is on the street level, the second floor of the Bhakti Center is a fully equipped and full-functioning yoga studio. Like most yoga studios in the United States, the yoga studio at the Bhakti Center is a simple, mostly unadorned space. Inside it are a number of tools designed to facilitate yogis' best possible postural practice—yoga mats, blocks, stretching straps, and so on. Besides the equipment, the otherwise simple space of the Bhakti Center's yoga studio is adorned with a single picture of Swami Prabhupada, whose smiling face looks out over the daily classes. There are also a few other decorations in the studio—a few small plants, candles, an incense holder, and a figure of Ganesh—all of which sit on the sills of the windows that line the front of the room, which overlooks the busy avenue.

Last but not least, the Bhakti Center's third floor is a relatively large, full-functioning ISKCON temple. Like all ISKCON temples, this temple has deities of Krishna—in particular, Sri Sri Radha Muralidhara—as well as a life-sized form of Swami Prabhupada. The temple also hosts a number of daily programs—*āratīs*, ISKCON scriptural classes, *kīrtans*, daily *darshans*, and so on—that characterize the typical programming at all ISKCON temples. The

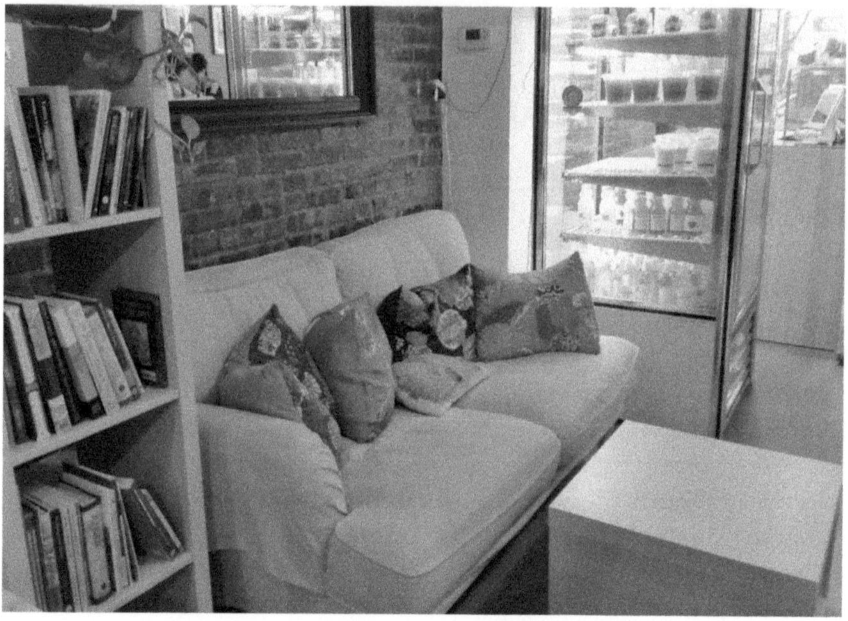

Figure 4.2 Bhakti Center restaurant and juice bar seating nook. August 2, 2015. Photo taken by author. New York, New York.

Figure 4.3 Greeting cards, scarves from India, and high-end yoga mats for sale at the Bhakti Center. August 2, 2015. Photo taken by author. New York, New York.

Figure 4.4 Gift shop on the first floor of the Bhakti Center. August 2, 2015. Photo taken by author. New York, New York.

Figure 4.5 Yoga Studio at the Bhakti Center. At the front of the room is a harmonium. August 3, 2015. Photo taken by author. New York, New York.

Figure 4.6 Yoga Studio at the Bhakti Center. A picture of Swami Prabhupada smiles over the room. August 3, 2015. Photo taken by author. New York, New York.

Figure 4.7 Entrance to the yoga studio. To the left is a rack for hanging clothes and storing shoes. At the front is a host and cashier stand. Studio door is at the front left. The yoga studio and entryway comprise the entire second floor of the Bhakti Center. August 3, 2015. Photo taken by author. New York, New York.

Figure 4.8 ISKCON temple on the third floor of the Bhakti Center. The entire third floor of the Bhakti Center is the temple and temple lobby space. August 4, 2015. Photo taken by author. New York, New York.

Bhakti Center has also recently begun a fundraising campaign for the installation of a new *mūrti* in the temple—Sri Gaurachandra (a form of Chaitanya)—although this *mūrti* has not yet been installed.

Finally, it bears mentioning that while the first-floor restaurant and gift shop and the second-story yoga studio can be accessed directly from the street, the temple can only be accessed from within the interior of the Bhakti Center; to access it, in other words, patrons not only need to know that it is there but also must enter it from inside the Bhakti Center.

Programs

The Bhakti Center serves the local East Village neighborhood with a number of different programs. These include "spiritual karate," Āyurvedic cooking classes, nutrition training, and a high-end restaurant that also does takeout and catering. However, the Bhakti Center primarily functions as a yoga studio, and it is the yoga classes around which the day's schedule there revolves.

Yoga classes at the Bhakti Center begin as early as 6:15 a.m. and end as late as 9:15 p.m. On any given day, one can find between four and six yoga classes on the Bhakti Center's programming. For example, there is Kundalini Yoga, advertised on the website as "a powerful practice which brings deep focus and clarity to the mind, uplifts the spirit, balances and aligns the chakras, detoxifies the organs, and flushes out the glandular system."[44] There is also Stretch and Restore class designed to "help you slow down with deep stretching and restorative poses."[45] Additionally, there are a number of *vinyāsa* and alignment-focused yoga classes offered each day, including Level 1 yoga, Level 2/3 yoga, All Levels yoga, and Community yoga, which is a donation-based class intended to be more widely available to newcomers and to the general public. Finally, there is even a Y12SR yoga class, which the Bhakti Center promotes as "a relapse prevention program that combines the timeless wisdom of yoga, the practical tools of 12-step programs, and the latest research on trauma healing."[46] More than this, the Y12SR yoga class is touted as "part of a holistic recovery program" that "works in tandem with traditional treatment to address the physical, mental and spiritual disease of addiction."[47]

Yoga classes at the Bhakti Center are very popular. For example, if one Googles "yoga East Village," the Bhakti Center comes up as the third hit from the top and boasts a review score of 4.9 out of 5. The Bhakti Center is also listed on Yelp's list of "The Best 10 Yoga [*sic*] near East Village, Manhattan, NY," coming in at number four on the list with fifty-five near-perfect reviews.[48] Moreover, the Bhakti Center is listed in the top thirty of "Classes and Workshops in New York City" on Trip Advisor in Manhattan and has near-five-star ratings not only on Yelp and Trip Advisor but also on Google and Facebook.[49]

Besides the yoga classes, the Bhakti Center also offers a number of other yoga-related courses and events. These include a number of seminars designed to help yogis cultivate their postures in a more focused way and delve deeper into their yoga practice. For example, there is the monthly Yoga 101, "a workshop designed as an introduction to the practice of yoga [that] is open for beginners as well as those who are seeking a better understanding on the fundamentals of alignment."[50] There is also a bimonthly workshop called Inversions 101, a seminar where more advanced yogis can learn yoga postures that invert the body upside down (the headstand, the forearm stand, and the handstand).[51] This inversions seminar is specifically designed for those who have an interest in standing on their heads more regularly during their practice but are scared to do so. "For many," the website notes, "going upside down in a yoga pose triggers feelings of doubt and fear in the mind."[52] The inversions seminar aims to help the yogis overcome this fear "by starting with the basics and working our way up to actually practicing the inversions" so that yogis "will learn to enter and exit poses safely and fearlessly!"[53] Finally, the Bhakti Center offers a seminar that is an introduction into a more relaxed form of yoga called Stretch and Restore, "a gentle, supported and healing form of yoga designed to release deep layers of tension stored in the physical and energetic body" and "allow the nervous system to relax and cells to regenerate."[54]

While all of the yoga classes, programs, and seminars offered at the Bhakti Center are typical postural yoga classes—that is, what one might find at a number of yoga studios across the United States—nearly all of the instructors at the Bhakti Center teach yoga in an effort to further Radhanath Swami's brand. In fact, most of the yoga teachers at the Bhakti Center are students and disciples of Radhanath Swami who promote his yoga brand as part of their devotional service within the ISKCON movement. As such, although their aim when they teach at the Bhakti Center is to instruct patrons in the forms and styles of postural yoga, their ultimate goal is to teach the yogis that there is more to yoga than just postures. Instead, they aim to teach them that the heart of yoga is devotion to Krishna. Toward this end—and in addition to the standard yoga postures—nearly every yoga class and program at the Bhakti Center also offers to attendees some dimension of ISKCON philosophy and practice. For example, most of the yoga classes that I attended at the Bhakti Center included the chanting of the *mahā mantra* in some form or another. Some teachers took the time to have students chant the mantra at the end of each class for several minutes, as a collective exercise; others walked around and sung the *mahā mantra* as they were calling out the yoga poses or helping to align the students' postures. Still other teachers played the *mahā mantra* on an audio recording during the class. More than this, most of the classes I attended also included a reading from, or discussion based on, the *Bhagavad-Gītā*. These discussions and readings varied but included topics such as one-pointed attention, "chastity" of intention, and the meaning of meditation. More than anything else, most of the yoga classes at the Bhakti Center encouraged attendees to practice yoga in a way that is true to its "deeper purpose"—that is, not just for exercise or stress relief but rather for cultivating love for Krishna.

Although attendees at the Bhakti Center's yoga classes are encouraged to pursue the "deeper purpose" of yoga, it is not the case that the yoga teachers there preach about Krishna Consciousness directly to class attendees. Instead, the encouragement to delve into the heart of yoga (by cultivating love of Krishna) comes through a number of subtler invitations. There are invitations, for example, to read and discuss the "yoga scriptures" with the teachers at the Bhakti Center (with the "yoga scriptures" being Prabhupada's *Bhagavad-Gītā As it Is*).[55] Attendees are also frequently invited to attend a number of programs hosted at the ISKCON temple, which is directly upstairs from the yoga studio.

For example, yoga patrons are invited to attend *kīrtan* nights at the temple, where they can feel the "deeper mood" of yoga. They are also invited to attend an event dubbed the Spiritual Recharge, which is the Bhakti Center's version of the ISKCON Sunday Feast. Last but not least, yogis are encouraged to attend Radhanath Swami's lectures when he comes to speak at the Bhakti Center (which he does quite frequently). All of these events are typically held in the temple room, and they therefore give patrons the opportunity to see a material conceptualization of Radhanath Swami's branding of ISKCON as the heart of yoga: namely, a traditional ISKCON worship space—complete with the devotional worship of Krishna in the form of Sri Sri Radha Muralidhara—right at the heart of the yoga studio they've been attending regularly as patrons.

History of the Bhakti Center

Before proceeding to a discussion of the Govardhan Eco Village and the ways in which it, too, materially operationalizes Radhanath Swami's rebranding of ISKCON as the heart of yoga, the curious reader might be interested in learning more about the Bhakti Center's somewhat complicated history, both in terms of the broader New York City ISKCON landscape in which it finds itself a part and in terms of its own real estate story. A careful observer will note that the Bhakti Center is situated immediately around the corner from another ISKCON center located at 26 Second Avenue. This Second Avenue location is the site of the very first ISKCON center—the place from which Prabhupada started and grew his worldwide movement and taught his earliest disciples the ropes of ISKCON devotional life. Although the Bhakti Center and the Second Avenue location now enjoy a separate set of programming, their histories (and even their finances) are inextricably connected.

Prior to coming into Radhanath Swami's hands, the Bhakti Center was called the Sanctuary and was a religious center built and financed by the disciples of ISKCON's most infamous outlaw guru, Swami Bhaktipada (also known as Kirtanananda). From 1979 through 1990, Swami Bhaktipada had been the guru in charge of ISKCON's New Vrindaban community in rural West Virginia, which at that time was a large and thriving residential community housing a number of ISKCON projects, including a number of theme park–like attractions and an opulent temple complex called Prabhupada's Palace of Gold. Although this community was initially thriving (and also immensely lucrative), it was eventually rocked by a number of scandals, including numerous acts of child molestation and even two murders. These crimes eventually led to the ousting of Bhaktipada from the community (and from ISKCON). They also led to his ultimate conviction on mail fraud and racketeering, crimes for which he eventually served eight years in prison.[56]

Despite the fact that he had committed morally and criminally atrocious acts, however, many of Bhaktipada's followers remained loyal to him, even after his imprisonment. These followers—who had by then formed an ISKCON splinter group known as the Interfaith League of Devotees—were the ones who built up and financed the Sanctuary. And upon Bhaktipada's release from prison, they had the Sanctuary prepared for him so that it could be a comfortable devotional place for his return. And when he was released from prison, he did, in fact, return there.

Over time, Radhanath Swami and his disciples came to inherit the Bhakti Center from Bhaktipada and the Interfaith League of Devotees. The gist of the story is that at around the same time that Bhaktipada and his Interfaith League of Devotees were residing in the Sanctuary (upon Bhaktipada's release from prison), another group of devotees had been living a monastic life around the block, at an ashram affiliated with the 26 Second Avenue ISKCON center. Because their rent was too high and because they had outgrown the worship space of both 26 Second Avenue and their affiliated ashram, Bhaktipada invited them to come and live with him and his disciples in the Sanctuary, offering to let them live there at a reduced rent. Somewhat surprisingly, the devotees took him up on his offer, and before long, all of the devotees and programs from the 26 Second Avenue location and its ashram shifted to the Sanctuary. Over time, however, the devotees did not just continue to shift to the Sanctuary, they ultimately also took over its management, eventually asking Bhaktipada and his disciples to leave. As a long-time devotee at the Bhakti Center explained to me:

> Bhaktipada . . . yeah, his disciples got that place [the Sanctuary], financed it, they started a very successful restaurant there for several years, and—it was a B and B actually—for some time. . . . When he was released from prison around 2006, I think it was, he came back to the Sanctuary. And it was *he* who invited [the devotees] into the Sanctuary. "You guys should come in and take part in this." So they—and this is a nutshell version—but they did move in and they started the whole thing, the morning program, they had a temple room, with the deities there that you saw—Radha Muralidhara. The temple room was on the second floor, though, where the yoga studio is now. And bit by bit they were encouraged to get on the board of directors. And while this was happening, it was also becoming apparent that Bhaktipada and his followers were not really following the principles very strictly, and so—just by momentum it seems—the ISKCON devotees took on a bigger role in that place, and the others took on less of a role until it just sort of switched hands. And then Bhaktipada had to be asked to leave.[57]

This is, of course, a contested history. The party on the other side of this story—the disciples of Bhaktipada who were asked to leave—claim that they were unjustifiably evicted and that the disciples at the ashram—with Radhanath Swami directing them—stole the Sanctuary from them, essentially taking the building that they worked so hard to build and pay for out from under their noses.[58] Needless to say, whichever account of the story one accepts, the disciples of Bhaktipada no longer have possession of the Sanctuary (now called the Bhakti Center). Instead, it is run under the direction of Radhanath Swami and administered by a board of ISKCON devotees who are largely under his discipleship. In the meantime, the original 26 Second Avenue location is still recovering from the exodus of devotees and programs. "Once everything moved over to the Bhakti Center [then still called the Sanctuary]," one devotee told me, "we were just holding onto 26 Second Avenue *strictly* for historical purposes. *Literally* nothing was going on there for years. And it was just being maintained by some donors, and nothing was going on. So then one program started up, must have been 2011 or so . . . and for several years his [one devotee's] program was the only thing happening there."[59]

As it stands right now, the small community of devotees at the 26 Second Avenue location is trying to expand their programming, but they struggle to find relevance in the shadow of the Bhakti Center as well as the funds to stay open (although they do receive both institutional support and donations from the Bhakti Center). Recently, there has been a move to turn the Second Avenue Center into a museum glorifying Prabhupada and his early days of the movement in New York City—a museum that would serve as a place where visitors and pilgrims alike can see where Prabhupada himself worshipped and spent his time.[60] In this regard, the Second Avenue location stands in stark contrast to the Bhakti Center. Whereas the Second Avenue location largely represents and even memorializes ISKCON's past, the Bhakti Center, at least in ISKCON's Manhattan landscape, represents ISKCON's future—a future that rests on Radhanath Swami's yoga brand.

The Govardhan Eco Village

Just like the Bhakti Center, the Govardhan Eco Village is an ISKCON-run yoga center with a temple to Krishna at its heart.[61] The Eco Village, too, is a physical operationalization of Radhanath Swami's rebranding of ISKCON. But although Radhanath Swami's two projects share these features, they are otherwise very palpably different from each other; while the Bhakti Center is a six-story yoga studio and temple located in the loud and bustling metropolitan center of New York City (with earsplittingly loud temple programs to match), the Govardhan Eco Village is a quiet, ninety-acre yoga retreat complex located in the rural and serene mountainous countryside of Palghar, Maharashtra, several hours outside the humming city limits of Mumbai.

The Govardhan Eco Village is one of ISKCON's—and certainly one of Radhanath Swami's—most successful projects. Founded in 2010 by Radhanath Swami and a number of his disciples, the Eco Village has been recognized with a number of awards and honors, including a recent Smart Cities India Award in the Smart Village category, a Skoch Development Foundation Skoch Award, and a Spirit of Humanity Award in the Livelihood category.[62] The Govardhan Eco Village is also routinely listed as one of the top attractions in or nearby Mumbai on the popular travel site Trip Advisor and has an uncommonly high five-star rating on a number of other travel and review sites, including Google, Facebook, and the Indian review site Just Dial.[63]

As an attraction, the Govardhan Eco Village advertises itself as "a model farm community & retreat center highlighting our need to live in harmony with ourselves, nature and the sacred."[64] As a model "farm community" where visitors can "live in harmony" with themselves and nature, the Eco Village can be best described as an experiment in the design of a fully sustainable, off-the-grid cooperative. Toward this end, the Eco Village hosts a number of eco-friendly and sustainable facilities and projects. For example, the Eco Village features its own impressive, large-scale water reclamation facility, one in which local water is recycled and filtered to be drinkable. Further, all waste from the community is recycled and used for fertilizer, and all of the buildings are made of unfired bricks (which help to naturally heat and cool the rooms). Additionally, nearly all of the food that is cooked for the Eco Village's 250 community members (full-time ISKCON *brahmacārīs* and householder families alike) and the village's many visitors is grown on the premises—a further exercise in sustainability. Moreover, all of the community's unused food and waste materials are composted for further use. The community also eschews (unauthorized) vehicular transportation within the village itself, choosing instead to have residents and visitors alike navigate its trails and dirt roads on foot or by ox-pulled carts.

Residents of the Eco Village told me that the off-the-grid and self-sufficient nature of the community is the biggest draw for visitors to the Eco Village each year, giving those (especially from the city) an ideal place for "self-discovery," "introspection," and "tak[ing] a break for a much needed slower pace of life." Adding to this draw, however, is likely also the fact that the Eco Village powerfully markets itself to visitors and also offers them a host of modern amenities to facilitate their peace of mind and introspection. These amenities include

Figure 4.9 Ox-pulled carts on the unpaved roads of the Eco Village reduce vehicular traffic to near zero. January 15, 2016. Photo taken by author. Palghar, Maharashtra, India.

Figure 4.10 All buildings at the Eco Village are made of unfired bricks. January 15, 2016. Photo taken by author. Palghar, Maharashtra, India.

Figure 4.11 Composting and recycling station at the Eco Village. January 15, 2016. Photo taken by author. Palghar, Maharashtra, India.

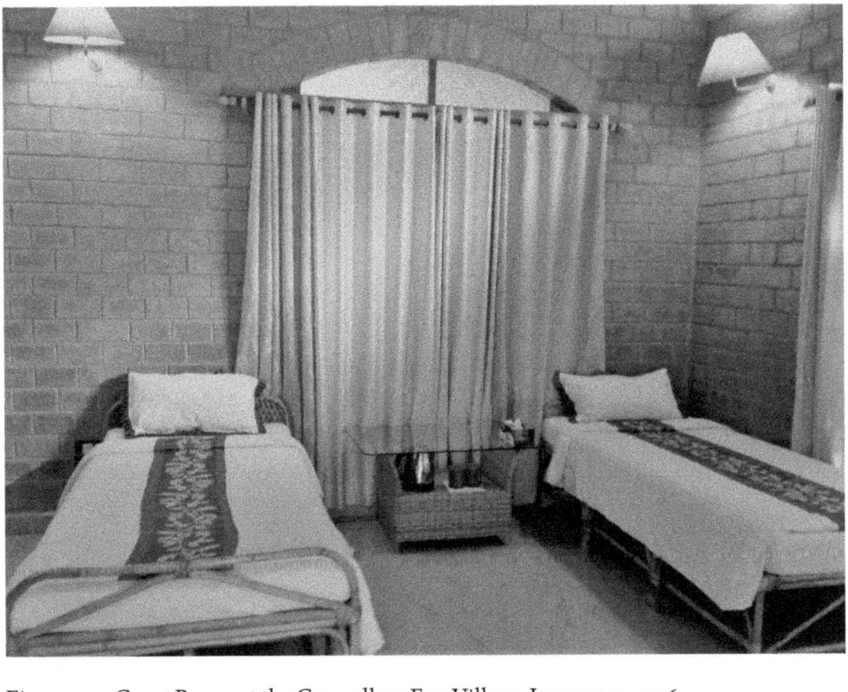

Figure 4.12 Guest Room at the Govardhan Eco Village. January 15, 2016. Photo taken by author. Palghar, Maharashtra, India.

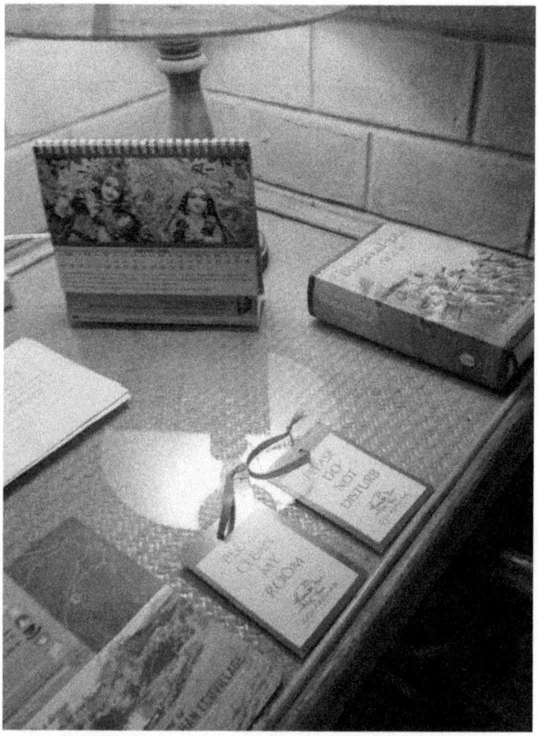

Figure 4.13 On the guest room tables are a picture of Radha and Krishna and a copy of Prabhupada's *Bhagavad-Gītā As It Is*. January 15, 2016. Photo taken by author. Palghar, Maharashtra, India.

immaculately maintained rooms that are well stocked for visitors' needs, a swimming pool, walking trails, and an Āyurvedic spa where patrons can get a massage, leech therapy, or other relaxation services. There is even an Āyurvedic doctor on site who specializes in *doṣa* (or body type) specific Āyurvedic treatments and who is available to meet with guests during their visits. Finally, there is also a beautifully maintained model of the sacred Vaishnava town of Vrindavan, complete with a footpath that weaves the visitor around replicas of Mount Govardhan, the Madan Mohan temple, and a recreated Yamuna River.

A Retreat Center Made for Yogis

Although the Govardhan Eco Village is, in some sense, marketed for all visitors wishing to find a peaceful retreat from hectic life (and for those who wish to see an award-winning model of sustainable living in action), it is particularly equipped for—and is especially marketed to—yoga practitioners. This is because it was built, in large part, to facilitate Radhanath Swami's rebranding of ISKCON as yoga.

One of the primary ways in which Radhanath Swami and his disciples market the Eco Village to practitioners of yoga is through the hosting of a number of different yoga training programs on the premises. Primary among these training programs are those that provide visiting yogis the opportunity to complete yoga teacher certification courses during their stay at the Eco Village. The Govardhan Eco Village hosts a number of these yoga teacher certification programs; in fact, it even has its own in-house yoga school—the Govardhan School of Yoga—which administers seven-, fifteen-, and twenty-eight-day residential programs that "train you to either begin your yoga journey with short programs or gain mastery by completing 200 hours yoga teachers training."[65]

At these programs, visiting yogis are taught by seven "faculty members," who are identified as either "yoga coaches" or "yoga philosophy teachers."[66] Although there are a few exceptions, most of these faculty members at the Govardhan School of Yoga are ISKCON *brahmacārīs,* and all of the teachers are disciples and students of Radhanath Swami who have been put in charge of the yoga programming at the Eco Village under his supervision. And while the curriculum at these programs varies, participants in them not only learn yoga techniques—including "asanas, pranayama, bandhas, kriyas and cleansing routines"—but they also learn yoga philosophy, such as the "8 limbs of yoga" and the "Yoga Sutras by Patañjali."[67] Moreover, they also learn anatomy and physiology, basic Sanskrit, Āyurveda, and the basics of the *Bhagavad-Gītā.*[68] Participants in the programs follow a tightly packed, daily monastic schedule: each day starts with a 5:15 a.m. wake-up call, followed by an hour of chanting the *mahā mantra* on *japa* beads before the yoga classes begin. In the evenings, there is also a *kīrtan* program that attendees are encouraged to attend.[69]

As a retreat center, the Govardhan Eco Village has a number of facilities built for the purpose of facilitating not only the practice of yoga but also these yoga teacher and other yoga training courses. Among these facilities, for example, is a large, state-of-the-art yoga studio. This yoga studio is an elevated, expansive, and beautiful yoga practice space that is surrounded on nearly all sides with wall-to-ceiling windows, allowing yogis to overlook the picturesque Sahyadri mountains as they practice yoga. Moreover, there is also a yoga *śālā* (yoga hut) that serves as a space for yogis to sit quietly in meditation, practice yoga on their own, or participate in small group yoga classes or discussions. Last but not least, yogis also have their own clustered accommodations in a series of cottages located at the Govardhan Eco Village, where they can stay nearby each other—especially convenient for those yoga practitioners traveling in groups.

Figure 4.14 Yoga *śālā* at the Govardhan Eco Village. January 15, 2016. Photo taken by author. Palghar, Maharashtra, India.

It is not just the Govardhan Yoga School that offers yoga teacher trainings and certifications at the Eco Village, however. On the contrary, the Eco Village frequently rents out its facilities to a number of other yoga studios for their own yoga and yoga teacher certification trainings. Some of these are ISKCON devotee-run yoga studios: yoga studios run by ISKCON devotees (most often disciples and students of Radhanath Swami) that have small-scale Bhakti Center–type programming. An example is Bhakti Yoga DC, a yoga studio run by a longtime ISKCON devotee and close associate of Radhanath Swami's in Washington, DC. With regularity, Bhakti Yoga DC offers a 200-hour yoga teacher training at the Govardhan Eco Village—a training called the 200-Hour Teacher Training: India Intensive. As Bhakti Yoga DC describes it:

> This training will take place at the Govardhan Ecovillage retreat center, north of Mumbai, India, at the foothills of the Sahyadri Mountains. Take yourself out of your conditioned environment and allow yourself to be surrounded by a culture where yoga philosophy, lifestyle and practices are organically woven into people's lives. The Ecovillage is peaceful, aesthetically beautiful and calming, an ideal setting for learning and contemplation.

Figure 4.15 Yoga Studio at the Govardhan Eco Village. Although the curtains are drawn, the entire studio is walled with windows. January 15, 2016. Photo taken by author. Palghar, Maharashtra, India.

> The food cooked daily by the monks is nourishing to soul and body, as are the daily yoga, meditation and pranayama sessions. Our 200 hour Teacher Training curriculum is a comprehensive study of yoga postures, art of sequencing, philosophy, mantra, anatomy and lifestyle. It empowers you to deepen your personal practice and heal and transform body and mind through breath and movement.[70]

Interestingly, even the Bhakti Center itself brings yoga students to the Eco Village each year, not for yoga teacher training per se (it hosts its own 100- and 200-hour teacher trainings at the Bhakti Center) but rather for a pilgrimage, which includes much yoga practice.[71] As the Bhakti Center describes the pilgrimage, it notes that attendees

> will fly into Mumbai and head straight to Govardhan Eco Village for the International Bhakti Yoga Festival—4 days of diving into the essence of

India's Yoga traditions with Radhanath Swami as well as other renowned teachers around the world. The Govardhan Eco Village is situated on 50 acres of pristine farmland and aims to demonstrate the principles of self-sufficiency and localized economy to the world. We will stay in eco-friendly cob houses in the naturally charming village, eat local dishes made from organic grains and vegetables grown on the land, and tour the facilities to see how a group of bhakti-yogis are making a difference towards a greener world. We will practice yoga daily, hear from Radhanath Swami, choose from an array of life changing workshops, swim in the inviting bio pool and have the option to receive Ayurvedic treatments at their world-class Ayurvedic Center.[72]

Last but not least, the Govardhan Eco Village also rents out its facilities to non-ISKCON-run yoga studios. Its most frequent non-ISKCON studio customer is the prestigious—and in some ways exclusive—Jivamukti Yoga School in Manhattan, the yoga studio owned and run by David Life and Sharon Gannon and where Radhanath Swami himself is often an invited speaker.[73] Each year, I was told, hundreds of students from Jivamukti come to the Eco Village to become trained and certified in Jivamukti's own brand of yoga through an intensive and immersive month-long, 300-hour teacher training program at the Eco Village. And the Jivamukti studio actively markets this training option to its students, selling them on both the value of the training itself and the optimal setting and location of the Eco Village.[74]

Through the active marketing of its various yoga courses and programs to yoga practitioners at studios in the United States and elsewhere, Radhanath Swami and his disciples try to draw yoga practitioners to come for a stay at the Govardhan Eco Village. But although the Eco Village rents out its facilities to these yogis so that they might have a serene space in which to cultivate and deepen their practice and training, it is important to remember why it is that Radhanath Swami and his disciples are running this yoga enterprise to begin with. As discussed at the beginning of this chapter, like his Krishna Brander peers, Radhanath Swami is saddened at the state of ISKCON in the world today—in particular, at the lack of ethnic, national, and racial diversity among its devotee constituency. As such, Radhanath Swami set out to rebrand ISKCON in order to attract more westerners to the movement, endeavoring to make it more diverse. He has primarily done this by rebranding ISKCON as yoga through efforts such as these at the Eco Village. The logic is simple: there are many westerners who practice yoga and who are yoga enthusiasts, especially in the United States and Europe, where Radhanath Swami's programs are primarily advertised. As such, he figures that if he can offer to these yogis high-quality yoga spaces—like the Eco Village—where they can practice and become trained in yoga, then they will come for a visit. And if they come for a visit—especially an extended residential one—then ISKCON devotees will have a chance to promote the movement to them, through the brand that pitches devotion to Krishna as the heart of yoga.

As he did at the Bhakti Center, what Radhanath Swami has done at the Eco Village to operationalize the brand that devotion to Krishna is the heart of yoga, is to put an ISKCON temple at the spatial and liturgical center of the Eco Village yoga complex, thereby physically instantiating the brand in the setup of the Eco Village space itself. This temple, which is home to Sri Sri Radha Vrindaban Behari ji, is a full-scale ISKCON temple, complete with elaborate daily worship of Sri Sri Radha Vrindaban Behari ji, as well as the rituals of *āratī*, *darshan*, and *puja* spread throughout the liturgical day. And just like they are at the Bhakti Center, yogis at the Eco Village are actively invited and encouraged to attend programs in the temple space during their stay, including *kīrtan*, *japa* chanting, and scriptural lectures.

But it is not just the fact that the temple sits at the center of the Eco Village that makes it a physical instantiation of Radhanath Swami's rebranding of ISKCON as the heart of yoga. Rather, it is also the architecture of the temple itself—along with the theological interpretation that underpins it—that most operationalizes Radhanath Swami's brand in the physical space. Painted onto the wooden floor of the temple, as well as on the staircase leading up to the temple, are a series of seven chakras: large painted squares in which sit intricate and overlapping stenciled lotus flower designs. Starting at the staircase outside of the temple, these chakras form a progressive path leading to the temple room. In other words, these chakras are arranged in a somewhat linear order, with each one bringing the visitor from the outside of the temple closer and closer to the altar space. As a resident at the Govardhan Eco Village explained it to me, "These are the different symbols of yoga—these chakras—and look how each of the chakras is successively taking you closer to Krishna."

Yoga chakras have a varied and complex set of interpretations within the yoga traditions, especially if one takes into account the many views of them that are operative in contemporary pop-cultural discussions. However, it is interesting to see how devotees at the Govardhan Eco Village theologize these chakras with respect to Radhanath Swami's rebranding of ISKCON. By painting the yoga chakras on the floor of the temple, with each one ultimately leading up to the altar, Radhanath Swami and his disciples are making the theological argument that with each chakra one moves through—or, as I was told, with each

Figure 4.16 Chakra on the floor of the temple of the Govardhan Eco Village. January 15, 2016. Photo taken by author. Palghar, Maharashtra, India.

progressive level of yoga that one achieves—one is getting closer and closer to Krishna himself, who is none other than yoga's ultimate goal. As a resident of the Eco Village put it:

> As one walks into the temple one will rise through the first three chakras which are situated on the stairs. In the yoga process we need the grace and blessings of advanced souls. So as an etiquette we bow down to Srila Prabhupada before we take darshan of the Lord. So the next three chakras are placed behind Srila Prabhupada's seat, so we rise above these chakras as we proceed to take blessings of the Founder-acharya. And as we move ahead to the center of the temple hall is the 7th chakra from where we can gaze upon the Lord. It is called the "drishti" point or the focal point in traditional temple architecture. If one stands on this 7th chakra, one will see Their Lordships Sri Sri Radha Vrindaban Behari and Sriman Mahaprabhu's gaze meet your eye exactly! So by anchoring one's mind on the beauty of the Lord and absorbing oneself in prayers for loving service one can attain the perfection of yoga.[75]

Figure 4.17 Seventh chakra located on the *dṛṣṭi* (*drishti*) point at the Govardhan Eco Village temple. This is the last chakra of seven that lead the visitor directly to Sri Sri Radha Vrindaban Behari ji. January 15, 2016. Photo taken by author. Palghar, Maharashtra, India.

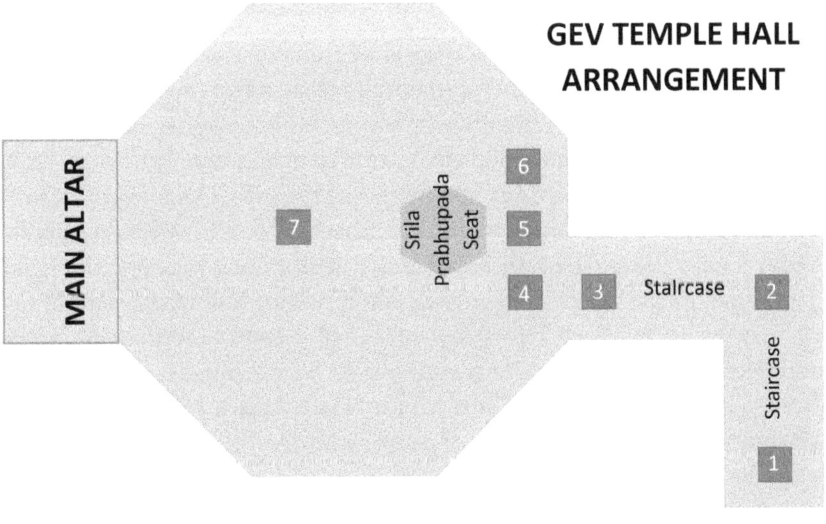

Figure 4.18 Diagram of the arrangement of the seven chakras on Govardhan Eco Village temple floor. Diagram by Govardhan Eco Village staff.

The material theology of the brand is clear, and it is etched onto and operationalized by the temple space itself: devotion to Krishna is the heart of yoga—its very goal and perfection—and it is this goal that awaits the visiting yogis should they cultivate their yoga practices to perfection. The whole experience at the Eco Village, in other words, is designed as an exercise to allow visiting yogis to not just practice and get certified in yoga but, more importantly, to get exposed to Radhanath Swami's conceptualization of it as a path to devotion to Krishna. And as disciples told me during my visit, all of this is by design. Radhanath Swami is the mastermind of it all, they said: "You can call him the chief architect of the whole village."

CONCLUSION

In response to the perceived need to attract more westerners to ISKCON, Radhanath Swami has developed a brand that promotes ISKCON—or ISKCON's devotion to Krishna—as the theological heart of yoga. This brand, as we've seen, is quite complex and has not only a conceptual arm—which equates surrender or devotion to Krishna with the *asamprajñāta samādhi* of the *Yoga Sūtras*—but also a material one. This material arm itself has many components—the Bhakti Center and the Govardhan Eco Village being just two of them—each of which consists of a state-of-the-art yoga center or complex with an ISKCON temple at its heart. Through these combined efforts, Radhanath Swami and his many disciples hope that they will be successful in attracting westerners not only to their yoga centers and complexes but eventually also to the ISKCON movement itself.

Before moving on to the next chapter of this book and to questions of whether or not brands such as this one (as well as that of Devamrita Swami from the previous chapter) will ultimately be successful in bringing westerners to ISKCON, I want to pause for a moment on a different question: Why yoga? That is, why is it that of all the options for rebranding the ISKCON movement that are available to him, Radhanath Swami has chosen to focus his western marketing efforts on developing a yoga brand aimed at attracting yoga practitioners, in particular, as the target market? Answered simply, Radhanath Swami focuses on yoga because he believes that yogis are the ripest western community for the reception of Krishna Consciousness. As he noted in a lecture entitled "Effective Models of Western Outreach for North America Today," the yoga community is "a large community of people who are like *this far* [putting his fingers close together to indicate an inch of space] from Krishna if we could just make that connection for them."[76] "The yoga community," he said, "[it's] *incredible, incredible* how many people could be completely transformed and accept Prabhupada's message."[77]

When Radhanath Swami speaks of the yoga community being just an inch away from Krishna, what he means is that he thinks their values and lifestyle choices match well with those of ISKCON's Vaishnavism. For example, he notes that many yogis are interested in "God Consciousness" and that many are also trying to live simply and maintain a vegetarian diet. His students and disciples—especially those who run his yoga programs—express similar beliefs about the receptivity of the yoga community to ISKCON, with many noting, like Radhanath Swami himself, that this receptivity stems from a close match in values and lifestyles. As one *brahmacārī* at the Eco Village told me, "The yoga/*kīrtan* audience is actually very finely tuned. [This is] like when Prabhupada had been to the west, [and] the hippie culture—that society—they took in the whole Krishna Consciousness philosophy. Now is the time when we see that *this* whole section of the society [e.g., the yoga community] seems to be more open and more receptive to hear this message of *Gītā* and *Bhāgavata*.... And, because you will see that many of these yoga followers, they are practically like a Vaishnava in their culture and lifestyle, so they are receptive."[78]

What this disciple is saying is that in terms of ISKCON's potential audience, yogis are the new hippies. Just as many in the American counterculture eagerly accepted the movement of Swami Prabhupada (as well as those of other Indian gurus) because these movements offered ideas and lifestyles that aligned with their own countercultural inclinations and values,[79] so too are today's western yoga practitioners believed to be attracted to ISKCON because the movement offers teachings and values that resonate with their own. In fact, as many devotees within ISKCON see it—especially those who are disciples of Radhanath Swami—the yoga community has now replaced the hippie community as ISKCON's dominant market. As such, these devotees believe that they should aim at yogis with full gusto in their efforts to rebrand ISKCON for westerners.

But beyond just the fact that those in the yoga community are believed to be receptive to ISKCON because of a well-matched set of values, Radhanath Swami and his yoga-branding disciples and students also cite another reason why they believe that yogis are more willing to accept ISKCON. This reason has to do with their belief that yogis have a highly developed mental poise and physical preparation—one that helps them in being open to receiving Krishna. That is, by virtue of having practiced yoga, yogis are presumed to have achieved the physical training, mental calm, and clarity of mind needed for (or at least helpful in) earnestly considering the message of Krishna Consciousness. As one of Radhanath Swami's yoga-studio-running students told me:

> I do really personally believe that yoga *āsana* prepares the body. It's like when you are gardening, you are gardening and you're digging. You're digging the earth, you're tilling the soil, and you plant a seed once the earth is ready. When we take care of our body . . . creating a *sāttvik* [pure] lifestyle . . . eating good . . . removing all the blockages . . . [then] yoga has an *incredible* powerful effect on the body and the mind. . . . It's like the mind has suddenly gone quiet, the body feels peaceful, all the noise has stopped. And it's like, this is the *perfect opportunity*, when the soul is ready to receive and hear the message of the soul [e.g., about Krishna]. . . . So for me it came very naturally to infiltrate the teachings of *bhakti* within the yoga community because I was a practitioner of yoga, and I knew so many yogis, and they were ready [to hear] because they've done all this work on their mind and their body that they were ready to receive [the message of the soul]. . . . Most of us are so restless mentally, we can't hear. Our minds are so agitated, we can't receive the message, we cannot, we're just not ready. So many people now from that physical practice and their lifestyle practice, they have hit a place where they are ready to go to the next level. And that's what I'm noticing in the yoga community all around. . . . That is why I was able to infiltrate and see how people are hungry for something deeper, because yoga practitioners are hungry. Because they're taking care of the body, and they are removing all the blockages, they're finding the peace of the mind, but the soul still hasn't found the connection.[80]

This devotee believes that the yoga community is ripe for ISKCON's message because their yoga practice has prepared their minds to be receptive to it. Most westerners, she claims, are too anxious, too busy, and too preoccupied with work, stress, and so on to even *think* about cultivating a deeper level of religiosity. Because of this, she believes, they simply cannot calm down enough to consider Krishna Consciousness. Yogis, on the other hand, have spent time learning how to train their bodies and minds to be calm and relaxed, and as a result, their minds are emptier, more focused, and less frenzied than those of their non-yogi western counterparts. They also purportedly have more mental room and capacity to contemplate ideas of God and the soul than do other westerners. It is for these reasons too—and not just because of their values—that Radhanath Swami believes that yogis are just an inch away from Krishna and why he believes that they are therefore the best target audience for ISKCON's western-focused marketing efforts. As he himself said in a lecture, "Yoga helps us to put our consciousness in harmony, where the body is in harmony with the mind and with the *ātmā*, with the soul. It helps us . . . the *āsanas* on a *physical level* make us in good health, but beyond that, it puts us in harmony with our mind and puts our mind in harmony with our *ātmā*, with the living force, with God within us."[81]

The question that remains, of course, is whether or not those who are attracted to yoga—and who are presumably ripe to be attracted to ISKCON—will, in fact, ultimately be attracted to the movement. After all, when Prabhupada argued that he wanted his movement to be a universal one, comprised of practitioners of all nationalities, races, and ethnicities, devotees typically interpret him to mean that he wanted these practitioners to become full ISKCON members—that is, initiated into the movement itself, and not just attendees at various programs (yoga and the like) that are run by ISKCON devotees. But will those people who are attracted to the yoga programs ultimately be attracted to ISKCON itself, enough so that they will make a meaningful transition to the movement?[82]

Radhanath Swami and his disciples, of course, point out that their enterprises are *already* successful and that while perhaps only a small number of western devotees have taken formal initiation into ISKCON each year as a result of them, the yoga-branding enterprise is still new, and only time can speak to its ultimate success. By way of indicating the promise of their yoga outreach, however, they note the enthusiasm that many yoga practitioners have for the ISKCON dimensions of the yoga centers and programs when they visit (enthusiasm for the temple, for the *kīrtans*, etc.), citing this enthusiasm as a positive sign. And this is an enthusiasm that I myself can confirm. From the yoga programs that I attended that were hosted by Radhanath Swami and his disciples—at the Bhakti Center, at the Eco Village, at a several-day retreat in Lanexa, Virginia, and elsewhere—it certainly seemed to be the case that the patrons there (nearly all of whom were westerners by ISKCON's definition of the term) seemed to enjoy the ISKCON programming. I even saw patrons' enthusiasm for ISKCON practices and ideas grow over the course of a single weekend: as when, by the last day of the retreat (called The Heart of Yoga) in Lanexa, Virginia, a group of thirty to forty western yoga practitioners ended the weekend by joyfully singing the *mahā mantra* in an open field, dancing enthusiastically while doing so to the beats of a *mṛdaṅga* drum, a harmonium, and *karatālas*.

Although this initial enthusiasm may be the case, however, it nonetheless remains to be seen whether or not Radhanath Swami's yoga branding programs will work in attracting these westerners into the movement formally or in the long run. And there are certainly some in the ISKCON movement who have their doubts, including—most notably—the Krishna Brander at the focus of the next chapter: Hridayananda Das Goswami. Although Hridayananda Das Goswami acknowledges the success of the rebranding programs of his fellow ISKCON gurus Radhanath Swami and Devamrita Swami, he believes that programs like theirs can be successful in attracting westerners to ISKCON only for an initial short period. To make ISKCON more demographically diverse in the long run, he believes something much more dramatic must be done. It is to his worldwide project and ISKCON's newest brand—Krishna West—that we now turn.

NOTES

1. Delaware Yoga Society. Accessed July 24, 2018. http://delawareyogasociety.com/home/. *Patañjali* is the typical spelling. Original text quoted as it appears.
2. A small form of Swami Prabhupada has since been added to the temple room space.
3. By using the term *conceptual brand*, my aim is not to say that other Krishna Branders are not doing conceptual work. Rather, my aim here is specifically to delineate the more textual and philosophical arm of Radhanath Swami's brand from the architectural and material arm of it.
4. Radhanath Swami. 2010. *The Journey Home: Autobiography of an American Swami*. San Rafael: Mandala.
5. Ibid., 6–7.
6. Ibid., 323.
7. Ibid., 325.
8. Ibid., 323.
9. Radhanath Swami. Interview by Nicole Karapanagiotis. In person, Lanexa, Virginia, June 13, 2016. Emphasis in original.
10. Radhanath Swami. Interview by Nicole Karapanagiotis. In person, Chowpatty, Mumbai, January 15, 2016. Emphasis in original.
11. Ibid.
12. Radhanath Swami 2016, Interview, June 13.
13. Ibid. Emphasis in original.
14. Radhanath Swami 2016, Interview, January 15.
15. Discussion with devotee. In person, Palghar, Maharashtra, India. January 15, 2016.
16. Radhanath Swami is involved in a number of marketing projects designed to draw the attention of westerners to the ISKCON movement (although his yoga brand is by far his chief and largest project). He also has various marketing projects that he himself does not directly administer but that he oversees in

a supervisory capacity. For example, he oversees the projects of his disciples Gadadhara Pandit Dasa and Jay Shetty (both of whom were discussed in the introduction), which seek to rebrand ISKCON for westerners by presenting it as mindfulness for work-life balance and as a meditative lifestyle brand, respectively.

17. RadhanathSwami.com. "Radhanath Swami's Bestseller *The Journey Within* Lights up Broadway." Accessed June 4, 2019. http://www.radhanathswami.com/2017/05/radhanath-swamis-bestseller-the-journey-within-lights-up-broadway/.

18. Dermot Killingley. 2014. "Manufacturing Yogis: Swami Vivekananda as a Yoga Teacher." In *Gurus of Modern Yoga*. Mark Singleton and Ellen Goldberg, eds. New York: Oxford University Press.

19. Mark Singleton and Ellen Goldberg, eds. 2014. *Gurus of Modern Yoga*. New York: Oxford University Press.

20. Andrea R. Jain. 2015. *Selling Yoga: From Counterculture to Pop Culture*. Oxford and New York: Oxford University Press, 71.

21. Ibid., and Mark Singleton and Ellen Goldberg. 2014. "Introduction." In Singleton and Goldberg 2014, 3.

22. Jain 2015, xi–xii.

23. Andrea R. Jain. 2014. "Muktananda; Entrepreneurial Godman, Tantric Hero." In Singleton and Goldberg 2014, 192. Jain notes that Muktananda was also successful in part because of his "godman" persona (using Fuller's definition of the term). C. J. Fuller. 2004. *The Camphor Flame: Popular Hinduism and Society in India*. Revised and Expanded Edition. Princeton: Princeton University Press.

24. Jain 2014, 197.

25. Ibid., 200. Lola Williamson defines *śaktipāt* within Siddha Yoga as "an initiation . . . in which the spiritual energy (*kundalini*) of the aspirant is awakened and then guided from within." Lola Williamson. 2005. In *Gurus in America*. "The Perfectability of Perfection: Siddha Yoga as a Global Movement." Thomas A. Forsthoefel and Cynthia Ann Humes, eds. Albany: State University of New York Press, 149.

26. Jain 2014, 198.

27. Joanne Punzo Waghorne. 2014a. "Engineering an Artful Practice: On Jaggi Vasudev's Isha Yoga and Sri Sri Ravi Shankar's Art of Living." In Singleton and Goldberg 2014, 284. Waghorne's argument here also applies to other gurus in Asia's large and quickly globalizing cities; in her chapter, however, she focuses on Sadhguru Jaggi Vasudev and Sri Sri Ravi Shankar in Singapore.

28. Carl Swanson. 2016. "Talking to the Hare Krishna Leader Who's Bringing the Movement Into the Age of Lululemon." *New York Magazine*, May 18. Accessed November 16, 2017. http://nymag.com/daily/intelligencer/2016/05/talking-to-hare-krishna-leader.html.

29. I do not mean to suggest that there is only one kind of postural yoga or that postural yoga is a monolith. Instead, I recognize that there are many different styles of practice and sets of ideas that make up what are, instead, many *postural yogas*. My use of the singular here and throughout this chapter refers only to the postural yoga "movement" as Radhanath Swami and his disciples understand it (which they see as largely singular and which they see to be based in an *aṣṭāṅga* yoga rooted in Patañjali's *Yoga Sūtras*). For scholarly discussions on the term postural yoga, see Elizabeth De Michelis. 2004. *A History of Modern Yoga: Patañjali and Western Esotericism*. New York: Continuum; Jain 2015; and Mark Singleton. 2010. *Yoga Body: The Origins of Modern Posture Practice*. New York: Oxford University Press.

30. I fondly remember Gerald Larson reiterating this point near daily during our graduate course on yoga philosophy at Indiana University. See also Mark Singleton and Tara Fraser (2014), who themselves cite Larson (and Johannes Bronkhorst) in this regard. Mark Singleton and Tara Fraser. 2014. "T. Krishnamacharya, Father of Modern Yoga." In Singleton and Goldberg 2014, 100. Gerald James Larson. 1989. "An Old Problem Revisited: The Relation between Sāṃkhya, Yoga, and Buddhism." *Studien zur Indologie und Iranistik* 15: 129–146; Gerald James Larson. 1999. "Classical Yoga as Neo- Sāṃkhya: A Chapter in the History of Indian Philosophy." *Asiatische Studien* 53, no. 3: 723–732; and Johannes Bronkhorst. 1981. "Yoga and Seśvara Sāṃkhya." *Journal of Indian Philosophy* 9: 309–320.

31. Sāṁkhya-yogāchārya Swāmi Hariharānanda Āraṇya (rendered into English by P. N. Mukerji). 1983. *Yoga Sūtras* I:2. In *Yoga Philosophy of Patañjali: Containing His Yoga Aphorisms with Vyāsa's Commentary in Sanskrit and a Translation with Annotations Including Many Suggestions for the Practice of Yoga*. Albany: State University of New York Press, 6.

32. Christopher Key Chapple. 2005. "Yoga and the Gita: Isvara-Pranidhana and Bhakti." *Journal of Vaishnava Studies* 14, no. 1: 29–42.

33. Āraṇya 1983, *Yoga Sūtras* I:18, 45.

34. Edwin Bryant. 2005. "Patañjali's Theistic Preference, Or, Was the Author of the *Yoga Sūtras* a Vaishnava?" *Journal of Vaishnava Studies* 14, no. 1: 7–28.

35. Ibid., 8. Brackets in original text.

36. Chapple 2005, 34.

37. Ibid., 31.

38. Radhanath Swami. 2012. "His Holiness Radhanath Swami Speaking at the Cambridge Union Society on 15/10/12." Cambridge Union YouTube channel, October 22. 1:17:39–1:18:35. Accessed November 17, 2017. https://www.youtube.com/watch?v=cKr27yOa57U.

39. *Brahma Saṃhitā* 5.1 is widely quoted in ISKCON literature, including in Prabhupada's own letters and talks. It also appears on numerous occasions in

the *Caitanya Caritāmṛta*. See Edward C. Dimock Jr. 1999. *Caitanya Caritāmṛta of Kṛṣṇadāsa Kavirāja: A Translation and Commentary*. Tony K. Stewart, ed. Cambridge: Harvard University Press.

40. Radhanath Swami. 2016. *The Journey Within: Exploring the Path of Bhakti, A Contemporary Guide to Yoga's Ancient Wisdom*. San Rafael: Mandala, 69.

41. Ibid., 78–79. In Radhanath Swami's text, these parentheses appear as brackets. However, I changed them to avoid confusion to the reader in my quoting of his passage. Italics in original.

42. Radhanath Swami. Lecture delivered at the Heart of Yoga Retreat, Day 1. June 11, 2016. Lanexa, Virginia.

43. Bhakti Center website. Accessed November 16, 2017. http://bhakticenter.org/.

44. Bhakti Center website. "Yoga Classes." Accessed November 16, 2017. http://bhakticenter.org/yoga/classes/. Clicking on a Kundalini Yoga class brings you to a pop-up window with a text description of the class.

45. Ibid. Clicking on a Stretch and Restore class brings you to a pop-up window with a text description of the class.

46. Ibid. Clicking on a Yoga for 12 Step Recovery class brings you to a pop-up window with a text description of the class.

47. Ibid.

48. Yelp.com. "The Best 10 Yoga near East Village, Manhattan, NY." Accessed November 16, 2017. https://www.yelp.com/search?cflt=yoga&find_loc=East+Village%2C+Manhattan%2C+NY.

49. TripAdvisor.com. "Classes & Workshops in New York City." Accessed November 16, 2017. https://www.tripadvisor.com/Attraction_Review-g60763-d8389845-Reviews-The_Bhakti_Center-New_York_City_New_York.html.

50. Bhakti Center website. "Yoga 101." Accessed November 16, 2017. http://bhakticenter.org/yoga-101/.

51. Bhakti Center website. "Inversions 101." Accessed September 1, 2017. http://bhakticenter.org/inversions-101/.

52. Ibid.

53. Ibid.

54. Bhakti Center website. "Stretch & Restore Yoga Class." Accessed November 16, 2017. http://bhakticenter.org/stretch-restore-yoga-class/.

55. For a discussion of ISKCON devotees' use of the label *yoga text* to describe the *Bhagavad-Gītā*, the reader is encouraged to refer back to pages 108 and 111 (and endnote 71).

56. Margalit Fox. 2011. "Swami Bhaktipada, Ex-Hare Krishna Leader, Dies at 74." *The New York Times*, October 24. Accessed May 17, 2019. https://www.nytimes.com/2011/10/25/us/swami-bhaktipada-ex-hare-krishna-leader-dies-at-74.html.

57. Discussion with devotee. By telephone, Wilmington, Delaware. May 13, 2019.

58. For details from those on this side of the story, see *Sun* Staff. "Kirtanananda Forms Alliance with ISKCON Devotees." *The Sampradaya Sun-Independent Vaishnava News.* Accessed May 17, 2019. https://www.harekrsna.com/sun/features/09-05/features47.htm; and Satchitananda Das. "A Plea from the New York Sanctuary." *The Sampradaya Sun-Independent Vaishnava News.* Accessed May 17, 2019. http://www.harekrsna.com/sun/editorials/06-07/editorials1640.htm. Another source, which includes an article and video that both contain profanity and inflammatory language, is Staff Member. 2011. "Radhanath and Yajya Purusha, The Sanctuary Hijackers." *Prabhupāda News,* April 24. Accessed May 17, 2019. http://www.prabhupadanugas.eu/news/?p=19290#more-19290.

59. Discussion with devotee. By telephone, Wilmington, Delaware. May 13, 2019.

60. Madhava Smullen. 2011. "First Ever ISKCON Temple Extends Plea for Help." ISKCONNews.Org, November 11. Accessed May 17, 2019. https://iskconnews.org/first-ever-iskcon-temple-extends-plea-for-help,2968/. ISKCON News Staff. 2011. "ISKCON In Danger of Losing 26 2nd Avenue." ISKCONNews.Org, November 2. Accessed May 17, 2019. https://iskconnews.org/iskcon-in-danger-of-losing-26-2nd-avenue,2947/.

61. Govardhan Eco Village website. Accessed November 17, 2017. https://www.ecovillage.org.in/.

62. Ibid. See also Jivamukti Yoga School website. "Govardhan Eco Village, India." Accessed November 17, 2017. https://jivamuktiyoga.com/general/11418/.

63. TripAdvisor.com. "Things to do in Mumbai (Bombay)." Accessed November 18, 2017. https://www.tripadvisor.com/Attraction_Review-g304554-d6949190-Reviews-Govardhan_Ecovillage-Mumbai_Bombay_Maharashtra.html.

64. Google Search descriptor that appears under the Eco Village on a Google search.

65. Govardhan Eco Village website. "About: Govardhan School of Yoga." Accessed November 18, 2017. https://ecovillage.org.in/yoga/intl/.

66. Govardhan Eco Village website. "Faculty." Accessed November 18, 2017. https://ecovillage.org.in/yoga/faculty/. Previously the yoga philosophy teachers were called yoga masters.

67. Govardhan Eco Village website. "About Us." Accessed November 18, 2017. https://ecovillage.org.in/yoga/about-us/.

68. Ibid.

69. Govardhan Eco Village website. "Schedule." Accessed November 18, 2017. https://ecovillage.org.in/yoga/schedules/.

70. Bhakti Yoga DC website. "200HR Teacher Training: India Intensive." Accessed November 18, 2017. http://www.bhaktiyogadc.com/ytt-200-india-2018/.

71. The Bhakti Center also hosts a 200-hour teacher training in Alachua, Florida, at an ISKCON-devotee-run Āyurvedic retreat center.

72. Bhakti Center website. "India Pilgrimage 2018." Accessed November 18, 2017. http://bhakticenter.org/india-pilgrimage/.

73. Jivamukti Yoga School website. Accessed November 18, 2017. https://jivamuktiyoga.com/.

74. Jivamukti Yoga School website. "Teacher Training: 300 Hour in India." Accessed November 18, 2017. https://jivamuktiyoga.com/teacher-training/teacher-training-in-india/. The Jivamukti Yoga School also hosts 300-hour trainings in Costa Rica and Germany.

75. Email correspondence with resident of Eco Village. November 7, 2017.

76. Italics in Original. Radhanath Swami. "Western Outreach by Radhanath Swami." 2015. YouTube video, June 9. 11:55–12:15. Accessed November 18, 2017. https://www.youtube.com/watch?v=oYFBvhdB-Io. This lecture was delivered at the May 1–3, 2015, conference at ISKCON Chicago discussed in the previous chapter: Reaching the Hearts and Minds of the Western Public (Effective Models of Western Outreach). For a list of all the lectures that were delivered there, see Sachin Mittal. 2015. "Seminar on Reaching the Hearts and the Minds of the Western Public." *Dandavats.* Accessed July 2, 2017. http://www.dandavats.com/?p=17198.

77. Italics in Original. Swami 2015.

78. Discussion with devotee. In person, Palghar, Maharashtra, India. January 15, 2016.

79. Jain 2015, 43.

80. Discussion with devotee. In person, Lanexa, Virginia, June 11, 2016.

81. Italics in original. Swami 2012.

82. It is up for debate, of course—as I will discuss in the conclusion—what counts as a "meaningful transition to the movement."

FIVE

KRISHNA WEST

ISKCON Must Be Reinvented, Not (Just) Rebranded

On a chilly evening in early October 2017, I was standing outside of ISKCON of Philadelphia with a devotee who through the years has become a friend of mine. We had both just attended the Sunday evening program at the temple and had stopped to chat outside on our way to the parking lot. As we stood outside talking, a crowd of about one hundred or so devotee families packed into their cars to leave the temple and head back home after what had been a long but devotionally charged Sunday feast and *kīrtan* (devotional singing) event. Besides the regular Sunday program crowd, the visitors at the temple on this particular evening also included a class from a neighboring university: a group of roughly thirty students, of mixed ages and ethnic, racial, and national backgrounds, who had come to the temple to learn about the ISKCON movement for their religion class.

Given his highly respected position at the temple, my devotee friend had been the host for the class that evening, which meant that he'd been put in charge of showing the students around the temple, answering their questions, and generally assuring that they felt comfortable during their stay. From the outside looking in, it seemed that the class visit had gone well; the students had seemed to enjoy the program, had had a number of thoughtful questions about it, and had appeared content and comfortable as they'd walked around the temple taking photos of the *mūrtis* (embodied forms, or *deities* in ISKCON parlance). They also seemed to enjoy glancing through the book packets they had been given, and eating the *prasādam* they had been served. Despite the visit's seeming success, however, in our conversation after the program, my friend began expressing to me what had become by that time in my research an all-too-familiar sentiment—a sense of shame about the present-day ISKCON movement. In particular, the shame he shared had to do with his vague sense that "our best ISKCON movement" was not presented to the students on their visit as well as his nagging concern that there had to be a better way to have introduced the movement to them. "The temple is not doing enough to appeal to the interests of diverse crowds of people," he said. "My biggest hope for ISKCON, and what Prabhupada wanted, was to build a house for the whole world to live in. And right now, I just don't see that happening. It hasn't happened. But I want to see it happen."[1]

What my friend was referring to, of course, is the fact that the ISKCON movement at present regularly attracts a predominantly Indian audience at what seems to many in the movement to be the exclusion of various other groups of people. More than this, he was expressing his sadness at the role of his own home temple in perpetuating this "problem." "ISKCON of Philadelphia," he told me, "is only relevant to one population of people—[Indian people]—many of whom drive for hours to get here." But, he said, "the temple is totally irrelevant to the people right around us, the residents of Philadelphia. These people don't come to the temple because there is nothing that draws them here." Then, pausing for a moment and gesturing at what he seemed to think might be a solution to the dilemma, he said shyly, almost hesitatingly, "You know, Prabhupada may have wanted to build a house that the whole world can live in, but that doesn't mean that the house doesn't have different rooms. The house can have different wings even, ya know. Like an Eastern wing, a Western wing. We can have different rooms and still include the whole world in the house."[2]

What he was suggesting was that if devotees want to draw in and retain westerners to the movement, the best way forward might not be trying to accommodate all devotees to worship together. Instead, the best way forward might be to create a religious space for westerners—a room in the ISKCON house, so to speak—that could be all their own and that could resonate with and accommodate their own interests and cultural styles of worship.

Although my friend is not a disciple of Hridayananda Das Goswami (or even a Krishna Brander himself), his suggestion for how to remedy ISKCON's current "diversity problem" resonates quite well with that of Hridayananda Das Goswami, this chapter's Krishna Brander. Hridayananda Das Goswami argues that ISKCON's biggest—nay, its only—hope for sustainably attracting westerners to the movement is to create an ISKCON "sub-movement" for them: a "western Hare Krishna movement," as he calls it, that caters specifically to westerners' religio-cultural tastes and preferences and that coexists alongside of, but separate from, ISKCON's traditional programs and centers. He calls this sub-movement, which still remains under the larger ISKCON umbrella, Krishna West.

HRIDAYANANDA DAS GOSWAMI AND HIS VIEWS ON ISKCON'S TRAJECTORY

Hridayananda Das Goswami was born in 1948 in Los Angeles, California. Having spent his childhood and young adult life in Los Angeles, the young Hridayananda Das Goswami moved in 1967 to attend college at the University of California, Berkeley. It was during his college years that he had his first encounter

Figure 5.1 *Saṃnyāsī* (renunciant) in a suit. Hridayananda Das Goswami (pictured above). Photo courtesy of KrishnaWest.com.[3]

with Swami Prabhupada, which occurred when he had an occasion to hear a lecture that Prabhupada delivered in 1969. So captured was Hridayananda Das Goswami by Swami Prabhupada, he notes, that within the span of one year of meeting him, he had not only joined an ISKCON temple as a full-time devotee, but had also taken formal initiation into the movement by Prabhupada himself. Just three short years later, in 1972, Hridayananda Das Goswami accepted *saṃ nyāsa* from Prabhupada—thereby entering the renounced order of life in order to devote himself full time to further the mission of his guru.[4]

By early 1977, Prabhupada knew that his days at the helm of the ISKCON ship were numbered, so he finalized an administrative plan for the movement's religious and organizational success into the future after his death. This future planning meant that he had to choose the successors who would run the movement after he was gone. It was in this way that Hridayananda Das Goswami got his start as a guru. In November of 1977, not too long before Swami Prabhupada passed away, he asked Hridayananda Das Goswami to be one of the eleven men to take disciples of his own and lead the movement after his death.[5] Hridayananda Das Goswami therefore rose to the top of the ISKCON ranks very quickly. Following his new status in the movement, Hridayananda Das Goswami had a tough road ahead of him, and he had to learn how to become a leader in a worldwide religious movement (that he had only just joined) in the prime of his youth. In fact, often raw in his own honesty, Hridayananda Das Goswami has spoken about the hardships of this early time in ISKCON—not just for himself but for all of the gurus that Prabhupada chose to succeed him. "It was just, ya know, a young age," he told me one afternoon via Skype as he reflected back on his early days as a guru in the movement. "It was just, I mean the stuff we went through was unbelievable in terms of the human toll it took."[6] Despite the hardships, however, and with a little help from an unlikely source—the writings of Jane Austin—Hridayananda Das Goswami persevered, forging a path for himself as a highly respected leader within ISKCON, with disciples and program initiatives all over the world. And he did so out of an eager commitment to Swami Prabhupada and to the vision that he brought for saving the world.

In many ways, the story of Hridayananda Das Goswami is similar to those of the other Krishna Branders discussed in this book thus far; it is the story of an ISKCON guru who believes that ISKCON is not reaching the full plan envisioned by Swami Prabhupada, specifically because it is not attracting westerners. As Hridayananda Das Goswami himself puts it, "there are two historical possibilities" for the ISKCON movement: "Number one, ISKCON simply continues to transform into basically a movement for people from a Hindu background. And of course there are other programs, there are devotees from other places, but overwhelmingly it is a movement for people from a Hindu background. It's going in that direction and it's—if it continues to go in that direction—then within a generation that's what it'll be. . . . This is *not* a criticism of people from a Hindu background," [he notes, but] "rather, it's just a fact, it's just a socio, historical, demographic fact that the movement is becoming dangerously unbalanced."[7]

The second option, according to Hridayananda Das Goswami, is that someone attempts to change the current demographic trend of the movement by rebranding ISKCON in order to attract more westerners. And this is what Hridayananda Das Goswami—like his Krishna Brander peers—is trying to do.

But the story of Hridayananda Das Goswami is also importantly different from those of the other Krishna Branders discussed in this book thus far; if not for the sheer degree of pain that he publicly expresses at the current demographic homogeneity of ISKCON, then for the bold degree and tremendous struggle to which is he is willing to go to draw westerners to the movement.

> History is moving in a certain direction. And I know that at the present time ISKCON, historically, is *not* moving in the direction that Prabhupada actually dreamed of. Because what Prabhupada dreamed of was a movement which is *truly* international. His mission, which is of course Gaura-Nitai's[8] mission, [is that ISKCON] becomes a *major, major* world religion, becomes a *powerful* spiritual cultural *force* in the West and transforms the world. And especially in western Europe and America. Prabhupada said it *again* and *again*—he said it every day—that America and Western Europe if they become Krishna Conscious [so too will the whole world]. . . . And so therefore there is something *very serious* at stake here. There is something at risk.[9]

What is at risk for Hridayananda Das Goswami is not just his fear that ISKCON will become even more demographically "unbalanced" than it is now, but more so his fear that if he allows this demographic shift to continue unchallenged, he will have violated his own commitment to be the servant of the servant of Krishna by serving the global aims of Swami Prabhupada.

> I joined the movement when the western mission was very powerful. *That's* the Hare Krishna movement I joined. *That's* the Hare Krishna movement I want to be part of. A movement where we are really transforming the western world. . . . *That's* the movement I fell in love with. *And that's the movement that Prabhupada loved.* And therefore my body now is 65 years

> old . . . I am now 65 years old and I don't know how many years I have left, only Krishna knows that, but *I have no choice*. I would be a *traitor to Prabhupada, I would betray my own eternal spiritual master* if I didn't at this point do *everything possible, use all of my energy, all of my time,* do *everything* possible, to help—'cause I can't do it alone—to help establish ISKCON as a *powerful, influential, major* spiritual force in the western world. There's nothing else for me to do in this world. . . . There's nothing else for me to do. There's nothing else for me to do.[10]

Hridayananda Das Goswami has always been somewhat of a maverick within ISKCON, as well as a leading voice of both academics and liberalism within the movement. For example, he went back to school to earn a PhD in Sanskrit and Indian Studies from Harvard (1996) and has since also actively encouraged his disciples to pursue graduate studies and to participate in academic discourses. He has also enthusiastically championed the rights of women to become gurus in ISKCON, despite the fact that this position has been contentious within the movement. More than this, he has also voiced one of the only (publicly) liberal positions on same-sex relationships within ISKCON—a position considered radical within the movement and one that earned him a significant degree of criticism therein.[11] It is perhaps no surprise, therefore, that Hridayananda Das Goswami has devised a solution for ISKCON's current demographic homogeneity that has ruffled the movement's waters in a way that no Krishna Brander's efforts before him have. In fact, his solution—a rebranding project that he calls Krishna West—has caused such alarm that it even earned him a temporary travel ban by ISKCON's GBC, meant to restrict his preaching (a ban that has since been lifted). But the fact that his endeavors have been criticized has not deterred Hridayananda Das Goswami, who retorts by asking, "What am I supposed to do, go against what Prabhupada said so that people don't criticize me on the Internet?"[12] On the contrary, Hridayananda Das Goswami remains stalwart in his faith that his Krishna West solution is both necessary to save the movement and also in line with what Prabhupada himself would do.

> I think just *objectively* any, any *objective* historian would say that our western preaching has *significantly* decreased in terms of how many devotees we make, in terms of our public influence, I mean, I think there's no question that an *objective* historian would say the western mission has significantly decreased. . . . The question [now is] if Prabhupada, let's say if we had the blessing of Prabhupada physically being with us right now and if Prabhupada saw that . . . what [would] Prabhupada [ ] say in response

> to that? . . . I think if we study Prabhupada, at every time that the movement was really in serious trouble or not doing well he would make an adjustment.[13]

Let us now turn to an exploration of Hridayananda Das Goswami's Krishna West—a rebranding project that rejects the methods of the previous two Krishna Branders as incapable of making the ISKCON movement demographically diverse in the long run. This is because while the other Krishna Branders rebrand ISKCON through yoga programs and meditation lofts, their ultimate aim is to bring the westerners they attract through these programs into the fold of ISKCON's traditional temple-based communities. But, like my devotee friend at ISKCON of Philadelphia, Hridayananda Das Goswami argues that this marketing method does not work. This is because, Hridayananda Das Goswami claims, westerners are not interested in participating in or worshipping at ISKCON's traditional temples, nor will they ever be. Instead, he argues, if ISKCON wants to not just attract but also reliably *retain* westerners, then the movement must be completely reinvented; ISKCON must create a set of spaces and centers where westerners will want to stay and participate for the long haul. In other words, Hridayananda Das Goswami believes that in order to create a house where the whole world can live, then more than just a shiny western-friendly exterior must be added to the house. Instead, ISKCON must create a set of rooms for westerners—their own wing of the house, so to speak, designed just for them. It is to a discussion of Krishna West that we now turn.

THE NEED FOR A NEW WAY

In chapter 3, I introduced the concept of the *bridge model* (also known as the *loft model*). As discussed therein, bridge programs in ISKCON (also known as loft programs) are those programs that seek to attract westerners to the movement by presenting them not with traditional "temple ISKCON"—or ISKCON as it is practiced in the majority of ISKCON centers—but rather with programs that focus on yoga, mindfulness, meditation, and so on. These programs are held not in the temple rooms of traditional ISKCON worship but rather in other more "innocuous" spaces, such as yoga studios, mantra lounges, and the like. The rationale of these bridge programs, from the perspectives of the leaders and devotees who run them, is simple: since westerners are not attracted to traditional ISKCON as it is, they must be drawn to ISKCON *through* other programs—programs that they are both excited about and familiar with. Through these programs (yoga, karate classes, vision boarding, etc.), westerners will become familiar with ISKCON's philosophy and comfortable with its devotees. And once they are familiar and comfortable with the movement and devotees, the argument goes, they will naturally take a liking to ISKCON and might also be drawn to participate in its heart—the temple worship programs to which they would have been otherwise unattracted. Although Devamrita Swami came up with the bridge (or loft) model concept, many others in the ISKCON movement operate programs based on a similar general framework. Most notably, Radhanath Swami's programs (as discussed in chap. 4) use a similar approach.

The basis for Hridayananda Das Goswami's Krishna West movement, however, rests on his belief that bridge programs do not work in the long run to attract westerners to ISKCON:

> A major point [of mine] is that relevant, accessible, user friendly Krishna Consciousness is not just a bridge to difficult, unnatural Krishna Consciousness. They have a common saying in America, it's a political term, they call it the bridge to nowhere.... And so there's this sense in which—and I don't want to be misunderstood—that this expression "bridge to nowhere" applies [to us] because [] you have a standard way that we present Krishna Consciousness which has completely *underwhelmed* the western world (almost everybody is not really interested in it, ya know, a few people are, but almost everyone is like, "no thank you"). So what we do is, "OK, let's have a little bridge program that's really nice and interesting and western and *draw* people in and, there's another expression called bait and switch. You know that expression? Bait is like when people are fishing... when you are fishing the thing you put on the hook to attract the fish... in other words you draw someone in with some bait and then you switch and give them something else. To me, I don't like to do that for various reasons. Number one, I just I like to be honest with people. But apart from that, it doesn't solve the problem. Let's say you go to a particular country... and let's say you're making maybe one devotee a year, or one devotee every two years, or couple devotees a year, and then you do some bridge program, which is very western, and it's maybe "oh my god, we made four devotees this year, or even five devotees this year." Statistically, it's irrelevant... because out of those five inevitably some of them will leave.... It's not that we go from irrelevance to relevance. It doesn't change that much.[14]

In these remarks, Hridayananda Das Goswami opens up his critique of ISKCON's bridge programs, such as the kind discussed in chapters 3 and 4 of this book. He begins by expressing his view that bridge programs are problematic because they are not straightforward with patrons. In fact, he likens them to a marketing ploy known as *bait and switch,* advertising methods whereby "a low-priced good is advertised but replaced by a different good at the showroom."[15] He repeats this criticism on a number of occasions, calling ISKCON's many bridge programs "tactics" and "baits."

But besides his belief that bridge programs are underhanded marketing methods, Hridayananda Das Goswami is also critical of them because he thinks they are ineffective. "The non-devotees," he explained in a formal interview delivered to a crowd in Germany,

> Many of them are not stupid. And if someone is going to join something, they want to know where does it lead. If I take this road, where will I go? If I get on this bus, where is it going? And so, it's a fact that when we go to the universities and so on, that we [do] have success. However, ultimately, these are bridge programs. And before people get on a bridge—most people—they want to know what's on the other side of the bridge. For example, in Los Angeles they have a house called the Bhakti House, which is meant to be like a bridge program. It's sort of modeled after—it's not identical to but it's modeled after—Devamrita Swami's programs. And so I've talked to some of the leaders, the main preachers at the Bhakti House in Los Angeles, and what they say is that most (ya know, I would say most) of the people that go to the Bhakti House, or a lot of them, at least half, or perhaps most of them, *do not want to go to the temple.* And therefore after some time they stop coming and they have to get new people *because people, they know where the bridge is going and most people don't want to go there.* In my opinion. That's my view.[16]

He elaborates on this point elsewhere, noting that "most of the people who come to [these bridge] program[s] *do not want to go to the main temple.* They don't feel comfortable. So the point of a bridge is people must desire to go to the other side of the bridge. People don't get on a bridge just because it's a beautiful bridge."[17]

On first glance, Hridayananda Das Goswami's argument seems straightforward. After some time has elapsed, he argues, westerners who were attracted to ISKCON through bridge programs—meditation clubs, yoga studios, and the like—will inevitably see that the movement into which they are being recruited is not, in fact, based in meditation centers, yoga studios and so on, but instead is based in temples. To some extent, even Devamrita Swami and Radhanath Swami acknowledge this problem with bridge-type programs, noting the difficulty westerners have in transitioning to temple worship, especially the ritual worship of the deities that characterizes it. However, unlike Devamrita Swami and Radhanath Swami, who believe that these westerners eventually come to accept the temples—provided that they are introduced to them gradually (and with theological sophistication and/or social comfort)—Hridayananda Das Goswami disagrees, citing the lack of westerners in the contemporary ISKCON movement as evidence to back up his view. Instead, he remains vehement that those who are drawn to the movement because of bridge programs will leave as soon as they see what's on the bridge's other side: the temple.

But for Hridayananda Das Goswami, it is not just the temples themselves—or the Vaishnava rituals of *mūrti puja* and *darshan* that take place there—that make westerners lose interest in joining or further entering the ISKCON movement that they find at the end of the bridge. Rather, there is also something much larger at play: "All these many programs that are sort of 'west friendly,'" he told me one day, "they're all bridges, they are bridges back to India."[18]

Congregations in the United States are notoriously homogenous in their constituencies across ethnic, national, racial, and linguistic lines. This trend in American religious groups has been long observed in public culture. In 1963, Dr. Martin Luther King, Jr. famously said that eleven o'clock on Sunday morning is "the most segregated hour in America."[19] This trend has also been observed in scholarship on religions in the United States; as early as 1970, Donald A. McGavran articulated the well-known "homogenous unit principle," which argued that "people like to become Christians without crossing racial, linguistic, or class barriers."[20] And many scholars today still echo these observations. For example, in 2003 Michael O. Emerson and Karen Chai Kim wrote that "congregations, like other voluntary organizations, tend to attract members who feel socially comfortable with one another. Given individual choice, it is natural for potential members to look for others like themselves, to seek 'homogenous units,' in their church."[21]

So common is this trend to congregational homogeneity among religious groups in the United States that only roughly 7 percent of US congregations can be considered meaningfully diverse.[22] While reasons for this homogeneity vary, some scholars have suggested that marketing forces play into these demographic trends. As Kevin D. Dougherty notes, "The competitive nature of the American religious marketplace forces churches to specialize and target their message to a particular market niche, thus driving religious groups toward internal similarity."[23] More than this, if those religious groups that are most attuned to and promoted for particular market niches are the most successful, "then successful congregations and parishes will continue to be homogenous."[24]

While most of the studies of congregational homogeneity in the United States focus on Christian churches, scholars note similar trends among non-Christian religious groups. In her lucidly argued book *Reflections of Amma,* for example, Amanda J. Lucia discusses the "congregational dynamics" of the Hindu guru Amma's communities of followers. She argues that "as new religious movements and Asian religions establish their foundations in the United States, they too (like their Christian peers) conform to de facto congregationalism and exhibit similar preferences for communal homogeneity."[25] In her book, Lucia suggests two broad categories through which to understand Amma's followers: those whom she calls *inheritors* and those whom she calls *adopters*. "Inheritors," she writes, "are those who were born into environments in which there were strong religio-cultural ties to Asian religions. Adopters," on the other hand, "are those who were not [born into such environments] and only later adopted various religio-cultural behaviors, ideas, material environments, and habits of Asian societies."[26] Although she is quick to point out that "the categories of inheritor and adopter are not contingent on race or cultural ethnicity," she nonetheless notes that "the majority of inheritors are Indian Hindus and the majority of adopters are whites of diverse, but non-Hindu, religious backgrounds."[27] And significantly, these two groups remain—to a large extent—congregationally separate.

All of this discussion on congregational homogeneity is to say that across religious traditions, religious practitioners tend to like to worship with people who are like them. For his part, Hridayananda Das Goswami is aware of this tendency, and his understanding of it informs his position that westerners do not want to take a "bridge to India." Put simply, he thinks that westerners do not want to join ISKCON at the end of the bridge because they do not want to join a culturally Indian church.

But besides his belief that westerners do not want to join a culturally Indian congregation, Hridayananda Das Goswami has more in mind when he says that westerners do not want to take a "bridge to India." Specifically, he believes that westerners do not want to join a religious movement that requires them to *themselves* take on a culturally Indian identity—which is precisely what he believes the traditional ISKCON movement at the end of the bridge requires of them. These bridge programs, he told me, are "just a tactic. . . . Sometimes they'll actually give a class on haṭha yoga, [etc.], but the ultimate goal is to Indianize you, to make you an ethnically Indian Hare Krishna."[28] This is why, he says, "I call [them] the bridge to nowhere, because basically trying to make everyone Indian in the West is a failed policy. And so the bridge programs are like, it's like bait and switch where, 'OK, hi we're just normal western people,' but then once they get you, once ya know [they bring you further into the movement], then [they say] 'Now let's go to India, ya know, now dress like an Indian, [etc.].'"[29]

What Hridayananda Das Goswami is referring to is the fact that much of the devotional culture that characterizes the ISKCON movement is rooted in an Indian Hindu cultural identity (albeit an idealized or romanticized one). For example, initiated devotees in ISKCON take Sanskrit devotional names (such as Vrajendra Das, Vrindavan Kishor Dasi, etc.[30]) and typically wear South Asian devotional clothing during their worship (*dhotīs* and *kurtās* for the men and sarees for women[31]). Additionally, most of the food that devotees eat in ISKCON centers is Indian cuisine—including dishes such as Gauranga potatoes (creamy potatoes), *khicaṛī* (rice and lentil porridge), and vegetable *koftā* (dumpling ball)—and all of the music that they play utilizes Indian instruments and melodies and is sung in Indian liturgical languages. Devotees also refer to one another through the use of Sanskrit reference terms, such as *prabhu* (my lord) for men and *mātā jī* (mother) for women. But it is precisely this adoption of an Indian identity and cultural framework—which Hridayananda Das Goswami argues westerners feel socially pressured to embrace—that he believes westerners find most off-putting about the movement. It is also why, Hridayananda Das Goswami believes, despite their interest in the bridge programs, westerners do not eventually join the movement at the end of the bridge. "We have a great philosophy," he says. "I mean frankly in terms of theology, this is like the gold medalist, and the practice is powerful. The problem is, people don't want to become Martians. And they don't want to commit social suicide."[32]

Hridayananda Das Goswami's concern with ISKCON's social pressuring of westerners to don Indian clothing (and to adopt an Indian cultural lifestyle, more broadly) is on the pulse of an important contemporary debate over cultural appropriation, even if being on this pulse is not his intention. Cultural appropriation is the practice of borrowing or adopting cultural artifacts from groups of which one is not a member. This borrowing can take a variety of forms, including but not limited to the wearing of clothing and accessories from another cultural group or the utilization of their symbols, practices, and iconography as one's own.

Though many borrowers believe that there is nothing wrong with their borrowing from other cultural groups—on the contrary, some believe that their imitation is a form of flattery—many experience reservations with their appropriations. In her book *Living in the Lap of the Goddess*, for example, Cynthia Eller argues that while many of the "spiritual feminists" in her study borrow freely from other cultures without concern, others of them experience hesitancy in doing so out of fear of being offensive. "The people spiritual feminists worry about offending," Eller writes, "are the people that white culture has already offended very deeply: Native Americans and African Americans. The concern is that European Americans have destroyed or appropriated nearly everything about these oppressed cultures, and are now scouring around to collect the last shred of precious spirituality they have left."[33]

At the heart of worries about cultural appropriation is a severalfold set of objections, all of which stem from concerns of exploitation. For starters, many critics of cultural appropriation have cited it as a form of fetishization—a process whereby "an object [is] abducted from its original context and social identity so that it may become available as a sign for [one's] own purposes."[34] Critics of cultural appropriation argue that many borrowers are less interested in the contexts and histories of the artifacts, objects, clothes, and ritual practices that they borrow and more interested in romanticizing them and piecing them together in ways that they believe will combat the sterility and ennui of their own lives.[35] But besides merely ignoring the contexts and social histories of these objects of borrowing, cultural appropriation also often *obfuscates* these contexts, especially the complicated histories of Western European colonial domination, imperialism, and orientalism that characterized them.[36] In fact, critics argue that cultural appropriation *extends* the uneven and hegemonic power dynamics of these histories, replicating and continuing them into the present. Of the Indian context, Lucia notes that Western appropriation of Indian clothing often "recalls the exploitative relationship between the West and India under colonialism," and that many "view [] contemporary Western appropriations of Indian culture as neocolonialism or at least neo-orientalism."[37] This is especially the case since such cultural borrowing often "provides a sense of entitlement for whites to continue to appropriate whatever they can grasp in their neocolonial gaze . . . [and] hides the fact that such 'sharing' exchanges exist within unjust power relations, and often . . . operates in unidirectional patterns. The sharing is not mutual," in other words; "rather, it is about whites appropriating the cultural symbols, artifacts, and objects of once-colonized peoples (Africans, Native Americans, Indians, and so on)."[38]

Although he does not cite the histories of imperialism and colonialism as the root of his own criticism of ISKCON's cultural appropriation, Hridayananda Das Goswami nonetheless frequently discusses his view that westerners are extremely uncomfortable with ISKCON's cultural borrowing, and it is likely that their reservations do stem from these histories. Because of this, Hridayananda Das Goswami says that rather than building bridge programs that only *initially* allow westerners to come as they are and be themselves, "We need to give people the opportunity not simply to take a *bridge to India,* but actually to be *German,* to be *American,* and to become pure devotees *as* Germans, *as* Americans. And if we insist that in order to be a first-class devotee, in order to be fully respected in ISKCON, and so on, in order to really be Krishna conscious, you have to immerse yourself in Indian culture, I think history shows that it's just not gonna work. And it's not working."[39] Instead, he asks, "Why not have relevant programs, programs that attract people, and then when people join, use that to develop larger relevant programs so that you can practice Krishna Consciousness your whole life? You can go back to Godhead, you know the gates of heaven will open and you float into Krishna Loka and you did all that without having to *be Indian*. So the idea that western [e.g. bridge] preaching is just a lower stage and then when people get serious they graduate to the higher stage which is becoming Indian, I don't get it. It doesn't work."[40]

AIMING FOR PROGRAMMING THAT WORKS: KRISHNA WEST

Krishna West, the ISKCON sub-movement conceptualized by Hridayananda Das Goswami, aims to give westerners a space wherein they can comfortably be a part of the ISKCON movement for the duration of their devotional careers. Its goal is to provide westerners with a set of spaces wherein they can practice the teachings and rituals of the ISKCON movement in their "own cultural comfort zone."[41] As the sub-movement's mission statement reads, "we call this project Krishna West because we do everything possible to make bhakti-yoga easy, relevant and enjoyable for Western people, without in any way compromising, diluting, or diminishing the purity and power of a glorious ancient tradition. We do this by offering the essential spiritual teaching and practice in its entirety, *without requiring students and practitioners to embrace a new ethnicity composed of non-essential Eastern dress, cuisine, music etc.* People in the West need and deserve the chance to practice genuine bhakti-yoga *within an external culture that is comfortable and natural for them.*"[42]

As suggested by the mission statement, making ISKCON a culturally comfortable movement for westerners means creating religious spaces that feel "natural for them" or, as Hridayananda Das Goswami puts it, spaces in which they are "not required to embrace a new ethnicity." In Krishna West, the creation of such spaces is accomplished in three primary ways: reimagining what is acceptable for ISKCON practitioners to wear during devotional worship, redesigning the types of music they play during religious services and functions, and reenvisioning the varieties of devotional food that they eat and serve to others.

Of these three changes to the devotional culture of ISKCON that characterize Krishna West, Hridayananda Das Goswami spends the most time focusing on the clothing: namely, the fact that within Krishna West, devotees and visitors alike do not need to wear South Asian devotional clothing. This means that rather than wearing ISKCON's typical attire of *dhotīs*, *kurtās*, and sarees, those in Krishna West can instead participate in programs "as they are"—that is, dressed in conservative western clothing such as khakis, button-down shirts, blouses, trousers, and modest skirts and dresses. "The first thing you would find [in Krishna West]," Hridayananda Das Goswami told me one day, is that "you could come dressed as you are"; you could come and "be a western rational lady, without having to wear a saree."[43] It is problematic that Hridayananda Das Goswami equates wearing western clothing with being "rational" and also that he assumes a sort of standard and monolithic set of preferences that comprises western clothing taste (and tastes in food and music, as well). In fact, he makes a number of troubling statements and pronouncements when describing his Krishna West efforts. Nonetheless, Hridayananda Das Goswami builds his Krishna West project in large part on the idea that westerners should be able to practice in—and fully join—the ISKCON movement while wearing the clothing that ostensibly makes them comfortable, rather than the South Asian devotional clothing that he feels the movement's more traditional devotees and administrators socially pressure them to wear. As he told an audience in Denmark in 2015:

> Many leaders and devotees believe—what I consider to be a fiction—that if you take on Indian customs . . . if you take on Indian dress and all that stuff, you're actually a better devotee, that there's like ISKCON has first-class citizens and second-class citizens, and the first-class citizens are very Indian, and the second-class citizens are western . . . I think that's philosophically incorrect, historically incorrect, in every way it's incorrect. . . . They even say . . . in English they say that clothes don't make the man, and the way they say that in Italian, and Spanish, and I think even in French, and Portuguese, they say that like the habit, that the religious clothes don't make the monk. And so, I mean *everyone* in the world—except us—knows that. . . . I think if we cared as much about consciousness as we do about clothes, we'd probably be doing better.[44]

By "doing better," Hridayananda Das Goswami means that if devotees were given social leeway to wear the clothes that make them comfortable, there would be more westerners in ISKCON today. For his part Hridayananda Das Goswami models this approach in his own life by wearing khakis, polo shirts, V-neck sweaters, and even baseball caps in order to give those who might follow him the confidence to comfortably wear these western clothes themselves.

In addition to being able to wear the clothing that is culturally comfortable for them, devotees in and visitors to Krishna West are also given the opportunity to worship Krishna through devotional music that is also (ostensibly) culturally comfortable for them—namely western classical music and other forms of music that utilize western instruments, such as pianos, guitars, and the

Figure 5.2 Hridayananda Das Goswami speaking to a small group in Aarhus, Denmark. September 11, 2015. Screenshot by author.[45]

like. "Another difference about Krishna West," Hridayananda Das Goswami told me, "since you asked ya know, about week on week, is [that] . . . it's like we're open to culture. . . . The [standard ISKCON] idea is that Indian classical music is OK, but not Bach, or not Handel . . . [but] in fact, when I hear Handel or play it, it just takes me right to the spiritual world. . . . And frankly, Handel and Baroque music reminds me of Krishna much more than Indian classical music. It's just not my culture."[46]

This preference for western music that Hridayananda Das Goswami has, he says, is not just his own, but is one that he claims many other westerners whom he encounters in his role as an ISKCON guru also share: many westerners, he believes, simply are unable to feel connected to Krishna through Indian classical music. However, he claims that they are able to feel love for Krishna through music rooted in their own cultural traditions. "There was one Israeli really nice couple," he told me one day, who "came [to Krishna West] and because they're rediscovering themselves too [in this Krishna West process] . . . told me, 'Yeah, I loved classical music, but I thought it was bad or something.' And so I was playing for them, I was playing some Handel keyboard suites—this really exquisite keyboard music from Handel—and she was, ya know Krishna Dasi,[47] the lady, was really moved, and she said, 'I was just, like, envisioning Krishna's Rasa dance.'"[48]

Hridayananda Das Goswami shares a number of stories like this one—stories of people whom he claims had trouble accessing a deep emotional connection to Krishna through traditional ISKCON centers because the cultural barriers of the ISKCON movement were simply too much for them to break through. He argues, however, that the cultural accommodations that he is making in Krishna West—such as changes in the music—are allowing them to connect with Krishna in deeply felt emotional ways.

In many regards, the cultural changes that Hridayananda Das Goswami is bringing to ISKCON in his Krishna West program—especially those that involve music—stem from years of his own trial and error in trying to deepen his relationship to Krishna. As he shared with me on a number of occasions, he is an avid player of western classical music, and he often speaks of the hours that he spends playing Bach and Handel on his piano as being some of the times that he feels closest to Krishna. He believes, he says, that creating an ISKCON sub-movement in which other westerners can also feel close to Krishna through western music is a step in a positive direction for attracting them to the ISKCON movement and keeping them there.

There are several ways in which western music is incorporated into the liturgical programming of Krishna West. For starters, the *bhajans* (devotional songs) that are traditionally played in ISKCON centers worldwide are played in Krishna West on western musical instruments—pianos, guitars, harps, and the like. This gives Krishna West a different musical vibe than ISKCON's traditional centers, where the musical devotions are played on harmoniums, *karatālas*, and *mṛdaṅga* drums. In addition to utilizing western music in Krishna West liturgical programming, Hridayananda Das Goswami and his Krishna West disciples also *record* western-inflected *bhajans* to distribute to others. For example, on the Krishna West website, one can find a number of *bhajans* for download that feature traditional ISKCON songs in western-inflected musical renditions.[49] Finally, Hridayananda Das Goswami also writes and composes his own music for Krishna—that is, he creates *new* Krishna *bhajans* that are not part of the traditional ISKCON musical programming. This music is not intended to replace ISKCON's standard set of *bhajans* but rather to supplement it, and it is available for play on platforms such as SoundCloud. One such song, "Tears Falling From My Eyes," serves as an illustrative example.[50] The lyrics of this song, featured below, are an imaginative retelling of the immense joys of singing the names of Krishna (Hari). The song's lyrics are in English (unlike ISKCON's traditional *bhajans*), and the song is sung and recorded by Hridayananda Das Goswami himself, accompanied by a synthesized keyboard.

When I sing the holy name of Gauranga
There will be trembling in my body
Then I will be free

How happy I will be
And I'll sing "Hari, Hari!"
And love I'll realize
"Hari, Hari!"
Tears falling from my eyes
Like rain falls from the sky
When will I feel the mercy of Nitai?
For things of this world
I'll never laugh, I'll never cry
For my spirit will be free
To enjoy eternally
And I'll sing "Hari, Hari!"
And love I'll realize
"Hari, Hari!"
Tears falling from my eyes
Like rain falls from the sky
When will I know
That in this world all things must pass?
Life's like a dream
It all seems real but it won't last
But the spirit can be free
To enjoy eternally
If we sing "Hari, Hari!"
And love we'll realize
"Hari, Hari!"
Tears falling from our eyes
Like rain falls from the sky
When will I see
The holy land they call "Vrindavan"?
Boys and girls
Play with the Lord in Vrindavan
Forever young and free
How happy they must be
And they sing "Hari, Hari!"
And love they realize
"Hari, Hari!"
Tears falling from their eyes
Like rain falls from the sky[51]

Finally, if western clothes and western music are central to Krishna West, then so too is western food. Hridayananda Das Goswami and his Krishna

Figure 5.3 Hridayananda Das Goswami singing and playing western-inflected music in Krishna West. Screenshot by author.[52]

Figure 5.4 Hridayananda Das Goswami and devotees record western-inflected *bhajans* in Krishna West North Carolina. Photo courtesy of Krishna West North Carolina. Screenshot by author.[53]

Figure 5.5 Hridayananda Das Goswami singing western-inflected music in Krishna West North Carolina. Photo courtesy of Krishna West North Carolina. Screenshot by author.[54]

West disciples frequently note that there is no need to serve *only* Indian food at ISKCON centers (which is what has been the standard protocol in most ISKCON centers worldwide). Rather, they say ISKCON centers should serve food that is more akin to "western-style cuisine," especially if the movement hopes to attract more westerners. This is why, as a Krishna West administrator put it, the *prasādam* in Krishna West

> will not be in usually ethnically Indian *prasādam*. It's going to be *prasādam* or types of food that people can relate to. For example, we find sometimes devotees think that somehow or other Indian recipes are better than Western recipes and they go out on the street and they distribute *gulāb jāmuns* [honey-dipped fried donut holes] to people which, you know people

just they freak out if they get a *gulāb jāmun* in their hand. So, you know, we would prefer to distribute cookies to people, 'cause everyone can relate to cookies or crackers or something like that.[55]

Along with serving western food during their public preaching outings, however, Krishna West devotees also serve western food inside Krishna West centers during programs and other events. Dishes such as pizza, french fries, and salads, devotees told me, are popular. As one Krishna West disciple said, "I'm an American, and sometimes I just want french fries, ya know?"

Religious Adaptations

Hridayananda Das Goswami argues that if ISKCON devotees hope to attract westerners to the movement, they will have to create a separate space in the ISKCON house for them—a space of their own where westerners will feel comfortable to practice and stay in the movement for the long haul. As I have discussed thus far, part of what is involved in creating this space for westerners entails making *cultural* changes to ISKCON, such as designing centers wherein devotees can wear western clothes, worship by means of western music, and eat and serve western food.

However, equal in importance to making cultural changes in ISKCON for the sake of westerners' comfort, Hridayananda Das Goswami argues, is making several key *religious* adaptations to the movement—adaptations aimed at making ISKCON's ritual worship more comfortable for them. For Hridayananda Das Goswami, these adaptations mean that Krishna West centers will not have an emphasis on deity worship. In Krishna West, Hridayananda Das Goswami explains, "We are not going to have elaborate deity worship." Instead, "Krishna West devotees will . . . they will go to the traditional temples for deity worship."[56]

It is admittedly vague what Hridayananda Das Goswami means when he says that there will be no "elaborate deity worship" in Krishna West. This vagueness has to do, in part, with the fact that Krishna West is still a start-up. That is, despite the immense momentum that Krishna West has experienced in recent years, it is still a relatively new project on the ISKCON scene, having been started only in 2013.[57] As such, while there are a number of pilot centers that Krishna West disciples are heading up around the world, the path to building, staffing, and funding full-functioning Krishna West centers is a slow one.[58] It is therefore not entirely clear what a lack of elaborate deity worship will look like in these centers until they are fully running. Hridayananda Das Goswami is also slightly hesitant to give specifics about the place of deity worship in Krishna West centers, perhaps because he knows that it is a sensitive topic among devotees. He has even gone so far as to tell me that he thinks the topic is one that is "too hot to handle."[59]

Vagueness aside, however, when Hridayananda Das Goswami says that there will not be elaborate deity worship in Krishna West, what he seems to mean is that prominent three-dimensional *mūrtis* (embodied forms) of Krishna—especially the large ones that are typically housed in ISKCON temples—will not be present in Krishna West centers. This means there also won't be any of the associated rituals that characterize their intricate care (making sure their space is adequately adorned, feeding them, dressing them, putting them to sleep at night and waking them up in the morning, etc.). Rather, in Krishna West centers, there will be a simpler and more abridged set of ritual devotions, limited to song, *āratī*, incense offerings, and so on, as well as a simpler altar space that holds only a few pictures of Krishna, Chaitanya, Swami Prabhupada, and other figures of importance in ISKCON. "I mean, our centers will have *maṅgal āratī*, guru *puja*. It's a normal ISKCON program," Hridayananda Das Goswami says. "It's the same kind of program we did when Prabhupada was here . . . we do *kīrtan*, we have pictures of *paramparā*, *pañca-tattva*, Radha Krishna. . . . Again, devotees who really want to have a lot of deity worship, they'll go to the temples. So the temples should be happy."[60]

Hridayananda Das Goswami's decision to not have elaborate deity worship inside Krishna West centers is an effort on his part to transform ISKCON (a sub-movement of it, anyway) into a tradition with a "portable practice" and a "transposable message." Thomas J. Csordas argues that portable practices and transposable messages are necessary in order for religious traditions to "travel well" or move successfully beyond their cultural context of origin.[61] He writes:

> Two aspects of religions that must be attended to in determining whether or not they travel well, [are] what I will call portable practice and transposable message. By *portable practice*, I mean rites that can be easily learned, require relatively little esoteric knowledge or paraphernalia, are not held as proprietary or necessarily linked to a specific cultural context, and can be performed without commitment to an elaborate ideological or institutional apparatus. . . . By *transposable message*, I mean that the basis of appeal contained in religious tenets, premises, or promises can find footing across diverse linguistic and cultural settings.[62]

Put simply, religious groups that have portable practices and transposable messages travel well, whereas those without them tend to remain isolated to the particular cultures in which they originated. It is for these reasons, Csordas notes, that "the many forms of yoga are perhaps the archetypal instances of portable practice" because "explicit bodily practices [can be] accompanied by more or less spiritual elaboration and [] may or may not form the basis for communal commitments or transformation of everyday life."[63] Similarly, Chinese feng shui is also an example of a portable practice because it "can be applied in any cultural setting in which the felicitous orientation of energy in space can be construed as appealing."[64] By taking elaborate deity worship out of Krishna West centers, Hridayananda Das Goswami hopes that he can not only make ISKCON's practices similarly portable and its messages equally transposable but also that he can thereby make the ISKCON movement itself more sellable. "I am not anti-deity worship," he says. "I am pro-saving the world[65] . . . [and] the fastest growing religions in the world don't necessarily have elaborate deity worship."[66] Just as many global-reaching gurus know that in order to sell their religious traditions widely, they must downplay the ritual and culturally embedded practices of their traditions (as Joanne Punzo Waghorne, Amanda J. Lucia, Jeff Wilson, and others discussed in chap. 3 have shown us), Hridayananda Das Goswami also operates on a similar understanding.[67] As he himself explains it, the lack of elaborate deity worship in Krishna West is "not an attempt to create a new movement, it's not trying to change anything. It's just creating a space within ISKCON where large numbers of western people can become Vaishnavas."[68] Put differently, it is just creating a religiously comfortable room for westerners in the larger ISKCON house.

CONCLUSION: JUSTIFYING KRISHNA WEST

In its short history, Krishna West has stirred a lot of controversy and resistance within the ISKCON movement. Some of this resistance has consisted of heated criticism of Krishna West, levied at Hridayananda Das Goswami and his disciples by more conservatively leaning ISKCON members. Other resistance, however, has come from far more official ISKCON channels, most notably ISKCON's own Governing Body Commission (GBC).

The GBC has enacted its resistance to Krishna West in a number of ways. First and foremost, it has imposed travel bans on Hridayananda Das Goswami, meant to limit his preaching of Krishna West. In 2014, for example, Hridayananda Das Goswami wrote a letter to his disciples explaining that "based on GBC concerns about Krishna West, the GBC decided that I should not go to Europe at this time . . . 'until we can come to an agreement regarding these problems and misunderstandings.'"[69] The GBC has also enacted its resistance to Krishna West in other, subtler ways—such as by exerting social pressure on Hridayananda Das Goswami to stop his spreading of Krishna West. In 2016, just two years after he was banned from traveling to Europe in order to preach, Hridayananda Das Goswami posted a letter to his disciples on Facebook stating the following: "For two and a half years, I have tried my best to explain what I feel is the best way to spread our movement in the West," but in order to "make a greater effort to avoid disturbing [ ] people . . . I will focus on my personal creative writing . . . [which] will require me to live a somewhat secluded life."[70] This written statement came immediately after Hridayananda Das Goswami had a meeting with two high-level leaders in the ISKCON movement who were sent from Ireland and California to meet with him to officially discuss Krishna West.[71]

There are a number of reasons why the GBC body and other ISKCON members have criticized and actively resisted Krishna West. The issue that has raised the most controversy for them, however, is the fact that Hridayananda Das Goswami has repeatedly said that Krishna West is not a bridge but a destination. "I'm saying," he told me one afternoon, "and this is something which really rankled some people—really hit them in a nerve—I said Krishna West is not a bridge, it's a final destination."[72] The reason this has "rankled some people" or, as another Krishna West associate put it, that it "sometimes can be taken in a way that's a little controversial"[73] is because Krishna West as it has been conceived and piloted by Hridayananda Das Goswami looks and feels radically different from the ISKCON movement with which most contemporary devotees are familiar. Moreover, unlike other programs (such as the Mantra Lounge, Bhakti Center, etc.), which present a radically different (or rebranded) ISKCON to westerners in order to draw them into more traditional ISKCON centers (namely temples), Hridayananda Das Goswami's Krishna West is both the starting *and* the ending point of recruitment for westerners. And this raises fears in the eyes of many in the movement, including those in the GBC, who worry that Hridayananda Das Goswami is creating not an ISKCON submovement but another ISKCON movement—not a new room in the ISKCON house but a new house altogether.

But Hridayananda Das Goswami adamantly maintains that he is not creating a new ISKCON movement at all. As one of his Krishna West administrators puts it, "One of the things that Hridayananda Maharaj said sometimes can be taken in a way that's a little controversial: he says Krishna West is not a bridge, it's a destination. That doesn't mean it's not ISKCON: Krishna West *is* ISKCON, it's *fully* ISKCON."[74] But how does Hridayananda Das Goswami justify his position that Krishna West is fully ISKCON when it looks radically different from ISKCON as it is practiced in most worldwide ISKCON centers—that is, when it cuts out many of the cultural and religious characteristics that typify most other ISKCON centers?

In order to understand how Hridayananda Das Goswami justifies this view, it is helpful to examine closely how exactly he conceptualizes Krishna West. In order to do so, it is necessary to look at chapter 1.2 (first section, second chapter) of the *Bhaktirasāmṛtasindhu* of Rupa Goswami, a text that Hridayananda Das Goswami cites frequently. In *Bhaktirasāmṛtasindhu* 1.2.72, Rupa Goswami begins to list "to the best of his judgment" the sixty-four practices that are the most important dimensions of *Vaidhī Bhakti* ("rule-based" *bhakti*).[75] These practices include, among others, surrendering at the guru's feet, taking initiation, learning from, and trustingly serving the guru (*guru-pādāśrayastasmāt kṛṣṇa-dīkṣādi-śikṣaṇam/ viśrambheṇa guroḥ sevā*),[76,] as well as inquiring into true religious duty (*saddharma-pṛcchā*),[77] renouncing mundane enjoyment for Krishna (*bhogādi-tyāgaḥ kṛṣṇasya hetave*),[78] and singing Krishna's names (*nāmasaṅkīrtanaṁ*).[79]

Within ISKCON, devotees have their own rendition of the *Bhaktirasāmṛtasindhu*, which is Prabhupada's abridged translation and interpretation of the text, *The Nectar of Devotion* (with *Nectar of Devotion* being Prabhupada's English translation of the title *Bhaktirasāmṛtasindhu*). In *Nectar of Devotion*, Prabhupada also lists and discusses these sixty-four practices, albeit with his own gloss and in an abridged form. Before listing them, however, he first introduces them, providing the reader with an explanatory framework within which to understand them. He writes:

> Śrīla Rūpa Gosvāmī states that his elder brother (Sanātana Gosvāmī) has complied *Hari-bhakti-vilāsa* for the guidance of *Vaiṣṇavas*, and therein has mentioned many rules and regulations to be followed by the *Vaiṣṇavas*. Some of them are very important and prominent, and he will now mention these very important items for our benefit. The purport of this statement is that Śrila [*sic*] Rūpa Gosvāmī proposes to mention only basic principles, not details. For example, a basic principle is that one has to accept a spiritual master. Exactly how one follows the instructions of his spiritual master is considered a detail. . . . The basic principle of acceptance of a spiritual master is good everywhere, although the details may be different. Śrīla Rūpa Gosvāmī does not wish to enter into details here, but he wants to place before us only the principles.[80]

The way that Prabhupada introduces the sixty-four practices of *Vaidhī Bhakti* is extremely important for Hridayananda Das Goswami's conceptualization of—and ultimate justification for—the Krishna West sub-movement. This is because it provides the basis for his argument that within Krishna Consciousness, there are essential principles and there are nonessential principles (or, more aptly, there are basic principles and there are details). The basic principles, he argues, are the important and eternal dimensions of Krishna Consciousness—namely, the sixty-four practices that are mentioned in *The Nectar of Devotion* and in the *Bhaktirasāmṛtasindhu*. By contrast, the details are all of those dimensions that are ultimately unimportant for Krishna Consciousness: namely, those which Prabhupada points out that Rupa Goswami did not mention. Using this schema, Hridayananda Das Goswami justifies the changes he makes to ISKCON in his Krishna West sub-movement; since Rupa Goswami did not mention a preference for clothing type, food style, or musical instruments, then these dimensions of Krishna Consciousness must be details. As such, one can make changes to them at will while at the same time keeping the "true essence" or basic principles of the ISKCON movement intact. As Hridayananda Das Goswami explained in an intimate discussion that he led in Aarhus, Denmark, on September 11, 2015:

> We really need to understand this crucial distinction that Rupa Goswami makes in Chapter Six of *The Nectar of Devotion*. He distinguishes between basic principles and details. So, for example, chanting Hare Krishna, accepting a bona fide guru, honoring Tulsi Devi, reading *Bhāgavatam* [*Bhāgavata Purāṇa*], associating with devotees, these are basic principles, so we can't change that. Other things are details. So clearly, for example, how one dresses, or the particular music style, or what recipes you use, what architecture, and so on, those are clearly details. And so the idea, this, frankly I think somewhat mythological idea, that there is an ideal eternal architecture, cuisine, dress, music style, etc. which are most favorable for Krishna Consciousness—it would have been so much easier if Rupa Goswami would have *mentioned* that, or if the *Bhāgavatam* would have mentioned that or if *somebody* would have mentioned it. Prabhupada sometimes expressed his own preference for that, but *many* other times he said it's actually not important. It's actually not important, that the real point is Krishna Consciousness. So, there is something tragic in the International Society for Krishna Consciousness becoming the International Society for Indian ethnic traditions.[81]

Putting it all together, Hridayananda Das Goswami believes that there is an essential set of practices and dimensions of Krishna Consciousness *that alone* make up the ISKCON movement's core. These practices and dimensions, for him, are chanting the Hare Krishna *mahā mantra*, understanding and living the philosophy (or the basic teachings handed down to devotees by Prabhupada), eating *prasādam* and serving it to others, and following the four regulative principles. These alone, he argues, coupled with the other of the sixty-four dimensions, comprise the necessary components for a sub-movement to be fully ISKCON. Everything else is what he calls "ethnic trappings," or details that are external and not eternal: details that are unimportant, unnecessary, and expendable. In this way, his argument that in Krishna West we "tr[y] to distill just the purest spiritual science [of the ISKCON movement] and spare people the onerous and superfluous obligation of becoming ethnically Indian,"[82] encapsulates the crux of his conceptualization of Krishna West; he believes that Krishna West has captured the essence of the ISKCON movement and has cut out only the extraneous "ethnic trappings." Of course, this move of wanting to siphon out a pure essence of a Hindu religious tradition—especially so as to make it appealing to a predominantly western audience and western set of religious values—was also present in problematic colonial, missionary, and Orientalist criticisms of Hinduism as well as in the Hindu reform movements that they inspired. Moreover, it was operative in the essentialist theories of religion that characterized the field of religious studies' earliest interpretative foundations and that problematically attempted to separate religion from culture. Troubling though it is, however, for Hridayananda Das Goswami, this belief in the possibility of siphoning out ISKCON's pure essence is a critical move in his justification that Krishna West is fully ISKCON, different though it may be from what devotees call "standard" ISKCON. And importantly, he bolsters this position that Krishna West is fully ISKCON by suggesting that Prabhupada *himself* would also share it—noting, as he does frequently, that Prabhupada was not concerned about extraneous details either. For example, he makes use of a number of citations from Prabhupada that quote him telling his disciples that "dress you can have as you like" and that "if karmi dress is favorable, then go with karmi dress. We have to execute missionary activities; dress is not fundamental."[83] He even quotes Prabhupada saying that "our only concern is to attract people to Krsna [*sic*] consciousness. We may do this in the dress of sannyasis or in the regular dress of gentlemen. Our *only concern* is to spread interest in Krsna [*sic*] consciousness."[84]

The one tricky issue left to consider, however, is whether Hridayananda Das Goswami thinks that "elaborate deity worship" is also an "ethnic trapping" or an extraneous detail that can be cut unproblematically from a fully ISKCON sub-movement. As indicated earlier, Hridayananda Das Goswami's precise position on deity worship can be hard to tease out because he often remains vague in his discussions of it. I did, however, have the occasion to ask him this question directly during a formal interview that I conducted with him on June 15, 2015. In this conversation, he was amply clear on his view that according to ISKCON's philosophy, elaborate deity worship is a detail. "It *is* optional," he said.[85] "First of all, it *is* optional. Even the *Bhāgavatam* says that there's various processes [or] devotional services—they usually say nine—like *śravaṇam, kīrtanam*, hearing, [and] chanting. And so *pūjanam*—deity worship—is one of them, and it says you can perform one of these, two, three. So yeah, it is optional. According to our philosophy, it's optional."[86]

But not only is it optional according to ISKCON's textual foundations; Hridayananda Das Goswami also argues that elaborate deity worship did not have a prominent place in the ISKCON movement historically either and that its present prominence is only a result of the movement's large Indian Hindu demographic.[87] In fact, he says, in the early days of the movement, "Prabhupada said the temples exist as bases for preaching, and to keep the devotees strong, we do some deity worship."[88] However, "in America at least, and I suspect in other countries as well, this was *totally inverted*, [or] put on its head, so that [now] the temples exist for deity worship, and in order to pay for it, we do a little preaching."[89] He adds:

> At the same time, all these Indians came into the West and they love deity worship—you know, basically what they want is the deity worship—and [so it was a] perfect match. So the temples just became not places to preach, but places to do *puja*. And the more people that come to see the *puja*, the more we spread the movement, even if very few of the people coming to see the *puja* are actually from that [local] country originally. . . . And so you can see all these different ways in which we kinda got it backwards.[90]

In answer to the question regarding elaborate deity worship, then, Hridayananda Das Goswami not only thinks that it is a detail but also that it is a detail that is a relatively new addition to the ISKCON movement. From his perspective, therefore, it is not so much scandalous that he has cut out elaborate deity worship from Krishna West but rather that elaborate deity worship ever came to have such a prominent place in contemporary ISKCON in the first place. (The fact that various dimensions of deity worship are among the sixty-four principles that Prabhupada notes as being discussed by Rupa Goswami is something that Hridayananda Das Goswami conveniently does not mention.)

With these hard-argued justifications for Krishna West as fully ISKCON, Hridayananda Das Goswami has made great strides in convincing more and more ISKCON devotees of the legitimacy of his Krishna West sub-movement.

And while he still has a number of detractors, he has managed to make some headway with ISKCON's GBC. Just recently, in fact—in October of 2017—Hridayananda Das Goswami "met with the GBC body and a special subcommittee to discuss some mutual philosophical concerns and Krishna West."[91] Out of this meeting came one of the first official glimpses of hope for Krishna West in the form of the release of a "Shared Statement of the GBC Body and Hridayananda Das Goswami." It reads:

> The GBC Body and Hridayananda Das Goswami are jointly striving towards a better integration of Krishna West within the general ISKCON preaching strategy. The GBC body has requested Hridayananda Das Goswami to serve as the GBC for Brazil, provisional to confirmation at the AGM [Annual General Meeting]. . . . We are grateful for everyone's cooperation in this matter. While this group endeavors to come to a mutually beneficial and encouraging path forward, we request the assembly of devotees to maintain a respectful attitude towards all parties involved and avoid criticism on either side of the issue.[92]

With this shared statement, the GBC seems to have struck a somewhat reconciliatory tone with Hridayananda Das Goswami and offered hope that his Krishna West sub-movement can eventually find a comfortable place in the ISKCON home. At the very least, they have given him the official go-ahead to go forth and try to attract westerners to join his Krishna West sub-movement. And although only time will tell of its success, as one Krishna West administrator put it, "The proof [will be] in the pudding. Ya know, when we start to make a lot of devotees, then there'll be a mad rush to copy. . . . It'll be proven by success. And if it's not successful, whatever, I mean at least we are trying to spread Krishna Consciousness. That's the whole idea."[93]

NOTES

1. Discussion with devotee. In person, Philadelphia, Pennsylvania. October 1, 2017.

2. Ibid.

3. Krishna West website. "Who We Are: H. D. Goswami." Accessed June 4, 2019. https://krishnawest.com/who-we-are/h-d-goswami/.

4. Hridayananda Das Goswami. Interview by Nicole Karapanagiotis. Conducted via Skype, Wilmington, Delaware, June 15, 2015; Hridayananda Das Goswami. Interview by Nicole Karapanagiotis. Conducted via Skype, Wilmington, Delaware, October 23, 2015; ISKCONLeaders.Com. "ISKCON Leaders: Hridayananda Das Goswami." Accessed March 23, 2018.

http://iskconleaders.com/hridayananda-das-goswami/; HDGoswami.Com. "H.D. Goswami." Accessed March 23, 2018. http://hdgoswami.com/; Official Website of the Governing Body Commission of ISKCON. "Hridayananda das Goswami." Accessed March 23, 2018. https://gbc.iskcon.org/hridayananda-das-goswami/.

5. ISKCONLeaders.Com, "ISKCON Leaders." For more background on Hridayananda Das Goswami, see also Dr. Howard J. Resnick website. "Dr. Howard J. Resnick." Accessed March 23, 2018. http://www.howardjresnick.com/.

6. Goswami 2015, Interview, June 15.

7. Hridayananda Das Goswami. 2014. "KRISHNA WEST—The Interview, Vol. 1." 46:35–48:14. GourTube YouTube channel, March 20. Accessed March 27, 2018. https://www.youtube.com/watch?v=2EEO5_2HVdc. Italics in original.

8. Gaura-Nitai refers to Chaitanya and his close associate Nityananda, respectively. ISKCON devotees believe that Chaitanya was none other than Krishna himself, who descended to earth in human form in order to spread love of Krishna around the world. Nityananda is believed to be the human form of Krishna's brother, Balarama. Because they are believed to have spent their lives in perpetual devotion to Krishna and in the constant spreading of his names, Chaitanya and Nityananda are figures of both worship and emulation within ISKCON.

9. Goswami 2014, "The Interview, Vol. 1," 49:07–50:35. Italics in original.

10. Ibid., 50:37–52:14. Italics in original.

11. By liberal, I mean liberal for ISKCON. See Hridayananda Das Goswami. 2005. "Vaisnava Moral Theology and Homosexuality," February 2. Accessed March 27, 2018. http://hdgoswami.com/essays/vaisnava-moral-theology-and-homosexuality/. See also Hridayananda Das Goswami. 2015. "The Vaiṣṇavī Guru," May 19. Accessed March 27, 2018. http://hdgoswami.com/essays/the-vaisnavi-guru-essay/. Besides writing essays on same-sex relationships (and on women gurus) within ISKCON, Hridayananda Das Goswami has also spoken widely on these topics. In his talks, he has been critical of arguments that aim to suppress women's leadership rights. He is also widely reported to have given his blessing to a same-sex couple for their commitment ceremony in 2008.

12. Hridayananda Das Goswami. 2014. "KRISHNA WEST—The Interview, Vol. 2." GourTube YouTube channel, November 20. 1:11:35–1:11:43. Accessed May 11, 2017. https://www.youtube.com/watch?v=X3q7l5L_E5w&t=3360s.

13. Ibid., 6:48–8:05. Italics in original.

14. Hridayananda Das Goswami. 2015. "Ideal Vedic Culture—Krishna West Istagosthi with H. D. GOSWAMI." Daniel Laflor YouTube channel, September 29. 15:15–18:15. Accessed February 24, 2017. https://www.youtube.com/watch?v=YottYzI98_M. Emphasis in original.

15. Edward P. Lazear. 1995. "Bait and Switch." *Journal of Political Economy* 103, no. 4: 813–830, 813.

16. Goswami 2014, "The Interview, Vol. 2," 12:39–14:03. Italics added for emphasis.

17. Ibid., 1:14-37–1:15:02. Italics added for emphasis.

18. Goswami 2015, Interview, June 15.

19. This statement has become proverbially commonplace in the United States, but it can be traced to Dr. King's sermon "Remaining Awake Through a Great Revolution," which he most famously delivered at the National Cathedral in Washington, DC, on March 31, 1968. Kathleen Garces-Foley. 2007a. *Crossing the Ethnic Divide: The Multiethnic Church on a Mission*. New York: Oxford University Press, 79, 167.

20. Donald A. McGavran. 1970. *Understanding Church Growth*. Revised and edited by C. Peter Wagner (1990). Grand Rapids, MI: William B. Eerdmans, 163.

21. Michael O. Emerson and Karen Chai Kim. 2003. "Multiracial Congregations: An Analysis of Their Development and a Typology." *Journal for the Scientific Study of Religion* 42, no 2: 217–227, 218.

22. See Emerson and Kim 2003, 217, and Kathleen Garces-Foley. 2007b. "New Opportunities and New Values: The Emergence of the Multicultural Church." *The Annals of the American Academy of Political and Social Science* 612: 209–224, 210. This widely cited number is based on a definition of diversity, derived from George Yancey, Karen Chai Kim, and Michael Emerson's "Multiracial Congregations and Their Peoples" project, which defines a diverse congregation as "a congregation in which *no one racial group accounts for 80 percent or more of the membership*." Curtiss Paul DeYoung, Michael O. Emerson, George Yancey, and Karen Chai Kim. 2003. *United by Faith: The Multiracial Congregation as an Answer to the Problem of Race*. New York: Oxford University Press, 3. Italics in Original. Although this definition of diversity is based in particular on the category of race (referring specifically to congregations that are multiracial) and although the categories of race, culture, and ethnicity are by no means synonymous, this definition of diversity is nonetheless widely used in scholarship to discuss congregations that are diverse according to measures other than race (such as ethnicity and culture). One reason is because congregants themselves often do not distinguish between these categories. The reader will notice this lack of distinguishing between categories in the language of the Krishna Branders, as well as in the language of other ISKCON devotees more broadly (as the reader will notice in this chapter and others). See Garces-Foley 2007b, 211.

23. Kevin D. Dougherty. 2003. "How Monochromatic Is Church Membership? Racial-Ethnic Diversity in Religious Community." *Sociology of Religion* 64, no. 1: 65–85, 70.

24. Ibid., 82.

25. Amanda J. Lucia. 2014b. *Reflections of Amma: Devotees in Global Embrace*. Berkeley and Los Angeles: University of California Press, 186.

26. Ibid., 151.

27. Ibid., 151. Importantly, Lucia notes that African Americans and members of the Latinx community also "demonstrate a significant and increasing presence in spiritual communities derived from Asian religions."

28. Goswami 2015, Interview, June 15.

29. Goswami 2015, Interview, June 15.

30. Names made up for the sake of example.

31. *Kurtās* and sarees are not exclusively Hindu; they are worn in South Asia by a variety of religious practitioners, including Muslims, for example.

32. Goswami 2015, Interview, June 15.

33. Cynthia Eller. 1993. *Living in the Lap of the Goddess: The Feminist Spirituality Movement in America.* New York: The Crossroad, 77.

34. Laura E. Donaldson. 2001. "On Medicine Women and White Shame-ans: New Age Native Americanism and Commodity Fetishism as Pop Culture Feminism." In *Women, Gender, Religion: A Reader.* Elizabeth A Castelli, ed. (assisted by Rosamond C. Rodman). New York: Palgrave, 247.

35. Ibid.

36. Lucia 2014b.

37. Ibid., 215.

38. Ibid., 214.

39. Goswami 2014, "The Interview, Vol. 2," 14:10–14:45. Emphasis in original.

40. Goswami 2015, "Ideal Vedic Culture," 18:17–19:03. Italics added for emphasis.

41. Goswami 2015, Interview, June 15.

42. Krishna West website. "Krishna West Mission: Inspiring Purposeful Living." Accessed March 29, 2018. http://krishnawest.com/about/mission/. Italics added for emphasis.

43. Goswami 2015, Interview, June 15.

44. Goswami 2015, "Ideal Vedic Culture," 30:41–33:37. Emphasis in original.

45. Goswami 2015, "Ideal Vedic Culture," 18:17–19:03.

46. Goswami 2015, Interview, June 15.

47. Name has been changed to protect anonymity.

48. Goswami 2015, Interview, June 15.

49. Krishna West *bhajans* are featured on a SoundCloud site linked off of its main site. Krishna West SoundCloud. "Krishna West SoundCloud." Accessed March 29, 2018. https://soundcloud.com/krishna-west. See also Krishna West website. Accessed March 29, 2018. http://krishnawest.com/.

50. Krishna West SoundCloud.

51. Ibid.

52. Hridayananda Das Goswami—Friends and Disciples Facebook group (public). Posted June 20, 2015. Accessed April 4, 2018. https://www.facebook.com/groups/acharyadeva/.

53. Krishna West Inc. Facebook page (public). Posted May 28, 2014. Accessed April 4, 2018. https://www.facebook.com/pg/krishnawestinc/photos/?ref=page_internal.

54. Krishna West Inc. Facebook page (public). Posted July 12, 2014. Accessed April 4, 2018. https://www.facebook.com/pg/krishnawestinc/photos/?ref=page_internal.

55. Bir Krishna Dasa Goswami. 2014. "Krishna West Overview by Bir Krishna Dasa Goswami, Part 1." YouTube video, April 15. 7:47–8:19. Accessed February 19, 2017. https://www.youtube.com/watch?v=bShPRTP1IJw.

56. Goswami 2014, "The Interview, Vol. 2," 52:12–52:22.

57. Krishna West website. "Krishna West: Who Are We? H. D. Goswami is an Early Pioneer and Renowned Teacher of *Bhakti Yoga* in the Western World." Accessed March 30, 2018. http://krishnawest.com/who-we-are/h-d-goswami/.

58. A list of current worldwide Krishna West projects can be found at Krishna West website. "Projects." Accessed March 30, 2018. http://krishnawest.com/projects/.

59. Goswami 2015, Interview, June 15.

60. Goswami 2014, "The Interview, Vol. 2," 54:55–56:00.

61. Thomas J. Csordas. 2009. "Introduction: Modalities of Transnational Transcendence." In *Transnational Transcendence: Essays on Religion and Globalization*. Thomas J. Csordas, ed. Berkeley: University of California Press, 1–29, 4.

62. Ibid., 4–5. Italics in original.

63. Ibid., 4.

64. Ibid., 4.

65. Goswami 2014, "The Interview, Vol. 2," 1:12:32–1:12:39.

66. Ibid., 53:27–53:54.

67. Joanne Punzo Waghorne. 2014b. "From Diaspora to (Global) Civil Society: Global Gurus and the Processes of De-ritualization and De-ethnization in Singapore." In *Hindu Ritual at the Margins: Innovations, Transformations, Reconsiderations*. Linda Penkower and Tracy Pintchman, eds. Columbia: University of South Carolina Press, 186–207; Lucia, Amanda J. 2014a. "Innovative Gurus: Tradition and Change in Contemporary Hinduism." *International Journal of Hindu Studies* 18, no. 2: 221–263; and Jeff Wilson. 2014. *Mindful America: The Mutual Transformation of Buddhist Meditation and American Culture*. Oxford and New York: Oxford University Press. See also Jeremy Carette and Richard King. 2005. *Selling Spirituality: The Silent Takeover of Religion*. Abingdon and New York: Routledge.

68. Goswami 2014, "The Interview, Vol. 2," 54:21–54:33.

69. Hridayananda Das Goswami. 2014. "Hridayananda Dasa Goswami Responds to GBC Disapproval of Krishna West" (letter, retitled). Published on March 6. OneISKCON.com. Accessed September 19, 2014. http://www

.oneiskcon.com/hridayananda-dasa-goswami-responds-to-gbc-disapproval-of-krishna-west/.

70. Hridayananda Das Goswami. 2016. "Letter to Devotees." Hridayananda Das Goswami Facebook page, January 7. Accessed April 2, 2018. https://www.facebook.com/hridayanandadasgoswami/posts/1717759215121769.

71. Ibid. Immediately following this letter, Hridayananda Das Goswami posted another one on his Facebook page clarifying his position that by taking on a more secluded life, he did not mean that he was abandoning Krishna West. Rather, he noted that he is "NOT retiring from Krishna West" and that he "would continue to support those devotees who help me." (Emphasis in original.) In the time that followed these letters, Hridayananda Das Goswami continued to work quietly on his Krishna West projects, acting as an advisor to his many worldwide disciples who were heading up Krishna West projects on his behalf. Both letters can be found on his website. Hridayananda Das Goswami. 2016. "An Important GBC Update—January 6, 2016." Accessed April 3, 2018. http://hdgoswami.com/chronicals/letters/an-important-gbc-update-january-6-2016/.

72. Goswami 2015, Interview, June 15.

73. Bir Krishna Dasa Goswami. 2014. "Krishna West Overview by Bir Krishna Dasa Goswami, Part 2." YouTube video, April 15. 1:23–1:26. Accessed May 11, 2017. https://www.youtube.com/watch?v=TBYnL9rTfgc.

74. Ibid., 1:21–1:34. Emphasis in original.

75. *haribhaktivilāse'syā bhakterangāni lakṣaśaḥ/ kintu tāni prasiddhāni nirdiśyante yathāmati.* Rūpagosvāmī. *Bhaktirasāmṛtasindhu. The Bhaktirasāmṛtasindhu of Rūpa Gosvāmin.* Translated with Introduction and Notes by David L. Haberman. 2003. New Delhi and Delhi: Indira Gandhi National Centre for the Arts and Motilal Banarsidass Publishers, 1.2.72. In this verse, Rupa Goswami notes that the *bhakti* practices he will list are from the *Hari-Bhakti-Vilāsa.* The *Hari-Bhakti-Vilāsa* is a Gauḍīya Vaishnava text, attributed to Gopala Bhatta Goswami, that focuses on practices and rules for the ritual worship of Krishna. These practices and rules are typically identified in Vaishnava literature as part of the path of *Vaidhī Bhakti* or the path of devotion that is based on textual rules and injunctions. *Vaidhī Bhakti* is the other side of the spectrum from *Rāgānugā Bhakti,* the *bhakti* path wherein devotees cultivate love of Krishna by imitating the emotions and moods of his paradigmatic associates. Rupa Goswami discusses these two distinct types of *bhakti* throughout the *Bhaktirasāmṛtasindhu.* See also David. L. Haberman. 1988. *Acting as a Way of Salvation: A Study of Rāgānugā Bhakti Sādhana.* Delhi: Motilal Banarsidass Publishers. The *Hari-Bhakti-Vilāsa,* along with the practices of *Vaidhī Bhakti* more generally, is of central importance within the ISKCON movement. Within ISKCON, the *Hari-Bhakti-Vilāsa* is attributed to Sanatana Goswami, whom devotees believe wrote it pseudonymously in the name of Gopala Bhatta Goswami.

76. Rūpagosvāmī, 2.1.74.

77. Ibid., 2.1.75.

78. Ibid., 2.1.75.

79. Ibid., 1.1.92.

80. A. C. Bhaktivedanta Swami Prabhupada. 1970. *The Nectar of Devotion: The Complete Science of Bhakti Yoga.* New York: The Bhaktivedanta Book Trust, 53.

81. Goswami 2015, "Ideal Vedic Culture," 0:30–2:24.

82. Goswami 2015, Interview, June 15.

83. Hridayananda Das Goswami. 2015. "Reply to Senior Leader." Unpublished essay. Posted on Hridayananda das Goswami—Friends and Disciples Facebook page (public), October 24. Accessed May 11, 2017. https://www.facebook.com/groups/acharyadeva/permalink/10153917775293646/. In the early days of the movement, devotees used to refer to non-devotees as *karmis,* a term they used to mean "those who are bound up in mundane life in the 'material world.'" Moreover, it was often the case that when devotees went out in public to preach (in parks, etc.), they would do so dressed in *karmi clothes* or the *street clothes* of non-devotees. It has even been reported that devotees would don wigs in their public preaching so as to maximize the preachers' odds of recruiting outsiders. See E. Burke Rochford Jr. 2004. "Airport, Conflict, and Change in the Hare Krishna Movement." In *The Hare Krishna Movement: The Postcharismatic Fate of a Religious Transplant.* Edwin F. Bryant and Maria L. Ekstrand, eds. New York: Columbia University Press.

84. Ibid., 9.

85. Goswami 2015, Interview, June 15. Italics in original.

86. Goswami 2015, Interview, June 15. Italics in original. The practices Hridayananda Das Goswami mentions are collectively known in Hinduism as the *navdhā bhakti* (ninefold *bhakti*). These ninefold practices include: *śravaṇam* (hearing), *kīrtanam,* (singing), *smaraṇam* (remembering), *pādsevanam* (serving God's feet), *arcanam* (worship), *vandanam* (prostration), *dāsyam* (servitude), *sakhyam* (friendship), and *ātmanivedanam* (dedication of one's being/self-surrender). They can be found in *Bhāgavata Purāṇa,* 7.5.23: *Śravaṇam kīrtanam viṣṇoḥ smaraṇam pādsevanam/ arcanam vandanam dāsyam sakhyamātmanivedanam.* C. L. Goswami and M. A. Shastri. 2003. *Śrīmad Bhāgavata Mahāpurāṇa* (with Sanskrit text and English translation), Part 1 (book 1 to 8). Gorakhpur: Gita Press.

87. Goswami 2015, Interview, June 15. Italics in original. E. Burke Rochford Jr., argues a similar point in *Hare Krishna Transformed,* noting that many ISKCON temples in the United States would have failed if not for the financial contributions of the Indian Hindu community. This financial need, he suggests, drives temple practices (such as focus on the deities), as devotees want to ensure

that the wishes of their largest donors are satisfied. E. Burke Rochford Jr. 2007. *Hare Krishna Transformed*. New York: New York University Press. There are many devotees in the movement, however, who maintain that the deities have always had a central place in ISKCON, even during Prabhupada's time.

88. Goswami 2015, "Ideal Vedic Culture," 1:04:59–1:05:07.

89. Ibid., 1:05:08–1:05:20. Italics in original.

90. Ibid., 1:06:56–1:08:30.

91. Ananda Tirtha Das. 2017. "Shared Statement of the GBC Body & Hridayananda Das Goswami," October 19. ISKCONNews.Org. Accessed March 30, 2018. https://iskconnews.org/shared-statement-of-the-gbc-body-hridayananda-das-goswami,6325.

92. Ibid.

93. Bir Krishna Dasa Goswami. 2014. "Krishna West Overview by Bir Krishna Dasa Goswami, Part 3." YouTube video, April 16. 10:05–11:01. Accessed May 11, 2017. https://www.youtube.com/watch?v=4PrVXbMyNI8.

CONCLUSION

ISKCON of Philadelphia is one of the oldest ISKCON temples in North America. Although formally established in 1977, the building in which the community is located was constructed much earlier, just around turn of the century. The building, which currently houses two residential facilities and a temple, used to be the historic Cresheim Arms Hotel, a celebrated landmark within Philadelphia in the Mt. Airy section of the city, a neighborhood that advertised itself on old postcards as "the highest altitude and most salubrious residential section of Philadelphia."[1] The oldest wing of the Cresheim Arms Hotel, sources suggest, dates back to the 1890s, and this wing now serves as one of the temple's two residential halls.[2]

Although the historic nature of the ISKCON of Philadelphia building lends an old-world charm to the community, since the building is over 120 years old and has not been updated since devotees took up residence in the 1970s, it currently looks more old than old-world. Put frankly, the building has fallen into a state of serious disrepair in recent decades. In fact, with peeling paint, broken window screens, and chipped wood siding that runs the periphery of the building, it might be assumed to be abandoned by a passerby, if not for the cars that fill the parking lot on Sunday evenings for the highly attended weekly feast program.

Over the past few years, the temple community at ISKCON of Philadelphia decided that they wanted to revamp and renovate their building. Initially, there was great excitement over the possibilities for the project, and devotees met regularly and with enthusiasm to discuss their visions for it. However, as the planning developed and over time turned to particulars, there came to be many disputes over the renovation project. As these disputes grew in frequency

Figure 6.1 Exterior of New ISKCON of Philadelphia temple (middle building). October 9, 2018. Photo taken by author. Philadelphia, Pennsylvania.

and intensity, they led to rampant infighting within the community and to an eventual stalemate on the project.

In the summer of 2017, after several years of infighting, the temple appointed a new vice president—a longtime ISKCON devotee and Radhanath Swami disciple—in order to move the project forward.[3] With his new position, the vice president was charged with the incredibly difficult task of trying to bring the community together to decide on the contours of the renovation project and to bring the project to fruition. After much negotiation, the community at ISKCON of Philadelphia—with the new vice president at the helm—finally reached a verdict. Within nine months of taking his post, the vice president had not only helped decide on a project but had also raised millions of dollars for it and had made significant progress on its construction. What he and his team decided to do for the renovation project was to construct a brand-new temple for ISKCON of Philadelphia. After consulting a number of builders and engineers, the team decided that the temple would be positioned between the existing residential facilities of ISKCON of Philadelphia and that the old

Figure 6.2 Exterior of New ISKCON of Philadelphia temple. October 9, 2018. Photo taken by author. Philadelphia, Pennsylvania.

temple building would be transformed into a large community dining hall so that devotees would no longer have to eat in the temple room.

While the final touches on the new temple are not yet fully done, the interior space is nearly complete, including its new and magnificent tiling, lighting, and window fixtures. The temple room itself is a large space completely covered in ivory marble—a marble that gives the space a crisp and bright feel, as the room beams with a row of cut-out windows lining the slanted sides of the ceiling. At the center of the temple is a large stage, around which is a *parikramā* path, where devotees and visitors will be able to circumambulate the deities of Krishna, as they do in many ISKCON (and other) temples in India. On the floor is a tiled lotus flower design that sits at the center of the space, at the end of a marked-off, tiled path that will be used for a *darshan* line. The only part of the temple that is left to complete is the construction of the altar itself, which will sit on top of the stage. The altar has not yet been completed because devotees have not yet agreed upon whether they want to construct a new one or try to move the old one into the new temple. This means that the temple deities—Sri Sri Radha Saradbihari, Lord Jagannatha, Lord Balarama, Srimati Subhadra Devi,

Figure 6.3 Interior of New ISKCON of Philadelphia Temple. Temple is still under construction, hence the lack of deities on the stage where the altar will go. September 23, 2018. Photo taken by author. Philadelphia, Pennsylvania.

and Sri Sri Gaura Nitai—have not yet moved into their new temple home yet, either. Their relocation will happen when the temple has its official inauguration, which the vice president hopes will be before Thanksgiving of 2018.

It only took nine months for the new temple vice president and his team to get the temple built, and they raised millions of dollars to do so. In fact, nearly all of the fundraising for and work on the temple's construction has been during his tenure and under his supervision.

Although I last spoke with the temple vice president in October of 2018, before that meeting it had been just over a year since I had least seen him at Janmāṣṭamī 2017. I had first met him at one of Radhanath Swami's yoga retreats in the summer of 2016. During that trip, we bonded over our shared commutes through New Jersey traffic and about our shared interest in ISKCON's newest branding techniques. A seasoned ISKCON devotee, the vice president shared with me his ISKCON story—how he had come to fall in love with the movement during his PhD program in chemistry in the early 1980s, as well as how he had grown weary of ISKCON's institutional setup amid the political issues that confronted the movement in the mid-1980s surrounding the "zonal *ācārya*" scandals.[4] During that time, he had sworn off ever finding a guru on whom he could fully rely, and his passion for the movement (although not for Krishna or for Prabhupada) faded. But a chance encounter with Radhanath Swami's *Journey Home* just after it was published in 2008 made him reconsider his faith in ISKCON's gurus, and he became once again reinvigorated to the ISKCON movement with full gusto, joyfully taking formal initiation under Radhanath Swami shortly thereafter. This usual enthusiasm for the ISKCON movement is why, when I saw him at the Philadelphia temple in the early fall of 2018, I was surprised to see him looking sad and drawn, dejected even.

During this last meeting, I had just sat down to talk with the vice president and with Bhaktimarga Swami, an ISKCON *saṃnyāsī* who had come to visit ISKCON of Philadelphia for their annual Rathayatra festival. Throughout ISKCON, Bhaktimarga Swami is known as the "walking monk" because he regularly makes treks on foot across Canada and the United States to draw public attention to pilgrimage as a religious activity, as well as to the ISKCON movement itself.[5] After talking about his travels, Bhaktimarga Swami stepped outside of the room, leaving just the vice president and me. "This year I had a new position: vice president," he said solemnly. As our conversation progressed, however, I came to find out that despite his success in his new position and in the temple construction that defined it, the vice president had only occupied the post for a total of ten months (he took the position in the summer of 2017 but had resigned by the summer of 2018). And he'd done so, he told me, because the position had come with a lot of stress and had brought him a number of health problems in the months that he'd held it. "I became too tired from the stress," he said, in particular "the constant fighting" and the "nasty politics," which he said became "too much for" him.[6] It was only later that I would find out that the stresses to which he was referring had to do with the battles that had been long festering between two groups of devotees in the ISKCON of Philadelphia community over competing visions for the new renovation project of which he was put in charge.

TWO GROUPS, TWO IDEAS FOR ISKCON OF PHILADELPHIA

There are two distinct groups of devotees who have been battling it out over the new renovation project at ISKCON of Philadelphia. On the one hand are those devotees who are highly dissatisfied at the idea of spending the community's renovation money and efforts on the construction of a new temple. Many of the devotees in this camp have been at ISKCON of Philadelphia for years, decades even, and have been waiting just as long for the chance to renovate and revamp their dilapidated center. Furthermore, because of the length of time that they have been waiting, they do not want to squander the chance to build the new ISKCON of Philadelphia center of their dreams—one that they believe will draw in a diverse crowd of people to the center, primarily those whom they identify as westerners.

I got the chance to spend much time with the group of devotees on this side of the table. In their view, the worst possible way in which to renovate ISKCON of Philadelphia is to spend their available time and resources building a new temple. Instead, the devotees in this camp want the resources to go toward the building of a new, large, modern, and versatile community center space, one in which ISKCON of Philadelphia can host many different types of events. The hope is that this community center, and the myriad of events it can host, will draw diverse crowds of people from the surrounding residential suburbs, the nearby lively downtown neighborhood of Germantown, and the greater Philadelphia area at large. Examples of the kinds of programs they want to run in this community center include yoga programs and yoga classes, as well as meditation sessions and *kīrtan* nights, all of which, they said, would benefit from being held "in a space that is not necessarily in front of the deities." Some devotees in this group even suggested that a community center could be used for an even wider variety of events and courses, such as making ISKCON of Philadelphia a "millennium learning center affiliate," one where devotees could host a number of courses that might draw in people from the surrounding neighborhoods—courses ranging from CPR certification trainings to real estate licensing programs.

To state it simply, the devotees in this camp told me that they wanted ISKCON of Philadelphia to build a center with its renovation money that could be used as a "bridge," by which they meant a space that would help them reach out to people in the surrounding area of the temple who are not otherwise attending ISKCON of Philadelphia's programs already—namely westerners. As one devotee on this side of the debate put it, "This new temple is not going to draw the whole Philadelphia community here, just like the old one isn't drawing them in." Continuing, he said, "I just don't see why we need to build another bigger, newer, shinier space, just to attract the people we are already attracting. I think we should build something for the whole community. That way maybe we have a chance to give them a reason to visit."[7]

On the other side of the debate are devotees who do not want to build a yoga studio, a meditation center, or a community center space in which to hold CPR courses, real estate training seminars, or any other such programs. Instead, these devotees support the building of the new temple as the ideal renovation project for ISKCON of Philadelphia. In these devotees' view, a large new temple is the perfect space to host the current community that congregates daily and weekly at ISKCON of Philadelphia, as well as to draw in the broader surrounding community by virtue of the temple's splendor and beauty. Worth mentioning is not just the fact that the devotees in this group want to build this new temple; rather, they are also willing to pay for it. In fact, the group of devotees who prefer the temple model to the community center are the ones who have funded ISKCON of Philadelphia's renovation project almost entirely. Without these devotees, I have been told, *no* renovation project at ISKCON of Philadelphia would be possible at all, as only roughly five thousand dollars of the several million raised for the renovation project have been donated by the group favoring the community center.

The devotees on the two sides of the renovation project debate do not just differ with respect to their competing visions for the renovation of ISKCON of Philadelphia, however. Rather, they also differ with respect to the grounds of power for their respective positions. The devotees who want to build the community center in order to explicitly attract and cater to westerners have their power rooted in their proximity to Prabhupada: that is to say, a sizable number of the devotees in this group—many of whom are westerners themselves—are direct disciples of Prabhupada, and most of them who are not his direct disciples have nonetheless been in the movement for a significant amount of time. This type of power that derives from proximity to a guru is what Amanda J. Lucia has called "proxemic authority" or "the hierarchical system of authority within [a] movement [that] radiates from [the guru] as the central charismatic authority toward the periphery."[8] As Lucia notes of her own observations of devotees within the global guru Amma's movement, "Those devotees who have been with Amma the longest often occupy higher positions of proxemic authority than those who are newer to the movement."[9] The second group of devotees in the ISKCON of Philadelphia renovation debate—many of whom are of Indian descent—have their power rooted in numbers and in money (and the two are not unrelated). That is to say, those who favor the new temple renovation model have grounds in the debate by virtue of the fact that they are funding the project, and without their money, no renovation would be possible.[10]

For his part, the temple vice president, a Kerala-born, Radhanath Swami disciple, said it is his dream—"the dream of my life," as he put it—to try to attract more westerners to the ISKCON movement. "I am a sixty years old [*sic*] man, and I am now retired," he told me one day from his office. "It is my dream for the rest of my life to help my guru in what is his wish . . . to make ISKCON cosmopolitan."[11] In this regard, he told me that he can identify with the perspective of the group of devotees who wants the community center space for yoga, meditation, and other such courses. He even added that he thinks such spaces and programs should be added to every ISKCON temple. At the same time, however, he recognizes and in some sense has come to accept the constraints that the community is under: the group of devotees who are willing to fund the renovation project do not want to build this community center space, and the devotees who want to build a community center cannot fund it. "So what are we to do," he asked? "I cannot wait around for the money [for the community center] to someday come while in the meanwhile the current structure is falling apart, ya know, while it is getting rotten."[12] Although he tried his best to compromise and appease both groups, in the end, the group of devotees who was hoping for the community center—a group similar in leanings to the Krishna Branders of this book—lost the battle over the ISKCON of Philadelphia renovation project.

The other type of battle that groups like them are losing—in particular, groups of Krishna Branders—is the battle to draw westerners to the temples through bridge centers (independent ISKCON-affiliated centers, such as yoga studios and meditation lounges, that are run outside of the temples and are designed to draw westerners into temple communities). I discussed the bridge model (also called the loft model) earlier in this book as an ISKCON model of marketing based on the belief that if westerners can be provided with worship spaces and programs that resonate with their interests and within which they feel comfortable, then from these centers and programs they can be easily transitioned into the movement's more traditional worship spaces: notably, the temples. The Krishna Branders who promote this model recognize that there are dimensions of ISKCON's temples and temple life with which westerners initially struggle, such as the *mūrtis* (embodied forms) of Krishna, the rituals of *darshan* and *puja*, and the temples' predominantly Indian demography (which purportedly makes westerners feel socially and culturally out of place). However, bridge-model advocates believe that if westerners are appropriately "primed," then they can eventually come to appreciate ISKCON's temple life and even become active participants in it. In this regard, bridge centers such as the Mantra Lounge, the Bhakti Center, and the Govardhan Eco Village are believed to serve as "transcendental on-ramps,"[13] providing the priming westerners need to be drawn to the mainline movement and its devotional locus in the temples.

That the Krishna Branders are losing the battle of trying to draw westerners to the temples through the bridge programs can be easily seen by mere observation at a number of ISKCON temples, where the primary demographic makeup is still overwhelmingly Indian (a demographic trend that holds even for those temples near or tied with bridge centers). For example, in August of 2018, I attended a Janmāṣṭamī festival at a large ISKCON temple on the East Coast of the United States: ISKCON of DC. The festival was a lively occasion, jam-packed with devotees and visitors alike. The festival setup featured a number of different stalls, food and music options, and media stations, all intended to keep attendees of various ages and interests happy and entertained. For example, for children, there was a balloon-popping game, a ball toss, and a cow-petting station. For adults, there were a number of vendors selling clothing, books, CDs, and even cooking utensils. There was also a "mantra station," where visitors were taught how to chant a round of "Hare Krishna" on *japa* beads, a tented seating area where guests could watch ISKCON's latest film—*Hare Krishna! The Mantra, the Movement and the Swami Who Started It*—playing on a loop, a number of food stalls that served festival food ranging from *pakoṛās* (batter fried puffs) to pasta, and a grand feast of *prasādam* that was given out to all attendees free of cost. Throughout the night, there were also lively devotional songs being played in the temple room, where attendees could gather to see Madan Mohan and his entourage finely dressed for the occasion and to sing and dance in devotion before them.

All in all, the festival was a huge success, and I was told that there were approximately 5,000 people in attendance. Of these 5,000 people, however, only roughly fifty of them were westerners, at least from an observational perspective. This means that the number of western attendees at the event was only around 1 percent—an exceptionally low number, especially given that the DC temple actively markets itself for a western audience through its various media and social media forms, has an active welcome committee for westerners, and advertises events explicitly to attract them.[14] It is also especially low given the fact that a number of Radhanath Swami's Krishna Brander disciples and students live at or near the temple and actively run yoga bridge programs, studios, and retreats nearby to try to draw westerners to the temple community. Lastly, it is worth noting that attendance at ISKCON of DC's non-festival programs is only slightly more diverse than that of its festivals, and this demographic situation seems to hold at many other ISKCON temples, as well. For example, ISKCON of Philadelphia has a similarly predominant Indian demographic constituency, despite the Mantra Lounge bridge center being located in the same city as the temple. In fact, devotees at the Philadelphia temple claim that *no one* from the Mantra Lounge has ever visited the temple and that even the crew who run the Mantra Lounge do not visit anymore—not even, I was told, for Janmāṣṭamī.

FACING AN UNCERTAIN FUTURE

From the looks of a number of ISKCON's most recent projects, it seems that those interested in attracting westerners to the movement are losing this battle at the level of the temple; they are not able to succeed at or gain support for projects designed to bring westerners to ISKCON temples. This is not to say, however, that they are losing the western outreach battle altogether. On the contrary, the Krishna Branders are immensely successful at bringing large numbers of westerners to ISKCON-run bridge centers and programs, despite the fact that observations suggest these westerners never make it to the temples. For example, I have seen sizable groups of westerners sitting tightly packed in the Mantra Lounge, gleefully chanting rounds of *japa* on *tulasī*-beaded necklaces, singing the *mahā mantra* on *karatālas* and *mṛdaṅga* drums, eating *prasādam,* and gathering around the table talking about the ways in which chanting "Hare Krishna" helps to declutter their minds and reduce their stress and depression. More than this, I have seen that many of these westerners are regulars and that many come multiple times a week to associate with devotees and engage in ISKCON activities, not only visiting the lounge but also reading Prabhupada's *Bhagavad-Gītā As It Is* and even volunteering in cleanup and other such collective duties.

I have observed a similar set of circumstances at the Govardhan Eco Village in India and at the Bhakti Center in New York City. At the Bhakti Center, for example, I have seen rooms full of westerners practicing yoga in classes that are set to the tune of the *mahā mantra* and which begin and end with readings from Prabhupada's *Bhagavad-Gītā As It Is.* Moreover, I have seen that many westerners who regularly attend the yoga classes also attend the center's other programs, with some even helping to staff the center or volunteer in its various roles. Many also enroll in the Bhakti Center's yoga teacher training programs, where they study in an intensive curriculum that includes reading Prabhupada's *Bhagavad-Gītā As It Is,* Radhanath Swami's *Journey Home,* and Gadadhara Pandit Dasa's *Urban Monk.*[15] Some even attend retreats, sponsored by the Bhakti Center, where they spend the weekend (or longer) engaged in *kīrtan* and yoga and hearing lectures on love of Krishna.

These centers, therefore, raise a number of important questions for devotees in the ISKCON movement and will continue to do so well into the future. For starters, the fact that westerners seem to be drawn to but not out of these centers suggests that rather than operating as bridge centers, these newly branded ISKCON centers (such as the Mantra Lounge, the Bhakti Center, etc.) are actually functioning as what Hridayananda Das Goswami would refer to as destinations (or destination centers). Based on the model proposed by Hridayananda Das Goswami, the idea of destination centers rests on the belief that westerners will never be drawn to participating in, or worshipping at, ISKCON temples, no matter what amount of priming or preparation they receive. Instead, this model suggests, if ISKCON wants to not just attract but also reliably retain westerners, then the movement must create a set of spaces designed explicitly for them, where they will want to stay and participate for the long haul. Although the bridge centers' administrators did not intend their centers to be destination centers, it seems that this is how they have nonetheless turned out.

But this itself raises a number of important questions for the ISKCON movement going forward, many of which are existential in nature. Chief among them is the question of whether or not this kind of religious participation—participation that begins and ends in these newly rebranded centers like yoga studios, meditation lounges, and Krishna West centers—will constitute, for the Krishna Branders or for devotees in the movement at large, a legitimate way to practice ISKCON. That is, what will devotees in the movement make of the situation if the westerners who are attracted to practicing Krishna Consciousness in these new centers never want to leave them to join the movement's mainline congregations at the temples? Deeply wrapped up in this question will be bigger and much more difficult ones regarding whether or not devotees will be able to accept multiple ways of being in and practicing ISKCON—that is, whether they will be able to accept within their ranks the presence of what amounts to multiple, yet equally legitimate, ISKCONs. This is an important question, because if these centers prove to be the only way to draw westerners to (and keep them in) the ISKCON movement, then devotees in the movement will have to come to grips with the sheer degree of innovation required to fulfill Prabhupada's mission of universalism. That is to say, they will have to grapple with the fact that if they want westerners in their movement, they must accept that these westerners will almost inevitably be practicing their Krishna Consciousness in a religious setting and participatory culture that is radically different from that of the current mainline movement (which is presently located primarily in the temples).

I recall asking Radhanath Swami about this issue during one of my meetings with him. I had just spent the weekend at one of his many retreats—doing yoga, sitting at the swimming pool, and singing around a nightly campfire—when I began to reflect on the radically different subculture at the retreat as compared to that of many ISKCON temples that I had visited. The participatory culture at this retreat was so different than that of ISKCON's temples, in fact, that it felt to me like an alternate ISKCON world—a distinct ISKCON altogether, running parallel to the mainline movement. Curious as to what Radhanath Swami would say about this difference, I asked him directly. In particular, I asked about whether he was worried that ISKCON's western-focused rebranding programs—both his own and those of the other Krishna Branders—would create what might amount to two ISKCON's: two distinct ISKCON movements running parallel to each other yet distinct in the shape of the Krishna Consciousness that they offer. But laughing in his coy and humble way, his reply was telling, "There are already two ISKCONs," he said. "There are *more* than two ISKCONs." He continued, "And this is what Lord Chaitanya preached, actually." Nodding assuredly, he added, "I hope that we can activate his philosophy, this philosophy of simultaneous difference in nondifference."[16]

The philosophy Radhanath Swami was referencing was that of Acintya Bhedābheda, the system of Vedānta attributed to Chaitanya and the Vrindavan Goswamis who helped to champion it. This Vedānta philosophy is one that positions itself against both Advaita and Dvaita Vedānta by positing that there is an inconceivable identity-in-difference that obtains between the world of plurality (both the individual *jīvas* and the world itself) on the one hand and Brahman on the other. Put differently, rather than positing that the world of plurality is either completely separate from or completely identical to Brahman, the Acintya Bhedābheda school of Vedānta posits that the world of plurality is both simultaneously different from and identical to Brahman. How they can be both at the same time is what is "inconceivable" (*acintya*).

The parallel that Radhanath Swami was drawing had to do with his viewpoint that just like the *jīvas* and the world can be both different from and also identical with Brahman, so too can different worship styles, brands, and cultures of devotion coexist within ISKCON, each of which—though different from each other—is nonetheless fully and legitimately ISKCON. The parallel he was drawing, in other words, had to do not only with his understanding that western-focused rebranding efforts had already produced multiple ISKCONs, but also his view that *this is OK*—that is, that multiple modes of being a Hare Krishna can and should be accepted under the ISKCON umbrella.

Although this is the perspective that Radhanath Swami himself has, it is not necessarily one that is or will be shared by others in the movement. While the Krishna Branders themselves and many similarly leaning devotees in the movement support the view that the Krishna Branders' newly produced modes of participating in ISKCON are legitimate, many others in the movement do not share this view. In fact, there is a whole subculture of devotees within ISKCON who write at length about what they call ISKCON's "mission drift"—what they see to be the movement away from Prabhupada's ideals due in part to overly liberal outreach or proselytization efforts.[17] These devotees believe that in an effort to attract more converts to the movement, their ISKCON peers have engaged in "pandering to the crowd" and in so doing have changed the heart of Prabhupada's society simply so as to have more westerners in it. With this argument, devotees in this anti-mission-drift camp have extensively criticized those whom I call the Krishna Branders for being "populists." As one such devotee remarked, "Radhanath Swami provides a model for how to act if you are looking to be inclusive. Gone is the day when exclusivity was a marketable commodity in the eyes of most ISKCON leaders."[18] Another put it more harshly: "An ISKCON that chooses the path of populism is likely to end up going through what political philosopher Clifford Orwin has called the 'unraveling of Christianity' in America," which is ostensibly what happened to churches who "chose the path of populism" and "wanted to accommodate the prevailing culture and ideas in order to become popular."[19] This accommodation, anti-mission-drift devotees claim, "turned out to be a Faustian bargain for them [these churches]: to become popular (and hence mainline) they replaced their core ideas with secular equivalents. In doing so they lost their original reason for being—their original purpose and mission."[20] This position has much weight in the ISKCON movement. In fact, anti-mission-drift criticisms of those whom I call the Krishna Branders have become so prominent that the Krishna Branders often feel compelled to respond to them. For example, Hridayananda Das Goswami frequently cites them in his own essays, just so that he can rebut them.[21]

In the large scheme of things, however, the question over whether or not ISKCON's broader devotee base will accept multiple models of participation in ISKCON as legitimate really boils down to how different groups of devotees navigate the complicated conundrum of balancing tradition and innovation. Far from being new, this conundrum sits at the heart of the ISKCON movement, having been introduced to devotees by Swami Prabhupada himself.[22] On the innovation side, Prabhupada is known to have said repeatedly that in preaching, all adjustments should be made for "time, place, and circumstance." As noted scholar of ISKCON William H. Deadwyler III quotes Prabhupada as saying, "All the great *acaryas* or religious preachers or reformers of the world executed their mission by adjustment of religious principles in terms of time and place. There are different climates and situations in different parts of the world, and if one has to discharge his duties to preach the message of the Lord, he must be expert in adjusting things in terms of the time and place."[23] This side of Prabhupada harkens back to his discussions of *yukta vairāgya* (as discussed in chap. 3), whereby he encouraged devotees to use all means (novel, innovative, and otherwise) in the preaching service of Krishna. And this is what Prabhupada himself was said to do in his own preaching. As one devotee said, "Prabhupada used all of the technology available to him: he took a boat, he took planes, traveled in cars, used a Dictaphone, printed books," and so on; so, why should today's devotees not do the same?

On the other side of the spectrum, however, is a Prabhupada who was extremely rooted in tradition and who encouraged his disciples to be similarly rooted in it—without addition to or subtraction from his methods. As Deadwyler explains it, "This consciousness of the importance of tradition was instilled in his disciples by Srila Prabhupada, who taught fidelity to tradition as a primary virtue. The tradition must be received and transmitted purely. One hears from the spiritual master, and repeats what one has heard without addition or subtraction. One must grant the spiritual master 'submissive aural reception' and follow his instruction exactly. Only by doing so will one achieve success in spiritual life."[24]

Devotees faced with the challenge of deciding whether or not new and multiple modes of being and practice within ISKCON can count as legitimate and authentic modes of being a Hare Krishna have a challenging set of poles to navigate. On the one hand is the side of pure tradition, which makes little room for novel ways of practicing ISKCON, such as yoga and mindfulness. This side of the spectrum, however, also leaves little room for increasing the global diversity of the ISKCON movement. On the other hand is the side of pure innovation, which allows not only for multiple ways of being in ISKCON (even radically new ones) but also, therefore, for an increased likelihood that devotees will be able to enhance the diversity of their movement, because more and different groups of people might be inclined to take up the practice. This side of the spectrum, however, risks fears of "losing the core" of the tradition, so to speak, even though scholars of religion know that such conceptions of "the core" are shifting goalposts or mere rhetorical moves mobilized at different times and for different reasons. Devotees in the movement, therefore, will need to decide how to navigate this tricky space and figure out "how innovative is too innovative" when it comes to deciding how best to attract westerners to ISKCON. In this regard, the Krishna Branders will have a hefty role to play in developing a theological framework within which to contextualize these innovative new programs of ISKCON and in systematizing a hermeneutic of Prabhupada that allows these programs, different though they may be from what he developed, to fit squarely within his conservative theology of "submissive aural reception," or the position that devotees should not make changes in their received tradition.

Whether or not devotees in the movement at large accept these multiple modes of participation in ISKCON as legitimate ways of being a Hare Krishna will also have to do with how closely they believe the Krishna Branders are following Prabhupada, if not in letter, then perhaps at least in spirit. For their own part, the Krishna Branders discussed in this book certainly see themselves to be following the spirit of Swami Prabhupada, and in fact, if one looks back at the circumstances of Prabhupada's journey to the United States, one can certainly see the Krishna Branders in his own story.

When Prabhupada boarded the *Jaladuta* on August 13, 1965, the weight of the world must have been on his shoulders. At the age of sixty-nine, with nothing more than his complimentary ticket, some dry cereal, and a few reading materials, Swami Prabhupada set off from Calcutta on a cargo ship—a vessel not quite fit for passengers—on a thirty-five-day journey that would take him across the world to the United States. It is hard to imagine what would motivate an elderly man in poor health, with no money, and with not a great command of the English language to cross the ocean alone on a freighter into the United States. But his own diary gives us an entryway into his thinking: "I am feeling separation from Sri Vrindaban and my Lords Sri Govinda, Gopinath, Radha Damodar," he wrote on September 10. But "I have left Bharatabhumi [India] just to execute the order of Sri Bhaktisiddhanta Sarasvati in pursuance of Lord Chaitanya's order. I have no qualification, but I have taken up the risk just to carry out the order of His Divine Grace."[25]

As a disciple of Bhaktisiddhanta Sarasvati, Prabhupada was part of a lineage in which the primary religious task incumbent upon him was to serve his guru in the service of Krishna. For Prabhupada, this meant following Bhaktisiddhanta Sarasvati's instruction to go west and spread devotion to Krishna to people outside of India. Bhaktisiddhanta Sarasvati had tried to achieve this mission throughout his own life but had failed. He had even sent three of his disciples as missionaries overseas to Germany and England, but this had not worked, and he passed away with his mission unfulfilled. When A. C. Bhaktivedanta decided to board the *Jaladuta*, therefore, he did so because he knew that the mission of his guru Bhaktisiddhanta Sarasvati was in dire straits and that the only way to save it was to take on the task himself—and he was willing to try anything in order to do so.

This state of pain and crisis that motivated Prabhupada in his decision to depart for the United States in 1965 is the same state that motivated the three Krishna Branders at the heart of this book to have created their ISKCON brands. If the reader will recall, the three Krishna Branders discussed in this book all started their dedication to Prabhupada's mission early on in life. They all left college before matriculating or immediately thereafter and accepted an entirely new way of life in order to follow Prabhupada, changing not only their view of the world but also how they lived in it—including their names, their clothing, and their circle of friends. More than this, they all took a lifelong vow of celibacy and gave up a life of family and society so that they could dedicate themselves full-time to Prabhupada's mission of trying to bring westerners to Krishna—just like Prabhupada had done for his own guru. Believing now that they have failed in their attempt to actualize the vision for which they spent their entire lives working, they find themselves disappointed, saddened, and in a state of despair. Seeing themselves in the golden years of their lives, just like Prabhupada was in 1965, they are desperate to actualize his vision of ISKCON's global success and universality before it is too late. As Hridayananda Das Goswami put it:

> Prabhupada shared with me in a very intimate, powerful way what I know are his real wishes and dreams. . . . Therefore, because my body is getting older . . . [and because] those instructions not only entered my ears but my heart . . . I cannot—as they say, in good conscience—I cannot sit back and not try to do what I can to try my best.* . . . Not as the *ācārya* of ISKCON, but simply as one disciple of Prabhupada who, before he leaves this world, has to try. It's very important to me, when I leave this world, I have to be able to say to Prabhupada, I tried my best.[26]

The extent to which devotees in the ISKCON movement can see the similarity in spirit that the Krishna Branders have with Prabhupada himself will, I think, contribute to the extent to which they can accept the Krishna Branders' new modes of devotion as legitimate forms of ISKCON practice. This is because while Hindu gurus are typically valued insofar as they are able to "innovate[] and overthrow[] custom, law, and tradition in efforts to demonstrate a new and alternative means by which to attain the goal of salvation or release,"[27] ISKCON gurus are understood and valued differently by devotees in the movement because they are what one might call *lineage gurus* or gurus who serve as gurus *under their own guru*. As such, the legitimacy of their teaching and programming is judged by a standard that is not just pure innovation but is instead an innovation gauged by its fidelity to the spirit of their predecessor guru (Swami Prabhupada). If they are perceived to be out of line with that spirit, they are less likely to be accepted. As Daniel Gold argues:

> In many Indic traditions, individual gurus and their successors are felt to offer their devotees the same continuing means of salvation: a specific mantra, enlightening teaching, and/or spiritual power, which the successor

> has somehow assimilated from his or her predecessor. The actual human personalities of the predecessor and successor gurus, however, can be quite different. Although differences of culture-historical generation certainly come into play here, just as important are those of personal temperament and style. Together these can lead to obvious changes in apparently central areas of practice, such as modes of initiation and openness to worldly entanglements. From the outside these differences may be readily taken as aspects of the changes inevitably occurring in religious traditions, but from the inside those changes might appear problematic: aren't old devotees often jarred and puzzled by what seem to be the successor's new, sometimes quite different ways? Of course they are, but they often manage to accommodate themselves very nicely, reaching different understandings about the meaning of succession in the process.[28]

Only time will tell the extent to which the Krishna Branders' innovative and novel programs will be accommodated by devotees at large into the accepted corpus of ISKCON practice.

Last but not least, we cannot forget about the tremendous role that ISKCON's broader institutional body, the GBC, will have to fill in garnering support for the Krishna Branders' innovative programs, especially if these programs do not lead westerners eventually to the temples. This is because without the broader support of the GBC, the full success of these programs cannot fully materialize. The critical question here, though, is whether or not a single institution can support multiple kinds of ISKCON: that is, multiple "orders" or branches of practice within the ISKCON movement.[29] This is because, although there are many points of disagreement among ISKCON devotees, they are overwhelmingly committed to one central principle—namely that devotees and leaders in ISKCON should maintain their commitment to Prabhupada's wish that ISKCON remain one single institution, led by one governing body. What this means is that unlike other religious traditions, which have accommodated differing interpretations of theology and modes of practice by splintering into different denominations each run by different institutions or churches, ISKCON devotees do not see themselves as having this option. Instead, any subdividing into different "orders," sub-movements, or any other different branches or types of practice, must be done under the umbrella of one institutional body. Maintaining an institutional ecosystem that can support a variety of branches of practice, therefore, will be essential not only for the full acceptance but also for the flourishing of the Krishna Branders' centers, programs, and modes of devotion.

Historically, the GBC has struggled with maintaining such an ecosystem. In fact, over the years, there have been many groups and individuals alike who have been exiled from ISKCON by the GBC and/or who have been deemed to be "heretical" by the movement. Consider, for example, the ISKCON Revival Movement (IRM), a group of devotees so called for their reconceptualization of ISKCON's understanding of the guru-disciple relationship.[30] In the years following Prabhupada's death, nearly all of the eleven men whom Prabhupada had chosen to succeed him as gurus in the movement "fell down," as devotees say—that is, they failed to honor their ISKCON devotional vows through acts that were considered sexual (and in some cases, criminal) misconduct. As scholars of ISKCON have noted, this guru crisis left not only structural problems in the movement,[31] but it also resulted in a great many ISKCON devotees (two-thirds of the movement, on some counts) being "spiritually orphaned" (left without a guru).[32] More saliently, however, it left many in the movement with a complicated religious question on their hands, specifically in terms of how they understood Prabhupada's infallibility. How could Prabhupada have chosen such imperfect men to be his succeeding gurus? How had he not known that they would "fall down"? And further, how could devotees put their trust in other gurus after them, especially since the failure rate of ISKCON's gurus during the years after Prabhupada's death was significant?[33]

In response to this dilemma, the devotees who formed the ISKCON Revival Movement proposed a solution advancing the idea that Prabhupada was the only real guru and that all other gurus in the movement (both in the past and in the future) were only *ṛitviks*—proxies for or representatives of Prabhupada. This means that the gurus in the ISKCON movement were only meant to have a *functional* role therein: that is, they were there merely to execute Prabhupada's guru responsibilities (such as initiation) in his absence. *Religiously* speaking, Prabhupada himself was the only figure whose true status in the movement was "guru." By reconceptualizing the role of ISKCON's gurus vis-à-vis Prabhupada in this way, IRM devotees believed that Prabhupada could retain his infallibility, that devotees of fallen gurus could avoid being orphaned, and that future devotees would not be so devastated should their own gurus fall off the path. Devotees in the IRM found textual evidence to support their view, most saliently in a letter dated July 9, 1977. This letter had been approved by Swami Prabhupada and stated that prior to his death, "Shrila Prabhupada indicated that soon He would appoint some of His senior disciples to act as 'ritvik'—representative of the acharya [Prabhupada himself], for the purpose of performing initiations." It further stated that "the newly initiated devotees [those initiated by the *ṛitviks*] are disciples of His Divine Grace A. C. Bhaktivedanta

Swami Prabhupada . . . to be included in His Divine Grace's 'Initiated Disciples' book."[34]

Although much could be said about the specifics of the IRM's reconceptualization of the guru-disciple relationship within ISKCON, what matters for the present purposes is that the GBC effectively banned the IRM from ISKCON, fearing that the changes the IRM was suggesting to implement in the movement were too great to accept. The IRM movement, therefore, is a valuable example to consider because it showcases that the GBC does not always endeavor to foster an ecosystem of multiplicity within the ISKCON movement and the possibility that the GBC might not ultimately (or fully) accept the Krishna Branders and their new brands as legitimate forms of ISKCON under its rubric. This is especially the case if the GBC perceives that, doctrinally, the Krishna Branders are making changes to ISKCON's core theology, if they perceive that the Krishna Branders are trying to "poach" devotees away from ISKCON (which is what they believed about the IRM), or if they believe that the charismatic power of any of the Krishna Branders is becoming too big in the movement or having too much sway over large groups of devotees. As Irvin H. Collins notes in his essay "The 'Routinization of Charisma' and the Charismatic," this is precisely the concern that the GBC had about Gaura Govinda Maharaj, who "was an elderly Indian disciple of Bhaktivedanta Swami and Vaishnava by birth, [and] thus more senior, learned, exemplary, and inspirational than the younger westerners who comprised the majority of ISKCON's gurus."[35] Collins further notes that Gaura Govinda Maharaj was, therefore, "perceived as a threat [and that] the GBC was concerned about the devotees who were flocking to his ISKCON temple in India from other ISKCON temples."[36] In fact, he notes that "the GBC was on the verge of taking disciplinary action against the Maharaja for his outspoken opinions—defying the commission's decisions on such theological matters as *guru tattva* (the truth about guru) and the origin of the soul—when he passed away."[37]

The GBC has also exiled two other gurus—Sridara Maharaj and Narayana Maharaj—from the movement, effectively banning them from ISKCON activities and spaces. Though these two gurus were not officially ISKCON gurus (each man being an associate of Swami Prabhupada in the greater Gauḍīya lineage), they nonetheless drew enough ISKCON devotees to themselves to prompt concern on the part of the GBC.[38] Fearing their charisma and popularity, the GBC banned them from ISKCON. It is always possible, then, that the GBC might effect similar bans or sanctions on the Krishna Branders at some point in the future.[39] Should the GBC effect sanctions or a ban on the Krishna Branders or their programs and centers, the Krishna Branders' (and their programs') perceived legitimacy in the eyes of a significant number of devotees would be negatively impacted. This is what happened to the IRM once the GBC exiled them from ISKCON's official folds. In fact, to this day, many devotees are fearful about the IRM, railing against them online and protesting against their publications and other preaching efforts. Some devotees have even resorted to violence against the IRM in order to threaten IRM-leaning temples to recede into the ISKCON background.[40] This is not to say, however, that all devotees feel this way about the IRM or that a sanction (or even an exile) from the GBC would mean that the Krishna Branders' programs would fall away. For instance, one could look at ISKCON Bangalore, a community which—despite having been formally expelled from the GBC for its association with the IRM—is nonetheless a vibrant temple community. It is to say, however, that it would be difficult for many devotees in the ISKCON movement to consider the Krishna Branders' programs and centers to be legitimate without the endorsement of the GBC.

Last but not least, the onus of accepting ISKCON's multiple modes of practice will also lie with scholars, who themselves will be responsible for representing ISKCON in its fullness and multiplicity in their own work on the movement. Up until this point, the temple has been at the center of the story of ISKCON, especially as that story has been told in academic literature on the movement. For example, there have been a number of works that examine the liturgical structure of ISKCON's temple life, explaining in detail not only the practices that are performed therein but also what they mean ritually and theologically.[41] Scholars have also traced the history of the growth of ISKCON temples—not only in the United States but also throughout Europe and back into India—following the spread of the movement to the west.[42] In addition to examining the liturgical dimensions and historical spread of ISKCON temples, scholars have also studied the social and personal reasons that lead many devotees to join temple life, as well as reasons for which they leave.[43] More than this, scholars have paid attention to the social dimensions of temples, especially the social dynamics between congregants within temple communities.[44]

Prior to the 1980s, many ISKCON devotees used to reside inside the temples full-time, renouncing life in the world for a monastic-style devotion. In recent scholarship, however, scholars have focused on the massive shift in ISKCON residential life, noting the sheer number of devotees who have moved out of ISKCON temples to pursue their ISKCON religious lives out in society at large. Examining this exodus from temple residency, scholars have argued that an increased legitimacy for married life within the movement and "the advent of the nuclear family within ISKCON society" played a role,[45] as did a number of financial factors that forced many devotees to quit full-time temple life and join the workforce.[46] But what is important to note is that even scholarship that discusses the exodus of devotees from ISKCON's residential temple life still tells the story of ISKCON through the temple. This is because such scholarship typically focuses on the religious life of congregational devotees—"lay people who live[] beyond the confines of the temple" but close enough to be "able to take advantage of [the temple's] daily religious functions and contribute to the temple's expenses while otherwise living independent lives."[47] These religious functions include attending the Sunday Feast, festivals, and various *darshan* and *ārati* services, all of which occur at and are sponsored by the temples.

It was one of my hopes in writing this book to showcase that the religious geography of the contemporary ISKCON movement is heterogeneous and diverse and that it is characterized by a multiplicity of worship spaces, not just temples. This diversity consists of devotional programs and activities, centers, and spaces that have been unrepresented in contemporary scholarship on the movement. For example, as we have seen in this book, within the global ISKCON landscape, there are meditation lounges, yoga studios, mindfulness studios, luxury retreat resort spots, and a variety of other devotional spaces that are decidedly different from temples. More than this, the primary programs at these centers include yoga classes, karate courses, meditation sessions, vision-boarding activities, cooking classes, guitar and piano musical programs, lectures on ecology and sustainable living, and even classes in acrobatics. Devotees based at these centers even venture into the corporate sphere to run seminars on work-life balance, stress management, and getting along with others in diverse workplace settings.[48] These diverse centers and the programs that they host, in other words, differ markedly from the temples and their mainstay programs of *darshan* and *puja*, and are run by Krishna Brander devotees and gurus far beyond just those discussed in this book. What is more, many of these diverse centers and programs have been around for a number of years, and they are only becoming increasingly prominent and numerous on the ISKCON landscape. It was my aim, therefore, to highlight for readers some of this diversity and introduce them to the multidimensionality of ISKCON's religious landscape that has gone largely under the radar in scholarship on ISKCON. The ISKCON field is no longer characterized (just) by temples; it is therefore time for our scholarly maps to reflect that.

Importantly, it was also my aim to show that it is through the lens of marketing that we are best able to not only see this diversity but also *understand* it, as well as account for its rise and contemporary presence. This is because, as I have shown, many of these diverse worship spaces stem from rebrandings of the ISKCON movement: ones aimed at attracting more westerners to ISKCON by reenvisioning, reconceiving, and redesigning the spaces in which (and programs through which) the movement is promoted to them. Taken together, these programs and spaces have set into motion a transformation of the ISKCON landscape by adding much variation to the movement's temple-based topography. And in so doing, they also collectively necessitate a shift in our scholarly paradigms for the study of ISKCON.

NOTES

1. Cresheim Arms Hotel Postcard. No Postmark. Photo Credit: The Paul J. Gutman Library Digital Collections. Old Images of Philadelphia Facebook page. Accessed October 27, 2019. https://www.facebook.com/oldimagesof philadelphia/photos/a.115711028491844/603114709751471/?type=3&teater.
2. Elizabeth Farmer Jarvis. 2008. *Images of America: Mount Airy*. Charleston, Chicago, Portsmouth, San Francisco: Arcadia Publishing, 108.
3. The vice president's name is omitted throughout for the sake of anonymity.
4. For a discussion of these zonal *ācārya* scandals, see E. Burke Rochford Jr. 2007. *Hare Krishna Transformed*. New York: New York University Press; and Federico Squarcini and Eugenio Fizzotti. 2004. *Hare Krishna*. Salt Lake City: Signature Books.
5. The Walking Monk website. "The Walking Monk: Bhaktimarga Swami." Accessed October 27, 2018. https://www.thewalkingmonk.net/.
6. Discussion with ISKCON of Philadelphia Temple Vice President. In person, Philadelphia, Pennsylvania. September 23, 2018.
7. Discussion with devotee. In person, Philadelphia, Pennsylvania. September 23, 2018.
8. Amanda J. Lucia. 2014b. *Reflections of Amma: Devotees in Global Embrace*. Berkeley and Los Angeles: University of California Press, 206.
9. Ibid., 206.
10. This is not to say devotees in the temple-favoring group are not disciples in the ISKCON movement.
11. ISKCON of Philadelphia Temple Vice President. Interview by Nicole Karapanagiotis. In person, Philadelphia, Pennsylvania, October 9, 2018.
12. Ibid.
13. Sita-pati. Das. 2006. "Loft Preaching Article." *Dandavats*. Accessed July 21, 2017. http://www.dandavats.com/?p=1840.
14. Nicole Karapanagiotis. 2018. "Of Digital Images and Digital Media: Approaches to Marketing in American ISKCON." *Nova Religio: The Journal of Alternative and Emergent Religion* 21, no. 3: 74–102.
15. A. C. Bhaktivedanta Swami Prabhupada. 1986. *Bhagavad-Gītā As It Is: Complete Edition Revised and Enlarged with Original Sanskrit Text, Roman*

Transliteration, English Equivalents, Translation, and Elaborate Purports. Los Angeles: The Bhaktivedanta Book Trust; Radhanath Swami. 2010. *The Journey Home: Autobiography of an American Swami.* San Rafael: Mandala; and Gadadhara Pandit Dasa. 2013. *Urban Monk: Exploring Karma, Consciousness, and the Divine.* New York: Pankaj Srivastava.

16. Radhanath Swami. Interview by Nicole Karapanagiotis. In person, Lanexa, Virginia, June 13, 2016.

17. Vastavika Das. 2012. "The Radhanathization of ISKCON." *The Sampradaya Sun-Independent Vaishnava News,* September 16. Accessed May 31, 2020. http://www.harekrsna.com/sun/editorials/09-12/editorials9062.htm; Krishna Kirti Das. 2012. "Preaching According to Time, Place, and Circumstance with Adhikara is Trouble." *The Sampradaya Sun-Independent Vaishnava News,* September 15. Accessed May 31, 2020. http://www.harekrsna.com/sun/editorials/09-12/editorials9051.htm; Murari Das. 2012. "Maintaining the Purity." *The Sampradaya Sun-Independent Vaishnava News,* September 15. Accessed May 31, 2020. http://www.harekrsna.com/sun/editorials/09-12/editorials9050.htm; Gopinath Dasa. 2012. "Radhanathardation: Opportunistic Nuevo ISKCON." *The Sampradaya Sun-Independent Vaishnava News,* September 22. Accessed May 31, 2020. http://www.harekrsna.com/sun/editorials/09-12/editorials9088.htm; *Sun* Staff. 2011. "Radhanatha Swami's 'Preaching Strategies.'" *The Sampradaya Sun-Independent Vaishnava News,* July 6. Accessed May 31, 2020. http://www.harekrsna.com/sun/editorials/07-11/editorials7442.htm; and Rocana Dasa. 2011. "Vancouver Ratha Ruined." *The Sampradaya Sun-Independent Vaishnava News,* August 6. Accessed May 31, 2020. http://www.harekrsna.com/sun/editorials/08-11/editorials7599.htm.

18. Das 2012, "The Radhanathization."

19. Das 2012, "Preaching."

20. Ibid.

21. See, for example, Hridayananda Das Goswami. 2015. "Reply to a Senior Leader." Unpublished essay. Posted on Hridayananda das Goswami—Friends and Disciples Facebook page (public), October 24. Accessed May 11, 2017. https://www.facebook.com/groups/acharyadeva/permalink/10153917775293646/. Others in the movement, including Hridayananda Das Goswami himself, respond by noting that the structure of the temples today—with their elaborate *pujas* and emphasis on *darshan* and the intricacies of deity worship—are themselves a form of "mission drift," a fall from grace, so to speak, from Prabhupada's wishes that also resulted from "pandering to crowds." E. Burke Rochford Jr. argues this point in *Hare Krishna Transformed,* noting that many ISKCON temples in the United States would have failed if not for the financial contributions of the Indian Hindu community. This financial need, he suggests, drives temple practices (such as focus on the

deities), as devotees want to ensure that the wishes of their largest donors are satisfied. Rochford 2007.

22. A special issue of the *International Journal of Hindu Studies* takes up the conundrum of the relationship between tradition and innovation within the Hindu traditions more broadly. See, for example, Jonathan Edelmann. 2014. "Introduction: Innovation in Hindu Traditions." *International Journal of Hindu Studies* 18, no. 2: 113–118; and Amanda J. Lucia. 2014a. "Innovative Gurus: Tradition and Change in Contemporary Hinduism." *International Journal of Hindu Studies* 18, no. 2: 221–263.

23. William H. Deadwyler III (Ravindra Svarupa Dasa). 1989. "Patterns in ISKCON's Historical Self-Perception." In *Krishna Consciousness in the West.* David G. Bromley and Larry D. Shinn, eds. Lewisburg: Bucknell University Press and Associated University Presses, 73, citing Swami Prabhupada's purport on *Bhāgavata Purāṇa*, 1.2.

24. Ibid., 58.

25. Satsvarupa Dasa Goswami. 1983. *Prabhupāda: Messenger of the Supreme Lord.* Mumbai: The Bhaktivedanta Book Trust, 2–3. Brackets in original text.

26. Hridayananda Das Goswami. 2014. "KRISHNA WEST—The Interview, Vol. 1." GourTube YouTube channel, March 20. 34:31–36:43. Accessed March 27, 2018. https://www.youtube.com/watch?v=2EEO5_2HVdc. Asterisk indicates brief point in interview during which recording is fuzzy.

27. Lucia 2014a, 241.

28. Daniel Gold. 2012. "Continuities as Gurus Change." In *The Guru in South Asia: New Interdisciplinary Approaches.* Jacob Copeman and Aya Ikegame, eds. London and New York: Routledge, 241.

29. Thanks to Hridayananda Das Goswami for bringing this question to my attention.

30. See E. Burke Rochford Jr. 2009. "Succession, Religious Switching, and Schism in the Hare Krishna Movement." In *Sacred Schisms: How Religions Divide.* James R. Lewis and Sarah M. Lewis, eds. Cambridge: Cambridge University Press; and Rochford 2007. See also Krishnakant Desai, Sunil Awatramami (Adridharan Das), and Madhu Pandit Das. 2004. "The No Change in ISKCON Paradigm." In *The Hare Krshna Movement: The Postcharismatic Fate of a Religious Transplant.* Edwin F. Bryant and Maria L. Ekstrand, eds. New York: Columbia University Press; and William H. Deadwyler (Ravindra Svarupa Das). 2004. "Cleaning House and Cleaning Hearts: Reform and Renewal in ISKCON." In Bryant and Ekstrand 2004.

31. Deadwyler, 2004.

32. Irvin H. Collins. 2004. "The 'Routinization of Charisma' and the Charismatic: The Confrontation Between ISKCON and Narayana Maharaja." In Bryant and Ekstrand 2004, 218. See also Rochford 2009.

33. Rochford 2009.
34. Desai, Awatramami, and Das 2004, 195.
35. Collins 2004, 234.
36. Ibid., 234.
37. Ibid., 234.
38. Rochford 2009 and Collins 2004.
39. The presence of several Krishna Branders on the GBC might complicate this slightly, however.
40. Desai, Awatramami, and Das 2004.
41. Kenneth Russell Valpey. 2006. *Attending Kṛṣṇa's Image: Caitanya Vaiṣṇava Mūrti-Sevā as Devotional Truth*. London and New York: Routledge; William H. Deadwyler III (Ravindra Svarupa Dasa). 1985. "The Devotee and the Deity: Living a Personalistic Theology." In *Gods of Flesh, Gods of Stone*. Joanne Punzo Waghorne and Norman Cutler, eds. New York: Columbia University Press.; Kenneth Valpey (Krishna Kshetra Das). 2004. "Krishna in *Mleccha Desh*: ISKCON Temple Worship in Historical Perspective." In Bryant and Ekstrand 2004.
42. Bromley and Shinn 1989; Bryant and Ekstrand 2004; Charles R. Brooks. 1989b. *The Hare Krishnas in India*. Delhi: Motilal Banarsidass Publishers; Kim Knott. 2000. "In Every Town and Village: Adaptive Strategies in the Communication of Krishna Consciousness in the UK, the First Thirty Years." *Social Compass* 47, no. 2: 153–167.; and Malory Nye. 2015. *Multiculturalism and Minority Religions in Britain: Krishna Consciousness, Religious Freedom, and the Politics of Location*. London and New York: Routledge.
43. Bryant and Ekstrand 2004; Rochford 2007.
44. Travis Vande Berg and Fred Kniss. 2008. "ISKCON and Immigrants: The Rise, Decline, and Rise Again of a New Religious Movement." *The Sociological Quarterly* 49: 79–104; Nurit Zaidman. 2000. "The Integration of Indian Immigrants to Temples Run by North Americans." *Social Compass* 47, no. 2: 205–219; Nurit Zaidman. 1997. "When the Deities Are Asleep: Processes of Change in an American Hare Krishna Temple." *Journal of Contemporary Religion* 12, no. 3: 335–352; and Rochford 2007.
45. Squarcini and Fizzotti 2004, 29.
46. Rochford 2007.
47. Squarcini and Fizzotti 2004, 29–30.
48. Gadadhara Pandit Das and Jay Shetty (from the introduction) are two such devotees engaged in corporate outreach programs.

GLOSSARY

Ācaryā: Religious teacher and leader.
Acintya Bhedābheda Vedānta: System of philosophy in which the world of plurality is simultaneously different from and identical to Brahman (or in ISKCON, to Krishna).
Advaita Vedānta: Nondualist system of philosophy in which the world of plurality is only apparently real.
Ahaṁkāra: Ego.
Akṣara: Unchanging.
Āratī: Fire lamp offering to a god(s) or goddess(es).
Asamprajñāta samādhi (or nirvīja/nirbīja/nirvija/nirbija samādhi): The highest *samādhi* and goal of yoga in the *Yoga Sūtras,* a state of objectless and contentless awareness. Distinct from the penultimate goal of the *Yoga Sūtras*—*samprajñāta samādhi*—which is one-pointed awareness.
Āsana: A posture or sitting position in yoga.
Āśrama (Ashram): A place of religious residence or retreat.
Aṣṭāṅga (or Ashtanga) yoga: Eight-limbed yoga.
Ātmā (also Ātman): Ultimate Reality (Brahman) when referring to its presence within individual beings. In ISKCON, often translated as *soul.* Used by Radhanath Swami to mean *soul, living force,* or *God within us.*
Āyurveda: Traditional system of medicine rooted in treating different body types and balancing their energy constitutions.
Balarama: Krishna's brother.
Bandha: Literally, *body lock* (in yoga).
Bhadralok: Middle class.

Bhajan: Devotional song.
Bhakti: Devotion.
Bhakti vṛkṣa: In ISKCON, devotional home study groups.
Bhakti yoga: The path of devotion.
Brahmā: A creator god in Hinduism.
Brahmacārī: Celibate student (in ISKCON, celibate monk).
Brahman: Name for Ultimate Reality within Hindu traditions; understood variously across groups and traditions.
Chaitanya (or Chaitanya Mahāprabhu/Mahaprabhu): Gauḍīya Vaishnavas believe that Chaitanya was none other than Krishna himself, who descended to earth in human form in order to experience the love and bliss of life as his own devotee. ISKCON devotees believe that Chaitanya descended to earth in order to spread love of Krishna around the world.
Chakra: Literally, *wheel.* Often painted diagrammatically in Hindu religious spaces. In yoga, a body node through which various energies are channeled.
Daṇḍavat: Prostration.
Darshan: Seeing and being seen by god(s)/goddess(es).
Dās: Servant (m); in ISKCON, often spelled *Das.*
Dāsī: Servant (f); in ISKCON, often spelled *Dasi.* Also in ISKCON, *Devī dāsī* (honorific) is sometimes used and is often *devi dasi.*
Deva: Generic term for a god; in ISKCON, also used as an honorific.
Dharma: Duty.
Dhotī: Long, wrapped loincloth.
Doṣa: Body type as understood in Āyurveda.
Dṛṣṭi (or drishti): Sight; viewpoint, or focal point.
Dvaita Vedānta: Dualist system of Indian philosophy.
Gauḍīya Vaishnavism: Religious movement inspired by Chaitanya, sometimes called Bengal Vaishnavism or Chaitanya Vaishnavism.
Gauranga: A name for Chaitanya, meaning *the one with the golden body.*
Gaura-Nitai (or Gaur-Nitai): Refers to Chaitanya and his close associate Nityananda, respectively. ISKCON devotees believe that Chaitanya was none other than Krishna himself, who descended to earth in human form in order to spread love of Krishna around the world. Nityananda is believed to be the human form of Krishna's brother, Balarama.
Gopa: A cowherd friend of Krishna.
Gopī: A cowherd maiden and friend/lover of Krishna.
Gurukula: Traditional religious school.
Hari: literally, *yellow-* or *green-colored;* a name for Vishnu and Krishna.

Harināma (or harināma saṅkīrtana or nāmasaṅkīrtana): Public chanting of Krishna's names.

Haṭha yoga: A form of yoga.

Īśvara: In the *Yoga Sūtras*, a god concept on which to meditate; for Radhanath Swami, *īśvara* is Krishna.

Jagannath(a): Literally, *lord of the world*; a form of Krishna.

Janmāṣṭamī: The birthday of Krishna and the celebration festival for it.

Japa: Prayerful recitation of a mantra or incantation; *bead meditation* for Mantra Lounge devotees.

Japa mālā: Prayer beads.

Jīva: Individual self.

Karatālas: Cymbals.

Karmi: A term previously used by ISKCON devotees to refer to non-devotees or those whom devotees understood as bound up in mundane life in the material world.

Karuṇā Sindhu: Literally, *ocean of compassion*. Used by Radhanath Swami to mean *sea of God's love*.

Kholas: Drums.

Kīrtan: Devotional singing; used by Mantra lounge devotees to mean *music meditation*.

Krishna: A divinity understood variously within Hinduism; within ISKCON, the Supreme God.

Kriyā: Action done toward the goal of yoga.

Kṣara: Changing.

Kuṇḍalinī yoga: A form of yoga.

Kurma: The second incarnation of Vishnu (or Krishna, within ISKCON); believed to descend to earth in the form of a tortoise.

Kurtā: A long, loose shirt.

Līlā: *divine play*; Krishna's playful mythological engagements or exploits.

Mahā mantra: "Hare Krishna" mantra.

Maṅgal āratī: Early morning worship.

Mañjarī sādhana: Type of devotional practice within some Gauḍīya Vaishnava Hindu traditions wherein devotees imaginatively visualize themselves in the role of the adolescent girlfriends (*mañjarī*) of Krishna's divine consort Radha.

Mantra: Religious recitation or chant; used by Mantra lounge devotees to mean *that which delivers the mind*.

Mātā jī: Literally, *mother*; honorific form of address ISKCON devotees use for women.

Mokṣa: Hindu salvific goal of liberation, understood variously across traditions.

Mṛdaṅga: Drum.

Mūrti: Embodied form of god(s)/goddess(es). In ISKCON, also called a deity.

Mūrti puja: Ritual worship of embodied form of god(s)/goddess(es). In ISKCON, called deity worship.

Nāma Haṭṭa: Marketplace of the Name program.

Navdhā bhakti (ninefold *bhakti*): Nine practices of devotion that include *śravaṇam* (hearing), *kīrtanam* (singing), *smaraṇam* (remembering), *pādsevanam* (serving God's feet), *arcanam* (worship), *vandanam* (prostration), *dāsyam* (servitude), *sakhyam* (friendship), and *ātmanivedanam* (dedication of one's being/self-surrender).

Nitai: Nityananda, the human form of Krishna's brother, Balarama (see Gaura-Nitai).

Nityananda: The human form of Krishna's brother, Balarama.

Padayātrā: Foot journey. In ISKCON, this is a practice whereby devotees walk on foot singing Krishna's names and devotions.

Pañca-tattva: Chaitanya and his four principal companions.

Paramparā: Lineage.

Parikramā: Circumambulation.

Prabhu: Literally, *my lord*; honorific form of address ISKCON devotees use for men.

Prāṇa: Breath; vital breath. Often spelled *prana*. Used by Radhanath Swami to mean one's *essence*.

Prāṇāyāma: Breath control. Often spelled *pranayama*.

Prasād (or Prasādam): Food sanctified by having been offered to god(s)/goddess(es).

Puja: Ritual worship of god(s)/goddess(es).

Radha: The eternal lover and companion of Krishna.

Rāgānugā Bhakti Sādhana: A set of practices in which devotees imitate the actions and moods of the characters from Krishna's mythological associations.

Rathayātrā: A public devotional parade in which divine forms are pulled on carts or chariots.

Ṛitvik: A type of priest; in ISKCON, a proxy (for a guru).

Sabhā: Community, association, or committee.

Śaktipāt: Awakening of *spiritual energy*.

Samādhi: Intense concentration, the goal of yoga. Radhanath Swami defines *samādhi* as devotion and surrender to Krishna.

Samādhi: Memorial tomb.

Sāṃkhya: Literally, *number* or *enumeration*; system of Indian philosophy concerned with enumeration of principles or categories.

Saṃnyāsa: Fourth and final Hindu stage of life wherein an individual formally relinquishes their previous identity and societal standing in order to live a permanently celibate life devoted to religious pursuits.

Saṃnyāsī: One who enters into *saṃnyāsa* (see above).

Sampradāya: Denomination or tradition.

Saṅkīrtan(a): Public oratorio/chanting. In ISKCON, also the preaching activity of distributing ISKCON literature in public.

Śaraṇāgati: Approach for divine protection; Radhanath Swami defines this as surrender.

Saree: A wrapped, draped dress made of lengthy cloth.

Sāttvik: Endowed with goodness or purity.

Śikhā: Devotional tuft of hair.

Śloka: Verse.

Śrī/Sri/Śrīmatī/Srimati/Śrīman/ Śrīmān/: Honorific titles (of which there are various conventional spellings).

Śrīla (or Srila): An honorific title.

Subhadra: Krishna's sister.

Svarūpa: Essential nature or form; embodied form.

Tantra: A range of esoteric traditions.

Tīrthaṅkara: Literally, *ford-maker*; an exemplary figure in Jainism who has crossed over rebirths and has paved a road for others.

Tulasī: Holy basil. The material out of which the Hare Krishna prayer beads (*japa mālā*) are made. Also, a goddess.

Vaidhī Bhakti Sādhanā: The devotional path of rules.

Vaishnavism: Traditions surrounding devotion to Vishnu and Krishna; a Vaishnava is one who practices Vaishnavism.

Vedānta: Literally, *end of the Vedas*; a system of Indian philosophy.

Vinyāsa yoga: A form of yoga.

Vyāsāsana: In ISKCON, guru seat or the elevated seat on which gurus or other important figures or speakers sit.

Yoga śālā: Yoga hut.

Yogāsana (yoga + āsana): A posture or sitting position in yoga. See *āsana*.

Yukta vairāgya: In the *Bhaktirasāmṛtasindhu* of Rupa Goswami, a form of renunciation marked not by a rejection of the world and its objects but by detachment from and use of them in relationship with Krishna. In ISKCON, a practice whereby devotees use whatever materials exist in the world not only to worship Krishna but also to evangelize—that is, to spread the Hare Krishna movement. A *yukta vairāgī* is one who practices *yukta vairāgya*.

BIBLIOGRAPHY

Aditya, Ram N. 2001. "The Psychology of Deception in Marketing: A Conceptual Framework for Research and Practice." *Psychology & Marketing* 18, no. 7: 735–737.

Āraṇya, Sāṁkhya-yogāchārya Swāmi Hariharānanda (rendered into English by P. N. Mukerji). 1983. *Yoga Philosophy of Patañjali: Containing His Yoga Aphorisms with Vyāsa's Commentary in Sanskrit and a Translation with Annotations Including Many Suggestions for the Practice of Yoga*. Albany: State University of New York Press.

Arrington, Carl. 1983. "In a Landmark Case, Ex-Krishna Robin George Sues the Cult and Wins Big: $9.7 Million." *People Magazine*, September 12, 1983. http://people.com/archive/in-a-landmark-case-ex-krishna-robin-george-sues-the-cult-and-wins-big-9-7-million-vol-20-no-11.

Arvamudan, Srinivas. 2006. *Guru English: South Asian Religion in a Cosmopolitan Language*. Princeton: Princeton University Press.

Bennett, Peter. 1993. "Krishna's Own Form: Image Worship and Puṣṭi Mārga." *Journal of Vaishnava Studies* 1, no. 4: 109–134.

Berg, Travis Vande, and Fred Kniss. 2008. "ISKCON and Immigrants: The Rise, Decline, and Rise Again of a New Religious Movement." *The Sociological Quarterly* 49: 79–104.

Bhakti Center website. Accessed November 16, 2017. http://bhakticenter.org/.

———. "India Pilgrimage 2018." Accessed November 18, 2017. http://bhakticenter.org/india-pilgrimage/.

———. "Inversions 101." Accessed September 1, 2017. http://bhakticenter.org/inversions-101/.

———. "Stretch & Restore Yoga Class." Accessed November 16, 2017. http://bhakticenter.org/stretch-restore-yoga-class/.

———. "Yoga Classes." Accessed November 16, 2017. http://bhakticenter.org/yoga/classes/.

———. "Yoga 101." Accessed November 16, 2017. http://bhakticenter.org/yoga-101/.

Bhakti Yoga DC website. "200 HR Teacher Training: India Intensive." Accessed November 18, 2017. http://www.bhaktiyogadc.com/ytt-200-india-2018/.

Bhatia, Varuni. 2017. *Unforgetting Chaitanya: Vaishnavism and Cultures of Devotion in Colonial Bengal*. New Delhi: Oxford University Press.

Bromley, David G. 1989. "Hare Krishna and the Anti-Cult Movement." In *Krishna Consciousness in the West*. David G. Bromley and Larry D. Shinn, eds. Lewisburg: Bucknell University Press and Associated University Presses, 255–292.

Bromley, David G., and Larry D. Shinn, eds. 1989. *Krishna Consciousness in the West*. Lewisburg: Bucknell University Press and Associated University Presses.

Bronkhorst, Johannes. 1981. "Yoga and Seśvara Sāṃkhya." *Journal of Indian Philosophy* 9: 309–320.

Brooks, Charles R. 1989a. "A Unique Conjecture: The Incorporation of ISKCON in Vrindaban." In *Krishna Consciousness in the West*. David G. Bromley and Larry D. Shinn, eds. Lewisburg, PA: Bucknell University Press, 165–187.

———. 1989b. *The Hare Krishnas in India*. Delhi: Motilal Banarsidass Publishers.

Bryant, Edwin F. 2005. "Patañjali's Theistic Preference, Or, Was the Author of the *Yoga Sūtras* a Vaishnava?" *Journal of Vaishnava Studies* 14, no. 1: 7–28.

Bryant, Edwin F., and Maria L. Ekstrand. 2004. *The Hare Krishna Movement: The Postcharismatic Fate of a Religious Transplant*. New York: Columbia University Press.

Brzezinski, Jan. 1998. "What Was Srila Prabhupada's Position: The Hare Krishna Movement and Hinduism." *ISKCON Communications Journal* 6, no. 2: 27–49.

Calder, Bobby J. 2005. "Designing Brands." In *Kellogg on Branding: The Marketing Faculty of the Kellogg School of Marketing*. Alice M. Tybout and Tim Calkins, eds. Hoboken: John Wiley & Sons, 27–39.

Carette, Jeremy, and Richard King. 2005. *Selling Spirituality: The Silent Takeover of Religion*. Abingdon and New York: Routledge.

Chakravarti, Sudhindra Chandra. 1969. *Philosophical Foundations of Bengal Vaisnavism (A Critical Exposition)*. Calcutta: Academic Publishers.

Chander, Vineet. 2016. *The Washerman's Dog: Reflections on Liminality and ISKCON's Engagement with the Hindu Diaspora* (unpublished manuscript). Presented at The Worldwide Krishna Movement: Half a Century of Growth, Impact, and Challenge Conference. Harvard University, Cambridge, MA, April 22–24.

Chapple, Christopher Key. 2005. "Yoga and the Gita: Isvara-Pranidhana and Bhakti." *Journal of Vaishnava Studies* 14, no. 1: 29–42.

Chen, Chiung Hwang. 2011. "Marketing Religion Online: The LDS Church's SEO Efforts." *Journal of Media and Religion* 10: 185–205.

Collins, Irvin H. 2004. "The 'Routinization of Charisma' and the Charismatic: The Confrontation Between ISKCON and Narayana Maharaja." In *The Hare Krishna Movement: The Postcharismatic Fate of a Religious Transplant*. Edwin F. Bryant and Maria L. Ekstrand, eds. New York: Columbia University Press, 214–237.

Copeman, Jacob, and Aya Ikegame. 2012. "The Multifarious Guru: An Introduction." In *The Guru in South Asia: New Interdisciplinary Perspectives*. Jacob Copeman and Aya Ikegame, eds. New York: Routledge, 1–45.

Cresheim Arms Hotel Postcard. No Postmark. Photo Credit: The Paul J. Gutman Library Digital Collections. Old Images of Philadelphia Facebook page. Accessed October 27, 2019. https://www.facebook.com/oldimagesofphiladelphia/photos/a.115711028491844/603114709751471/?type=3&teater.

Csordas, Thomas J. 2009. "Introduction: Modalities of Transnational Transcendence." In *Transnational Transcendence: Essays on Religion and Globalization*. Thomas J. Csordas, ed. Berkeley: University of California Press, 1–29.

Dandavats. Accessed August 11, 2016. http://www.dandavats.com.

Darshan Deities Around the World Facebook page. Accessed August 11, 2016. https://www.facebook.com/darshanglobal/?fref=t.

Darshan Deities Around the World Tumblr. Accessed August 11, 2016. http://darshanglobal.tumblr.com/.

Das, Ananda Tirtha. 2017. "Shared Statement of the GBC Body & Hridayananda Das Goswami," October 19. ISKCONNews.Org. Accessed March 30, 2018. https://iskconnews.org/shared-statement-of-the-gbc-body-hridayananda-das-goswami,6325.

Das, Dayananda. 2006. "A Disciple's Perspective on the Hinduization of ISKCON." *Jagannatha's Chakra*. http://www.chakra.org/discussions/IntApr15_06.html. Accessed February 24, 2017.

Das, Jaya Madhava. 2014. "Surrounded by Indians." *The Sampradaya Sun-Independent Vaishnava News*, January 10. Accessed May 20, 2020. http://www.harekrsna.com/sun/editorials/01-14/editorials11247.htm.

———. 2013. "The Hare Krishna Movement Without Krishna/Prabhupada—Part 4." *The Sampradaya Sun-Independent Vaishnava News*, August 19. Accessed May 20, 2020. http://www.harekrsna.com/sun/editorials/08-13/editorials10516.htm.

———. 2006. "The Hinduization of ISKCON?" *Dandavats: Discussion*. Accessed May 20, 2020. http://www.dandavats.com/?p=127.

Das, Krishna Kirti. 2012. "Preaching According to Time, Place, and Circumstance with Adhikara is Trouble." *The Sampradaya Sun-Independent*

Vaishnava News, September 15. Accessed May 31, 2020. http://www.harekrsna.com/sun/editorials/09-12/editorials9051.htm.

Das, Murari. 2012. "Maintaining the Purity." *The Sampradaya Sun-Independent Vaishnava News*, September 15. Accessed May 31, 2020. http://www.harekrsna.com/sun/editorials/09-12/editorials9050.htm.

Das, Ragaputra. 2005. "The Hindufication of ISKCON." *Jagannatha's Chakra*. http://chakra.org/discussions/IntMar31_05.html. Accessed February 24, 2017.

Das, Satchitananda. "A Plea from the New York Sanctuary." *The Sampradaya Sun-Independent Vaishnava News*. Accessed May 17, 2019. http://www.harekrsna.com/sun/editorials/06-07/editorials1640.htm.

Das, Sikhi Mahiti. 2015. "Message from the Temple President—Sikhi Mahiti das." *ISKCON Philadelphia Newsletter*, October 15. Accessed July 2, 2017. http://iskconphiladelphia.com/wp-content/uploads/2015/10/Newsletter-101615.pdf.

Das, Sita-pati. 2006. "Loft Preaching Article." *Dandavats*. Accessed July 21, 2017. http://www.dandavats.com/?p=1840.

Das, Vastavika. 2012. "The Radhanathization of ISKCON." *The Sampradaya Sun-Independent Vaishnava News*, September 16. Accessed May 31, 2020. http://www.harekrsna.com/sun/editorials/09-12/editorials9062.htm.

Dasa, Gadadhara Pandit. "Conscious Living with Pandit Dasa." Accessed August 9, 2016. http://www.consciouslivingnyc.com/.

———. "NYC Pandit." Accessed October 2015. http://www.nycpandit.com. Page now redirects to Conscious Living NYC.

———. Pandit Dasa Facebook page. Accessed October 18, 2016. https://www.facebook.com/iskconjuhu/?fref=ts.

———. 2013. *Urban Monk: Exploring Karma, Consciousness, and the Divine*. New York: Pankaj Srivastava.

Dasa, Gopinath. 2012. "Radhanathardation: Opportunistic Nuevo ISKCON." *The Sampradaya Sun-Independent Vaishnava News*, September 22. Accessed May 31, 2020. http://www.harekrsna.com/sun/editorials/09-12/editorials9088.htm.

Dasa, Jaya Madhava. 2011. "Is ISKCON Shrinking or Growing?" *The Sampradaya Sun-Independent Vaishnava News*, April 3. Accessed May 20, 2020. http://www.harekrsna.com/sun/editorials/04-11/editorials7165.htm.

Dasa, Rocana. 2011. "Vancouver Ratha Ruined." *The Sampradaya Sun-Independent Vaishnava News*, August 6. Accessed May 31, 2020. http://www.harekrsna.com/sun/editorials/08-11/editorials7599.htm.

Dasa, Shukavak N. 1999. *Hindu Encounter with Modernity: Kedarnath Datta Bhaktivinoda Vaiṣṇava Theologian*. Los Angeles: Sanskrit Religions Institute.

Dasa, Subhananda, ed. *Śrī Nāmāmṛta—The Nectar of the Holy Name*. Accessed May 9, 2017. https://docs.google.com/file/d/0BzR876u4ZuxEYmE0YTg1NWEtZTI1YS00NTYyLThkYmYtMTQ4MzJhMGJmMzFk/view.

Dasi, Hare Krsna. 2004. "The Hinduization of ISKCON?" *Jagannatha's Chakra.* http://www.chakra.org/discussions/IntFeb12_04.html. Accessed February 24, 2017.

Dawson, Lorne L., and Douglas E. Cowan. 2004. "Introduction." In *Religion Online: Finding Faith on the Internet.* Lorne L. Dawson and Douglas E. Cowan, eds. New York: Routledge, 1–16.

DC Devotee. Interview by Nicole Karapanagiotis. In person, Lanexa, Virginia, June 11, 2016.Deadwyler, William H. (Ravindra Svarupa Dasa). 2004. "Cleaning House and Cleaning Hearts: Reform and Renewal in ISKCON." In *The Hare Krshna Movement: The Postcharismatic Fate of a Religious Transplant.* Edwin F. Bryant and Maria L. Ekstrand, eds. New York: Columbia University Press, 149–169.

———. 1989. "Patterns in ISKCON's Historical Self-Perception." In *Krishna Consciousness in the West.* David G. Bromley and Larry D. Shinn, eds. Lewisburg: Bucknell University Press and Associated University Presses, 55–75.

———. 1985. "The Devotee and the Deity: Living a Personalistic Theology." In *Gods of Flesh, Gods of Stone.* Joanne Punzo Waghorne and Norman Cutler, eds. New York: Columbia University Press, 69–87.

Delaware Yoga Society. Accessed July 24, 2018. http://delawareyogasociety.com/home/.

Delmonico, Neal. 2007. "Chaitanya Vaishnavism and the Holy Names." In *Krishna: A Sourcebook.* Edwin F. Bryant, ed. Oxford and New York: Oxford University Press, 549–575.

De Michelis, Elizabeth. 2004. *A History of Modern Yoga: Patañjali and Western Esotericism.* New York: Continuum.

Desai, Krishnakant, Sunil Awatramami (Adridharan Das), and Madhu Pandit Das. 2004. "The No Change in ISKCON Paradigm." In *The Hare Krshna Movement: The Postcharismatic Fate of a Religious Transplant.* Edwin F. Bryant and Maria L. Ekstrand, eds. New York: Columbia University Press, 194–213.

Devi Dasi, M. 2015. "Reaching the Hearts Day 2 Session 4." Kishorekishori YouTube channel, May 2. 45:57. Accessed July 2, 2017. https://www.youtube.com/watch?v=xL7_bQT1etc.

DeYoung, Curtiss Paul, Michael O. Emerson, George Yancey, and Karen Chai Kim. 2003. *United by Faith: The Multiracial Congregation as an Answer to the Problem of Race.* New York: Oxford University Press.

Dimock, Edward C., Jr. 1999. *Caitanya Caritāmṛta of Kṛṣṇadāsa Kavirāja: A Translation and Commentary.* Tony K. Stewart, ed. Cambridge, MA: Harvard University Press.

Donaldson, Laura E. 2001. "On Medicine Women and White Shame-ans: New Age Native Americanism and Commodity Fetishism as Pop Culture

Feminism." In *Women, Gender, Religion: A Reader.* Elizabeth A Castelli, ed. (assisted by Rosamond C. Rodman). New York: Palgrave, 237–256.

Dougherty, Kevin D. 2003. "How Monochromatic Is Church Membership? Racial-Ethnic Diversity in Religious Community." *Sociology of Religion* 64, no. 1: 65–85.

Dr. Howard J. Resnick website. "Dr. Howard J. Resnick." Accessed March 23, 2018. http://www.howardjresnick.com/.

Dwyer, Graham, and Richard J. Cole, eds. 2013. *Hare Krishna in the Modern World: Reflections by Distinguished Academics and Scholarly Devotees.* London: Arktos Media.

———, eds. 2007. *The Hare Krishna Movement: Forty Years of Chant and Change.* London and New York: I.B. Tauris.

Eck, Diana L. 1996. *Darśan: Seeing the Divine Image in India.* New York: Columbia University Press.

Edelmann, Jonathan. 2014. "Introduction: Innovation in Hindu Traditions." *International Journal of Hindu Studies* 18, no. 2: 113–118.

Einstein, Mara. 2008. *Brands of Faith: Marketing Religion in a Commercial Age.* New York: Routledge.

Ellenbogen, Josh, and Aaron Tugendhaft, eds. 2011. *Idol Anxiety.* Stanford, CA: Stanford University Press.

Eller, Cynthia. 1993. *Living in the Lap of the Goddess: The Feminist Spirituality Movement in America.* New York: The Crossroad.

Emerson, Michael O., and Karen Chai Kim. 2003. "Multiracial Congregations: An Analysis of Their Development and a Typology." *Journal for the Scientific Study of Religion* 42, no. 2: 217–227.

Finke, Roger, and Rodney Stark. 2005. *The Churching of America 1776–2005: Winners and Losers in Our Religious Economy.* New Brunswick and London: Rutgers University Press.

Fisher, Adjua. 2016. "These $10 Yoga-and-Dinner Classes Are One of Philly's Best Kept Secrets." *Philadelphia Magazine: Be Well Philly,* November 15. Accessed July 21, 2017. http://www.phillymag.com/be-well-philly/2016/11/15/mantra-lounge/.

Flood, Gavin. 1995. "Hinduism, Vaishnavism, and ISKCON: Authentic Traditions or Scholarly Constructions?" *ISKCON Communications Journal* 3, no. 2: 5–15.

Forsthoefel, Thomas A., and Cynthia Ann Humes, eds. 2005. *Gurus in America.* Albany: State University of New York Press.

Fox, Margalit. 2011. "Swami Bhaktipada, Ex-Hare Krishna Leader, Dies at 74." *The New York Times,* October 24. Accessed May 17, 2019. https://www.nytimes.com/2011/10/25/us/swami-bhaktipada-ex-hare-krishna-leader-dies-at-74.html.

Fuller, C. J. 2004. *The Camphor Flame: Popular Hinduism and Society in India.* Revised and Expanded Edition. Princeton: Princeton University Press.

Fuller, Jason Dale. 2009. "Modern Hinduism and the Middle Class: Beyond *Reform* and *Revival* in the Historiography of Colonial India." *The Journal of Hindu Studies* 2: 160–178.

———. 2005. *Religion, Class, and Power: Bhaktivinode Thakur and the Transformation of Religious Authority Among the Gauḍīya Vaiṣṇavas in Nineteenth-Century Bengal.* PhD Dissertation: University of Pennsylvania.

———. 2003. "Re-membering the Tradition: Bhaktivinoda Ṭhākura's *Sajjanaṇ osanī* and the Construction of a Middle-Class Vaiṣṇava Sampradāya in Nineteenth-Century Bengal." In *Hinduism in Public and Private: Reform, Hindutva, Gender, and Sampraday.* Antony Copley, ed. New Delhi: Oxford University Press, 173–210.

Gallagher, Eugene V. 2004. *The New Religious Movements Experience in America.* Westport and London: Greenwood Press.

Garces-Foley, Kathleen. 2007a. *Crossing the Ethnic Divide: The Multiethnic Church on a Mission.* New York: Oxford University Press.

———. 2007b. "New Opportunities and New Values: The Emergence of the Multicultural Church." *The Annals of the American Academy of Political and Social Science* 612: 209–224.

Gold, Daniel. 2012. "Continuities as Gurus Change." In *The Guru in South Asia: New Interdisciplinary Approaches.* Jacob Copeman and Aya Ikegame, eds. London and New York: Routledge, 241–254.

Goswami, Bir Krishna Dasa. 2014. "Krishna West Overview by Bir Krishna Dasa Goswami, Part 1." YouTube video, April 15. 9:32. Accessed February 19, 2017. https://www.youtube.com/watch?v=bShPRTP1IJw.

———. 2014. "Krishna West Overview by Bir Krishna Dasa Goswami, Part 2." YouTube video, April 15. 7:15. Accessed May 11, 2017. https://www.youtube.com/watch?v=TBYnL9rTfgc.

———. 2014. "Krishna West Overview by Bir Krishna Dasa Goswami, Part 3." YouTube video, April 16. 11:47. Accessed May 11, 2017. https://www.youtube.com/watch?v=4PrVXbMyNI8.

Goswami, C. L., and M. A. Shastri. 2003. *Śrīmad Bhāgavata Mahāpurāṇa* (with Sanskrit text and English translation), Part 1 (book 1 to 8). Gorakhpur: Gita Press.

Goswami, Hridayananda Das. 2014. "Hridayananda Dasa Goswami Responds to GBC Disapproval of Krishna West" (letter, retitled). Published on March 6. OneISKCON.com. Accessed September 19, 2014. http://www.oneiskcon.com/hridayananda-dasa-goswami-responds-to-gbc-disapproval-of-krishna-west/.

———. 2015. "Ideal Vedic Culture–Krishna West Istagosthi with H. D. GOSWAMI." Daniel Laflor YouTube channel, September 29. 2:56:20. Accessed February 24, 2017. https://www.youtube.com/watch?v=YottYzI98_M.

———. 2016. "An Important GBC Update—January 6, 2016." Accessed April 3, 2018. http://hdgoswami.com/chronicals/letters/an-important-gbc-update-january-6-2016/.

———. Interview by Nicole Karapanagiotis. Conducted via Skype, Wilmington, Delaware, June 15, 2015.

———. Interview by Nicole Karapanagiotis. Conducted via Skype, Wilmington, Delaware, October 23, 2015.

———. 2014. "KRISHNA WEST—The Interview, Vol. 1." GourTube YouTube channel, March 20. 1:46:35. Accessed March 27, 2018. https://www.youtube.com/watch?v=2EEO5_2HVdc.

———. 2014. "KRISHNA WEST—The Interview, Vol. 2." GourTube YouTube channel, November 20. 1:37:27. Accessed May 11, 2017. https://www.youtube.com/watch?v=X3q7l5L_E5w&t=3360s.

———. 2016. "Letter to Devotees." Hridayananda Das Goswami Facebook page, January 7. Accessed April 2, 2018. https://www.facebook.com/hridayanandadasgoswami/posts/1717759215121769.

———. 2015. "Reply to a Senior Leader." Unpublished essay. Posted on Hridayananda das Goswami—Friends and Disciples Facebook page (public), October 24. Accessed May 11, 2017. https://www.facebook.com/groups/acharyadeva/permalink/10153917775293646/.

———. 2015. "The Vaiṣṇavī Guru," May 19. Accessed March 27, 2018. http://hdgoswami.com/essays/the-vaisnavi-guru-essay/.

———. 2005. "Vaisnava Moral Theology and Homosexuality," February 2. Accessed March 27, 2018. http://hdgoswami.com/essays/vaisnava-moral-theology-and-homosexuality/.

Goswami, Mukunda, and Krishnarupa Devi Dasi, eds. 2016. *The Hare Krishnas: Celebrating 50 Years.* ISKCON Communications International.

Goswami, Satsvarūpa Dāsa. 1983. *Prabhupāda: Messenger of the Supreme Lord.* Mumbai: The Bhaktivedanta Book Trust.

Govardhan Eco Village website. "About: Govardhan School of Yoga." Accessed November 18, 2017. https://ecovillage.org.in/yoga/intl/.

———. "About Us." Accessed November 18, 2017. https://ecovillage.org.in/yoga/about-us/.

———. Accessed November 17, 2017. https://www.ecovillage.org.in/.

———. "Faculty." Accessed November 18, 2017. https://ecovillage.org.in/yoga/faculty/.

———. "Schedule." Accessed November 18, 2017. https://ecovillage.org.in/yoga/schedules/.

Haberman, David L. 2014. "The Accidental Ritualist." In *Essays in South Asia Rituals in Honor of Fredrick Clothey.* Penkower, Linda & Tracy Pintchman, eds. Columbia: University of South Carolina Press, 151–165.

———. 1999. "First Annual Robert C. Lester Lecture on the Study of Religion." Delivered February 11, 1999. University of Colorado.

———. 1994. "Divine Betrayal: Krishna Gopal of Braj in the Eyes of Outsiders." *Journal of Vaishnava Studies* 3, no. 1: 83–111.

———. 1993. "On Trial: The Love of the Sixteen Thousand Gopees." *History of Religions* 33, no. 1: 44–70.

———. 1988. *Acting as a Way of Salvation: A Study of Rāgānugā Bhakti Sādhana.* Delhi: Motilal Banarsidass Publishers.

HDGoswami.Com. "H.D. Goswami." Accessed March 23, 2018. http://hdgoswami.com/.

Hein, Norvin. 1994. "Chaitanya's Ecstasies and the Theology of the Name." *Journal of Vaiṣṇava Studies* 2, no. 2: 7–27.

Hendershot, Heather. 2004. *Shaking the World for Jesus: Media and Conservative Evangelical Culture.* Chicago and London: University of Chicago Press.

Herman, Phyllis K. 2010. "Seeing the Divine Through Windows: Online Puja and Virtual Religious Experience." *Online—Heidelberg Journal of Religions on the Internet* 4, no. 1: 151–178.

Hine, Christine. 2015. *Ethnography for the Internet: Embedded, Embodied and Everyday.* London: Bloomsbury.

———. 2000. *Virtual Ethnography.* Thousand Oaks, London, and New Delhi: SAGE Publications.

Holdrege, Barbara. 2015. *Bhakti and Embodiment: Fashioning Divine Bodies and Devotional Bodies in Kṛṣṇa Bhakti.* London and New York: Routledge.

Hopkins, Thomas J. 1989. "The Social and Religious Background for Transmission of Gaudiya Vaishnavism to the West." In *Krishna Consciousness in the West.* David G. Bromley and Larry D. Shinn, eds. Lewisburg: Bucknell University Press and Associated University Presses, 35–54.

Hridayananda Das Goswami—Friends and Disciples Facebook group (public). Posted June 20, 2015. Accessed April 4, 2018. https://www.facebook.com/groups/acharyadeva/.

Huffer (Lucia), Amanda J. 2011. "Backdoor Hinduism: A Recoding in the Language of Spirituality." *Nidān: International Journal for the Study of Hinduism* 23: 53–71.

Huffington Post Facebook page. 2016. "Changing the World Starts with You." Video by Jay Shetty, February 26. 3:09. Accessed August 9, 2016. https://www.facebook.com/HuffingtonPost/videos/10153699398631130/.

Humes, Cynthia Ann. 2005. "Maharishi Mahesh Yogi: Beyond the TM Technique." In *Gurus in America.* Thomas A. Forsthoefel and Cynthia Ann Humes, eds. Albany: State University of New York Press, 55–79.

ISKCON Alachua Facebook page. Accessed August 7, 2016. https://www.facebook.com/alachuatemple/?fref=ts.

ISKCON Communications Journal online. Accessed October 15, 2016. http://content.iskcon.org/icj/contents.html.

ISKCON Delhi Facebook page. Accessed August 7, 2016. https://www.facebook.com/iskcondelhi/?fref=ts.

ISKCON Juhu Facebook page. Accessed August 8, 2016. https://www.facebook.com/iskconjuhu/?fref=ts.

ISKCONLeaders.Com. "ISKCON Leaders: Hridayananda Das Goswami." Accessed March 23, 2018. http://iskconleaders.com/hridayananda-das-goswami/.

ISKCON London Facebook page. Accessed August 7, 2016. https://www.facebook.com/iskconlondon/?fref=ts.

ISKCON Mayapur head *pujārī* (priest). Interview by Nicole Karapanagiotis. In person, Mayapur, West Bengal, India. December 24, 2015.

ISKCON Mayapur (Public Group) Facebook page. Accessed August 7, 2016. https://www.facebook.com/groups/167861299929466/.

ISKCON New Jersey Facebook page. Accessed August 7, 2016. https://www.facebook.com/iskconofnj/?fref=ts.

ISKCONNews.Org. Accessed June 5, 2016. http://iskconnews.org/.

ISKCON News Staff. 2011. "ISKCON In Danger of Losing 26 2nd Avenue." ISKCONNews.Org, November 2. Accessed May 17, 2019. https://iskconnews.org/iskcon-in-danger-of-losing-26-2nd-avenue,2947/.

ISKCON of Philadelphia Temple Vice President. Interview by Nicole Karapanagiotis. In person, Philadelphia, Pennsylvania, October 9, 2018.

ISKCON Vrindavan Daily Darshan Facebook page. Accessed August 7, 2016. https://www.facebook.com/iskconvrindavandailydarshan/?fref=ts.

ISKCON Vrindavan Facebook page. Accessed August 7, 2016. https://www.facebook.com/vrindavan.tv/.

Jagannatha's Chakra. Accessed June 5, 2016. http://www.chakra.org/.

Jain, Andrea R. 2014. "Muktananda; Entrepreneurial Godman, Tantric Hero." In *Gurus of Modern Yoga*. Mark Singleton and Ellen Goldberg, eds. New York: Oxford University Press, 190-209.

———. 2015. *Selling Yoga: From Counterculture to Pop Culture*. Oxford and New York: Oxford University Press.

Jarvis, Elizabeth Farmer. 2008. *Images of America: Mount Airy*. Charleston, Chicago, Portsmouth, San Francisco: Arcadia Publishing.

Jivamukti Yoga School website. Accessed November 18, 2017. https://jivamuktiyoga.com/.

———. "Govardhan Eco Village, India." November 17, 2017. https://jivamuktiyoga.com/general/11418/.

———. "Teacher Training: 300 Hour in India." Accessed November 18, 2017. https://jivamuktiyoga.com/teacher-training/teacher-training-in-india/.

Karapanagiotis, Nicole. 2019. "Automatic Rituals and Inadvertent Audiences: ISKCON, Krishna and the Ritual Mechanics of Facebook." In *Digital Hinduism*. Xenia Zeiler, ed. New York: Routledge Press, 51-67.

———. 2013. "Cyber Forms, *Worshipable Forms*: Hindu Devotional Viewpoints on the Ontology of Cyber-Gods and Goddesses." *International Journal of Hindu Studies* 17, no. 1: 57–82.

———. "Digital Diaspora of Viṣṇu: Vaiṣṇava Digital *Darśan(s)* and the Internet." Forthcoming in *Vaiṣṇavisms: Many Varieties of the Worship of Viṣṇu*. Archana Venkatesan and Gavin Flood, eds. Oxford: Oxford University Press.

———. 2018. "Of Digital Images and Digital Media: Approaches to Marketing in American ISKCON." *Nova Religio: The Journal of Alternative and Emergent Religion* 21, no. 3: 74–102.

Kendall, Lori. 1999. "Recontextualizing 'Cyberspace': Methodological Considerations for On-Line Research." In *Doing Internet Research: Critical Issues and Methods for Examining the Net*. Steve Jones, ed. Thousand Oaks, London, New Delhi: SAGE Publications 57–74.

Killingley, Dermot. 2014. "Manufacturing Yogis: Swami Vivekananda as a Yoga Teacher." In *Gurus of Modern Yoga*. Mark Singleton and Ellen Goldberg, eds. New York: Oxford University Press, 17–37.

Kishorekishori YouTube channel. Accessed June 30, 2017. https://www.youtube.com/user/kishorekishori/videos.

Knott, Kim. 2000. "In Every Town and Village: Adaptive Strategies in the Communication of Krishna Consciousness in the UK, the First Thirty Years." *Social Compass* 47, no. 2: 153–167.

———. 1986. *My Sweet Lord: The Hare Krishna Movement*. Wellingborough: The Aquarian Press.

KrishnaPath.Org. *Śrī Padyavali*. http://www.krishnapath.org/Library/Goswami-books/Rupa/Rupa_Goswami_Sri_Padyavali.pdf. Accessed May 12, 2017.

Krishna West Chapel Hill Vimeo channel. "Krishna West Chapel Hill Introduction." 1:31. Accessed March 29, 2018. https://vimeo.com/100906068.

Krishna West Inc. Facebook page (public). Posted May 28, 2014. Accessed April 4, 2018. https://www.facebook.com/pg/krishnawestinc/photos/?ref=page_internal.

———. Posted July 12, 2014. Accessed April 4, 2018. https://www.facebook.com/pg/krishnawestinc/photos/?ref=page_internal.

Krishna West SoundCloud. "Krishna West SoundCloud." Accessed March 29, 2018. https://soundcloud.com/krishna-west.

Krishna West website. "Krishna West Mission: Inspiring Purposeful Living." Accessed March 29, 2018. http://krishnawest.com/about/mission/.

———. "Krishna West: Who Are We? H. D. Goswami is an Early Pioneer and Renowned Teacher of *Bhakti Yoga* in the Western World." Accessed March 30, 2018. http://krishnawest.com/who-we-are/h-d-goswami/.

———. "Projects." Accessed March 30, 2018. http://krishnawest.com/projects/.

———. "Who We Are: H. D. Goswami." Accessed June 4, 2019. https://krishnawest.com/who-we-are/h-d-goswami/.

Larsen, Elena. 2004. "Cyberfaith: How Americans Pursue Religion Online." In *Religion Online: Finding Faith on the Internet*. Lorne L. Dawson and Douglas E. Cowan, eds. New York: Routledge, 17–20.

Larson, Gerald James. 1989. "An Old Problem Revisited: The Relation between Sāṃkhya, Yoga, and Buddhism." *Studien zur Indologie und Iranistik* 15: 129–146.

———. 1999. "Classical Yoga as Neo-Sāṃkhya: A Chapter in the History of Indian Philosophy." *Asiatische Studien* 53, no. 3: 723–732.

Lazear, Edward P. 1995. "Bait and Switch." *Journal of Political Economy* 103, no. 4: 813–830.

Lee, Shayne, and Phillip Luke Sinitiere. 2009. *Holy Mavericks: Evangelical Innovators and the Spiritual Marketplace*. New York and London: New York University Press.

Lichtblau, Eric, and Matt Lait. 1992. "Court Orders Retrial of O.C. Krishna Case." *Los Angeles Times*, January 31. Accessed February 19, 2017. http://articles.latimes.com/1992-01-31/news/mn-1099_1_supreme-court.

Lövheim, Mia, and Alf G. Linderman. 2005. In *Religion and Cyberspace*. Morten T. Højsgaard and Margit Warburg, eds. London and New York: Routledge, 121–137.

Lucia, Amanda J. 2014a. "Innovative Gurus: Tradition and Change in Contemporary Hinduism." *International Journal of Hindu Studies* 18, no. 2: 221–263.

———. 2014b. *Reflections of Amma: Devotees in Global Embrace*. Berkeley and Los Angeles: University of California Press.

Mallapragada, Madhavi. 2010. "Desktop Deities: Hindu Temples, Online Cultures and the Politics of Remediation." *South Asian Popular Culture* 8, no. 2: 109–121.

Mantra Lounge Philadelphia Facebook page. Accessed July 22, 2017. https://www.facebook.com/mantraloungephiladelphia/.

———. July 31, 2018. Accessed June 4, 2019. https://www.facebook.com/mantraloungephiladelphia/photos/a.657394061001739/2175448702529593/?type=3&theater.

———. "Yoga Revolution Retreat—Being for Real in Bhakti." Retreat April 14–16, 2017. Accessed July 22, 2017. https://www.facebook.com/events/392039644490790/.

Mantra Lounge Philadelphia website. Accessed July 20, 2017. http://mantraphilly.com/.

———. Calendar Event page. "Kirtan Connection: Music Meditation & Dance." Accessed July 22, 2017. http://mantraphilly.com/events/mantra-meditation-mindfulness-5/.

———. Calendar Event page. "Monday—Power Yoga: Body Therapy." Accessed July 22, 2017. http://mantraphilly.com/events/mindful-mondays-breathe-stretch-mantra/.

———. Calendar Event page. "Tuesday—Kirtan Connection: Music Meditation & Dance." Accessed July 22, 2017. http://mantraphilly.com/events/mantra-meditation-mindfulness-5/.

———. "Find us on Campus." Accessed June 1, 2017. http://mantraphilly.com/find-us-on-campus/.

———. "Kirtan." Accessed July 22, 2017. http://mantraphilly.com/mantrameditation/.

———. "Retreat." Accessed July 22, 2017. http://mantraphilly.com/retreat/.

———. "Sustainability Circle." Accessed July 23, 2017. http://mantraphilly.com/sustainability/.

———. "Workshops." Accessed July 23, 2017. http://mantraphilly.com/workshops/.

———. "Yoga Classes." Accessed July 22, 2017. http://mantraphilly.com/yoga/.

Marcus, George E. 1995. "Ethnography in/of the World System: The Emergence of Multi-Sited Ethnography." *Annual Review of Anthropology* 24: 95–117.

McGavran, Donald A. 1970. *Understanding Church Growth*. Revised and edited by C. Peter Wagner (1990). Grand Rapids: William B. Eerdmans.

Mittal, Sachin. 2015. "Seminar on Reaching the Hearts and the Minds of the Western Public." *Dandavats*. Accessed July 2, 2017. http://www.dandavats.com/?p=17198.

Moore, R. Laurence. 1994. *Selling God: American Religion in the Marketplace of Culture*. New York and Oxford: Oxford University Press.

Nye, Malory. 2015. *Multiculturalism and Minority Religions in Britain: Krishna Consciousness, Religious Freedom, and the Politics of Location*. London and New York: Routledge.

Official Website of the Governing Body Commission of ISKCON. "Hridayananda das Goswami." Accessed March 23, 2018. https://gbc.iskcon.org/hridayananda-das-goswami/.

Patel, Urvashi. 2005. "Response to the Article 'The Hindufication of ISKCON.'" *Jagannatha's Chakra*. http://www.chakra.org/discussions/IntMay04_05.html. Accessed February 24, 2017.

———. 2006. "The Need for Diversity." *Jagannatha's Chakra: Discussions*. Accessed May 10, 2017. http://www.chakra.org/discussions/IntJun08_06.html.

Prabhupada, A. C. Bhaktivedanta Swami. 1986. *Bhagavad-Gītā As It Is: Complete Edition Revised and Enlarged with Original Sanskrit Text, Roman Transliteration, English Equivalents, Translation, and Elaborate Purports*. Los Angeles: The Bhaktivedanta Book Trust.

———. 1975. *Sri Caitanya-caritamrta, Madhya-lila: The Pastimes of Lord Caitanya Mahaprabhu*. Los Angeles: Bhaktivedanta Book Trust.

———. 1974. *Śrīmad-Bhāgavatam: With the Original Sanskrit Text, Its Roman Transliteration, Synonyms, Translation and Elaborate Purports by His Divine Grace A.C. Bhaktivedanta Swami Prabhupada Founder-Acarya of the International Society for Krishna Consciousness*. Fourth Canto, "The Creation of the Fourth Order" (part 4, chapters 25–31). Los Angeles: Bhaktivedanta Book Trust, 4.29.55. Official ISKCON digital book. Accessed May 10, 2017. http://vanisource.org/wiki/Srimad-Bhagavatam.

———. 1974. "Lecture Arrival—Mayapur," September 27. Accessed May 10, 2017. http://vanisource.org/wiki/Arrival_Lecture_--_Mayapur,_September_27,_1974.

———. 1973. "Lecture Festival Disappearance Day, Bhaktisiddhana Sarasvati—Los Angeles," December 13. Accessed May 10, 2017. http://vanisource.org/wiki/His_Divine_Grace_Srila_Bhaktisiddhanta_Sarasvati_Gosvami_Prabhupada%27s_Disappearance_Day,_Lecture_--_Los_Angeles,_December_13,_1973.

———. 1972. "Letter to Devotees Written from Los Angeles," August 26. Accessed May 10, 2017. http://vanisource.org/wiki/Letter_to_Devotees_--_Los_Angeles_26_August,_1972.

———. 1970. *The Nectar of Devotion: The Complete Science of Bhakti Yoga*. New York: The Bhaktivedanta Book Trust.

Prasad, Ramananda. 1995. *The Bhagavad-Gītā*. Delhi and Fremont: Motilal Banarsidass and The American Gita Society.

RadhanathSwami.com. "Radhanath Swami's Bestseller *The Journey Within* Lights up Broadway." Accessed June 4, 2019. http://www.radhanathswami.com/2017/05/radhanath-swamis-bestseller-the-journey-within-lights-up-broadway/.

Rochford, E. Burke, Jr. 1985. *Hare Krishna in America*. New Brunswick, NJ: Rutgers University Press.

———. 2004. "Airport, Conflict, and Change in the Hare Krishna Movement." In *The Hare Krishna Movement: The Postcharismatic Fate of a Religious Transplant*. Edwin F. Bryant and Maria L. Ekstrand, eds. New York: Columbia University Press, 273–290.

———. 2007. *Hare Krishna Transformed*. New York: New York University Press.

———. 2009. "Succession, Religious Switching, and Schism in the Hare Krishna Movement." In *Sacred Schisms: How Religions Divide*. James R. Lewis and Sarah M. Lewis, eds. Cambridge: Cambridge University Press, 265–286.

Roof, Wade Clark. 1999. *Spiritual Marketplace: Baby Boomers and the Remaking of American Religion*. Princeton, NJ : Princeton University Press.

Rūpagosvāmī. *Bhaktirasāmṛtasindhu. The Bhaktirasāmṛtasindhu of Rūpa Gosvāmin.* Translated with Introduction and Notes by David L. Haberman. 2003. New Delhi and Delhi: Indira Gandhi National Centre for the Arts and Motilal Banarsidass Publishers.

Sampradaya Sun. Accessed June 5, 2016. http://www.harekrsna.com/sun/.

Sarbadhikary, Sukanya. 2015. *The Place of Devotion: Siting and Experiencing Divinity in Bengal-Vaishnavism.* Oakland: University of California Press.

Sardella, Ferdinando. 2013. *Modern Hindu Personalism: The History, Life, and Thought of Bhaktisiddhānta Saravatiī.* Oxford and New York: Oxford University Press.

Sax, William S., ed. 1995. *The Gods at Play: Lila in South Asia.* Oxford and New York. Oxford University Press.

Scheifinger, Heinz. 2010. "Om-Line Hinduism: World Wide Gods on the Web." *Journal for the Academic Study of Religion* 23, no. 3: 325–345.

———. 2009. "The *Jagannath* Temple and Online *Darshan.*" *The Journal of Contemporary Religion* 24, no. 3: 277–290.

Sher, Shlomo. 2011. "A Framework for Assessing Immorally Manipulative Marketing Tactics." *Journal of Business Ethics* 102: 97–118.

Shinn, Larry D., and David G. Bromley. 1989. "A Kaleidoscopic View of the Hare Krishnas in America." In *Krishna Consciousness in the West.* David G. Bromley and Larry D. Shinn, eds. Lewisburg, PA: Bucknell University Press.

Singleton, Mark. 2010. *Yoga Body: The Origins of Modern Posture Practice.* New York: Oxford University Press.

Singleton, Mark, and Ellen Goldberg, eds. 2014. *Gurus of Modern Yoga.* New York: Oxford University Press.

Singleton, Mark, and Tara Fraser. "T. Krishnamacharya, Father of Modern Yoga." In *Gurus of Modern Yoga.* Mark Singleton and Ellen Goldberg, eds. New York: Oxford University Press.

Smullen, Madhava. 2011. "First Ever ISKCON Temple Extends Plea for Help." ISKCONNews.Org, November 11. Accessed May 17, 2019. https://iskconnews.org/first-ever-iskcon-temple-extends-plea-for-help,2968/.

———. 2016. "Urban Monks Present Spirituality for the Apple Generation." ISKCONNews.Org, May 20. Accessed August 9, 2016. http://iskconnews.org/urban-monks-present-spirituality-for-the-apple-generation,3524/.

Squarcini, Federico, and Eugenio Fizzotti. 2004. *Hare Krishna.* Salt Lake City, UT: Signature Books.

Srinivas, Smriti. 2008. *In the Presence of Sai Baba: Body, City, and Memory in a Global Religious Movement.* Leiden: Brill.

Srinivas, Tulasi. 2010. *Winged Faith: Rethinking Globalization and Religious Pluralism through the Sathya Sai Movement.* New York: Columbia University Press.

Staff Member. 2011. "Radhanath and Yajya Purusha, The Sanctuary Hijackers." *Prabhupāda News,* April 24. Accessed May 17, 2019. http://www.prabhupadanugas.eu/news/?p=19290#more-19290.

Sternthal, Brian, and Angela Y. Lee. 2005. "Building Brands Through Effective Advertising." In *Kellogg on Branding: The Marketing Faculty of the Kellogg School of Marketing.* Alice M. Tybout and Tim Calkins, eds. Hoboken: John Wiley & Sons, 129-149.

Strauss, Amy. 2016. "Listen to My Mantra: New Fishtown Studio Fueled by Mantra Meditation and Travelling Monks." *Spirit News,* August 25. Accessed July 21, 2017. https://spiritnews.org/articles/listen-to-my-mantra-new-fishtown-studio-fueled-by-mantra-meditation-and-travelling-monks/.

Sun Staff. n.d. "Kirtanananda Forms Alliance with ISKCON Devotees." *The Sampradaya Sun-Independent Vaishnava News.* Accessed May 17, 2019. https://www.harekrsna.com/sun/features/09-05/features47.htm.

———. 2011. "Radhanatha Swami's 'Preaching Strategies.'" *The Sampradaya Sun-Independent Vaishnava News,* July 6. Accessed May 31, 2020. http://www.harekrsna.com/sun/editorials/07-11/editorials7442.htm.

Swami, Devamrita. n.d. "Devamrita Swami, Reaching the Hearts Day 2 Session 3." ISKCON Online YouTube channel, May 27. 1:29:20. Accessed June 30, 2017. https://www.youtube.com/watch?v=pnXkLkVasfI.

———. n.d. "Introduction to Devamrita Swami." DevamritaSwami.Com. Accessed July 2, 2017. http://devamritaswami.com/.

———. 2012. "Devamrita Swami Seminar—Urban Preaching 1." Accessed June 1, 2017. http://iskconleaders.com/seminar-on-urban-preaching-audio-lecture-by-devamrita-swami/#sthash.ZUVANtLP.dpuf.

———. 2012. "Devamrita Swami Seminar—Urban Preaching 2." Accessed June 1, 2017. http://iskconleaders.com/seminar-on-urban-preaching-audio-lecture-by-devamrita-swami/#sthash.ZUVANtLP.dpuf.

———. 2012. "Devamrita Swami Seminar—Urban Preaching 5." Accessed June 1, 2017. http://iskconleaders.com/seminar-on-urban-preaching-audio-lecture-by-devamrita-swami/#sthash.ZUVANtLP.dpuf.

———. 2015. "Nrshima Caturdasi & Reaching the Hearts Day 2." Kishorekishori YouTube channel, May 2. 1:52:52. Accessed July 21, 2017. https://www.youtube.com/watch?v=YZC6ewjG2bE.

———. 2016. Interview by Nicole Karapanagiotis. In person, Potomac, Maryland, March 28, 2016.

Swami, Radhanath. n.d. "His Holiness Radhanath Swami Speaking at the Cambridge Union Society on 15/10/12." Cambridge Union YouTube channel, October 22. 1:20:20. Accessed November 17, 2017. https://www.youtube.com/watch?v=cKr27yOa57U.

———. Interview by Nicole Karapanagiotis. In person, Chowpatty, Mumbai, January 15, 2016.

———. Interview by Nicole Karapanagiotis. In person, Lanexa, Virginia, June 13, 2016.

———. Lecture delivered at the Heart of Yoga Retreat, Day 1. June 11, 2016. Lanexa, Virginia.

———. 2010. *The Journey Home: Autobiography of an American Swami*. San Rafael: Mandala.

———. 2016. *The Journey Within: Exploring the Path of Bhakti, A Contemporary Guide to Yoga's Ancient Wisdom*. San Rafael: Mandala.

———. "Western Outreach by Radhanath Swami." 2015. YouTube video, June 9. 46:13. Accessed November 18, 2017. https://www.youtube.com/watch?v=oYFBvhdB-Io.

Swanson, Carl. 2016. "Talking to the Hare Krishna Leader Who's Bringing the Movement Into the Age of Lululemon." *New York Magazine*, May 18. Accessed November 16, 2017. http://nymag.com/daily/intelligencer/2016/05/talking-to-hare-krishna-leader.html.

The Official Website for the International Society for Krishna Consciousness. Accessed August 11, 2016. http://www.iskcon.org.

The Pluralism Project. "The Rush of Gurus." Harvard University. Accessed February 11, 2017. http://pluralism.org/religions/hinduism/hinduism-in-america/the-rush-of-gurus/.

The Walking Monk website. "The Walking Monk: Bhaktimarga Swami." Accessed October 27, 2018. https://www.thewalkingmonk.net/.

TripAdvisor.com. "Classes & Workshops in New York City." Accessed November 16, 2017. https://www.tripadvisor.com/Attraction_Review-g60763-d8389845-Reviews-The_Bhakti_Center-New_York_City_New_York.html.

———. "Things to do in Mumbai (Bombay)." Accessed November 18, 2017. https://www.tripadvisor.com/Attraction_Review-g304554-d6949190-Reviews-Govardhan_Ecovillage-Mumbai_Bombay_Maharashtra.html.

Urban, Hugh B. 2003. "Avatar for Our Age: Sathya Sai Baba and the Cultural Contradictions of Late Capitalism." *Religion* 33, no. 1: 73–93.

———. 2005. "Osho, from Sex Guru to Guru of the Rich: The Spiritual Logical of Late Capitalism. In *Gurus in America*. Thomas A. Forsthoefel and Cynthia Ann Humes, eds. Albany: State University of New York Press, 169–192.

Valpey, Kenneth Russell. 2006. *Attending Kṛṣṇa's Image: Caitanya Vaiṣṇava Mūrti-Sevā as Devotional Truth*. London and New York: Routledge.

———. 2013. "Interview with Dr. Kenneth R. Valpey." In *Hare Krishna in the Modern World*. Graham Dwyer and Richard J. Cole, eds. London: Arktos Media.

———. 2004. "Krishna in *Mleccha Desh*: ISKCON Temple Worship in Historical Perspective." In *The Hare Krishna Movement: The Postcharismatic Fate of a Religious Transplant*. Edwin F. Bryant and Maria L. Ekstrand, eds. New York: Columbia University Press, 45–60.

Waghorne, Joanne Punzo. 2014a. "Engineering an Artful Practice: On Jaggi Vasudev's Isha Yoga and Sri Sri Ravi Shankar's Art of Living." In *Gurus of Modern Yoga*. Mark Singleton and Ellen Goldberg, eds. New York: Oxford University Press, 283–307.

———. 2014b. "From Diaspora to (Global) Civil Society: Global Gurus and the Processes of De-ritualization and De-ethnization in Singapore." In *Hindu Ritual at the Margins: Innovations, Transformations, Reconsiderations*. Linda Penkower and Tracy Pintchman, eds. Columbia: University of South Carolina Press, 186–207.

———. 1985. "Introduction." In, Waghorne, Joanne Punzo and Norman Cutler, eds. 1985. *Gods of Flesh Gods of Stone*. New York: Columbia University Press, 1–7.

Wallis, Roy. 1982 "Charisma, Commitment and Control in a New Religious Movement." In *Millenialism and Charisma*. Roy Wallis, ed. Belfast: The Queen's University, 73–140.

Warrier, Maya. 2005. *Hindu Selves in a Modern World: Guru Faith in the Mata Amritanandamayi Mission*. London: RoutledgeCurzon.

Williamson, Lola. 2005. "The Perfectability of Perfection: Siddha Yoga as a Global Movement." In *Gurus in America*. Thomas A. Forsthoefel and Cynthia Ann Humes, eds. Albany: State University of New York Press, 147–167.

Wilson, Jeff. 2014. *Mindful America: The Mutual Transformation of Buddhist Meditation and American Culture*. Oxford and New York: Oxford University Press.

Wuthnow, Robert. 2005. *America and the Challenges of Religious Diversity*. Princeton and Oxford: Princeton University Press.

Yelp.com. "The Best 10 Yoga near East Village, Manhattan, NY." Accessed November 16, 2017. https://www.yelp.com/search?cflt=yoga&find_loc=East+Village%2C+Manhattan%2C+NY.

Zaidman, Nurit. 2000. "The Integration of Indian Immigrants to Temples Run by North Americans." *Social Compass* 47, no. 2: 205–219.

———. 1997. "When the Deities Are Asleep: Processes of Change in an American Hare Krishna Temple." *Journal of Contemporary Religion* 12, no. 3: 335–352.

INDEX

Page numbers in *italics* indicate photos.

NICOLE KARAPANAGIOTIS is Assistant Professor of Religion at Rutgers University, Camden.

Lightning Source UK Ltd.
Milton Keynes UK
UKHW012036040321
379797UK00001B/43

9 780253 054890